THE INVENTION OF DIONYSUS

JAMES I. PORTER

The Invention of Dionysus

An Essay on **The Birth of Tragedy**

STANFORD UNIVERSITY PRESS

STANFORD, CALIFORNIA

2000

Stanford University Press
Stanford, California

Printed in the United States of America

Library of Congress Cataloging-in-Publication Data

Porter, James I.
The invention of Dionysus : an essay on The birth of tragedy / James I. Porter.
p. cm.
Includes bibliographical references and index.
ISBN 0-8047-3699-5 (alk. paper)—ISBN 0-8047-3700-2 (pbk. : alk. paper)
1. Nietzsche, Friedrich Wilhelm, 1844–1900. Geburt der Tragèdie. 2. Metaphysics—History—19th century. 3. Plato. 4. Dionysus (Greek deity) I. Title.
B3313.G43 P67 2000
111'.85—dc21 00-022875

∞ This book is printed on acid-free, archival quality paper.

Original printing 2000
Last figure below indicates year of this printing:
09 08 07 06 05 04 03 02 01 00

Typeset by Robert C. Ehle in 10/14 Janson.

For Gabriel,
the best birth of all

Acknowledgments

My debts for this book can be read out of the acknowledgments to *Nietzsche and the Philology of the Future*. Some of the present study appeared in an earlier form as "The Invention of Dionysus and the Platonic Midwife: Nietzsche's *Birth of Tragedy*" in the *Journal of the History of Philosophy* 33.3 (1995), pp. 467–97. Special thanks go again to Helen Tartar, in particular for smiling on my last-minute decisions, and to the University of Michigan and the Alexander von Humboldt-Siftung for their generous support. Thanks also to John Pedley, for pointing me to "Dionysus in the Vineyard"; to the Museum of Fine Arts for permissions; to Camilla MacKay for editorial assistance; and to Chris Luebbe for help in preparing the index.

Contents

Abbreviations xi
Introduction 1
The Problem of Periodization: Nietzsche's Appearances 6
Abyssal Metaphysical Surfaces: F. A. Lange 9
The Appearance of Metaphysics in *The Birth of Tragedy* and Beyond 16
The Complication of Appearances 33
Anticipations: The Physiology of Dreams 36
"Delicate Boundaries" 47
"On Schopenhauer" 57
Transfiguration 74
Beyond Metaphysics—To Its Banality 77
Narrative Appearances 86
"Raving Socrates" 88
The Platonism of *The Birth of Tragedy* 94
"The Goal of the Antipodes" 105
The Socratic Fallacy 110
"Eternal" Phenomena: Culture's Illusions 120

Primordial Fairy Tales 123
Classical Mythologies in the Present Tense 131
Power and Appearances 142
The Myth of Mythlessness 148
Notes 167
Works Cited 213
Index 221

Abbreviations

NIETZSCHE

German Editions*

BAW	*Historisch-kritische Gesamtausgabe. Werke*
KGB	*Kritische Gesamtausgabe. Briefe*
KGW	*Kritische Gesamtausgabe. Werke*
KSA	*Kritische Studienausgabe. Sämtliche Werke*

See Works Cited for further details and for conventions used in citations.

Early Essays and Lectures

"DW"	"The Dionysian Worldview" (1870) *KSA* 1, 553–77
"ECP"	"Encyclopedia of Classical Philology" (1871/74) *KGW*, 2.3, 341–437
"GrS"	"The Greek State" (1872) *KSA* 1, 764–77
"HC"	"Homer's Contest" (1872) *KSA* 1, 783–92
"HCP"	"Homer and Classical Philology" (1869) *KGW* 2.1, 248–69
"ISPD"	"Introduction to the Study of the Platonic Dialogues" (1871–72) *KGW* 2.4, 7–188

*The textual and critical apparatus and supplements to the materials most relevant to the present study, now published in *KGW*, 3.5.1–2 (*Nachbericht zur dritten Abteilung*, edited by Michael Kohlenbach and Marie-Luise Haase [Berlin: De Gruyter, 1997]), fell into my hands only as this study was going to press. I regret that I could not make fuller use of these two copious volumes.

"IST"	"Introduction to Sophoclean Tragedy" (1870) *KGW* 2.3, 7–57
"OS"	"On Schopenhauer" (1867/68) *BAW* 3, 352–61
"OT"	"On Teleology" (1867/68) *BAW* 3, 371–72
"PP"	"The Preplatonic Philosophers" (1869/70[?]–76) *KGW* 2.4, 211–362
"PTG"	"Philosophy in the Tragic Age of the Greeks" (1873) *KSA* 1, 801–72
"R"	"Description of Ancient Rhetoric" (1874) *KGW* 2.4, 415–502
"TL"	"On Truth and Lying in an Extra-Moral Sense" (1872/73) *KSA* 1, 875–90; trans. C. Blaire, in Gilman et al. 1989, 246–57
"TSK"	"Teleology since Kant" (1867/68) *BAW* 3, 372–94
"WPh"	"We Philologists" (1875) *KSA* 8, 1–96, 121–27

Works in Translation*

A	*The Anti-Christ*
"Attempt"	"Attempt at a Self-Criticism" (second preface to *BT*; 1886)
BGE	*Beyond Good and Evil*
BT	*The Birth of Tragedy*
D	*Daybreak*
EH	*Ecce Homo*
GM	*On the Genealogy of Morals*
GS	*The Gay Science*
HA	*Human, All Too Human*
TI	*Twilight of the Idols*
UM	*Untimely Meditations*
*WP**	*The Will to Power*
Z	*Thus Spoke Zarathustra*

*Cited by section numbers, with "Pref." representing "Preface"

KANT

CR *Critique of Pure Reason*

SCHOPENHAUER

P&P *Parerga und Paralipomena*
W *Die Welt als Wille und Vorstellung*

OTHER

DK Diels-Kranz, *Die Fragmente der Vorsokratiker*

*Note on *WP*: This posthumous edition of the late fragments is used only for the sake of its convenience of reference for nonspecialists. Incomplete and by no means authoritative (its organization was contrived by its editors), *WP* remains for now the only existing translation of the later *Nachlass*. Cross-references to the German editions will be found in *Nietzsche-Studien* 9 (1980): 446–90, a concordance compiled by Marie-Luise Haase and Jörg Salaquarda.

The souls of men see their own images as in the mirror of Dionysus.

—PLOTINUS

It is not gods who create evil, but only men.

—NIETZSCHE

But I am *not* a God, not a God's hell: deep is *your* pain.

—ZARATHUSTRA

Introduction

Oh, it is wicked and offensive! Read it furtively in your closet.

—NIETZSCHE TO GUSTAV KRUG, 31 DECEMBER 1871

This study is about Nietzsche's first book, around which an imaginary Nietzsche—or rather two imaginary Nietzsches—have been constructed from both sides of his readership, classical philologists and nonphilologists. The work itself has consequently become something like a leftover, a phantom object. Intractable from either angle, it is a work without a clear home.

For classical philologists who care to read it, *The Birth of Tragedy out of the Spirit of Music* (1872) is anathema: it represents a departure from narrow philological ways and an opening toward a speculative and threatening philosophy. What it augurs is not a philology of the future but the annulment of philology and of the classical heritage. The trouble with this view is that its anxieties are misplaced: it misconstrues Nietzsche's commitments to philology prior to 1872 and underestimates the continuity of those commitments after the publication of *The Birth of Tragedy*. As I argue in a separate study, Nietzsche's earliest philological projects are in fact provocative reflections upon the problem of "classical antiquity" and its significance to the modern world. And that remained the thrust of his later interest in the problems of the classical inheritance, which he never in fact abandoned. Nietzsche had developed a thoroughgoing critique of philology well before he wrote his first book; and the ends of cultural critique and of philological critique were for him indissolubly linked already at that time. By the same token, Nietzsche's later critique of culture is in effect an extended form of this critical philology (of reading and deciphering meaning, transmission, tradition, falsification, and the like). And so, *The Birth of Tragedy*, far from breaking with his earlier philology, instead flows logically from it, and often in unsuspected ways. Be that as it may, making the argument of continuity with Nietzsche's philology will not be the main burden of what follows.

For nonphilologists and readers of Nietzsche's later writings, for whom the present study is principally conceived, *The Birth of Tragedy*, an early work, inevitably elicits momentary shows of discomfort, embarrassment, little apologies, a slight bemusement—as if the familiar and recognizable Nietzsche had temporarily blinded himself to his customary shibboleths (Wagner, the Teutonic spirit, metaphysical seductions), had not yet acquired the wisdom to see *beyond* them, with a gaze that would show itself to be more profound, more critical, darker. It is as though, with the later writings, we can breathe a heavy sigh of relief ("Fresh air!") and rejoice at the fate (but when was fate ever less surprising?) of now being comfortably at home in a landscape that at least appeases our sense of the rightness of mental action. Here, at last, we may experience that delicious, unconditional surrender to knowledge and insight under certain, well-marked, and acceptable conditions—free of those little metaphysical and philological worries that trouble the surface of Nietzsche's earliest writings.

And yet *The Birth of Tragedy* is not a turning point in Nietzsche's career, as his readers on both sides of the disciplinary divide might prefer to think. It is partly because the images of Nietzsche in circulation today are in some respects so elaborately controlled that it will be necessary to raise the question of Nietzsche's acceptability, if only to underscore the simple fact that "Nietzsche" is a construct. Roped off within secure bounds, vigilantly policed and contained, "Nietzsche" is confined between his earliest missteps or half-steps (who would admit that these are blunders? Preferably they are to be seen as precocious first steps on the road to future academic or philosophical glory) and eventual delirium. (Speaking of Nietzsche's youthful efforts, Friedrich

Ritschl, his mentor, wrote in a letter from 1869 that would eventually secure him a post at the University of Basel at the age of twenty-four, "I have *never before* known a young man . . . who *so* early and *so* young was already *so* mature as this Nietzsche. If he lives a long life, god willing, I prophesy that he will stand one day in the front ranks of German philology." Walter Kaufmann, more sympathetic than Ritschl to the budding philosophical talents of the young Nietzsche, could write of the latter's first book: "This book as a whole . . . has a touch of genius," even despite its being "marred by the faults that Nietzsche enumerates in his 'Attempt at a Self-Criticism'" from 1886 and sets to rights in his more mature philosophy.)[1]

This, then, is the institutionalized Nietzsche, who is permitted to wander aimlessly, if not freely, between two doorways, that of the philological seminar and that of the sanatorium, an allowance that protects Nietzsche and his readers from traveling too far in either direction.[2] The incomprehensible otherness of a text like *The Birth of Tragedy*, rather than acting as an incentive to read on with a diminished appreciation, might instead serve a more useful purpose—like the sounding of a siren or alarm. Happily, one can choose to ignore these indications (how disturbing it can be to read in the presence of an alarm!). Or else one can embrace the disquieting possibility, which disarms every hermeneutic operation carried out upon Nietzsche and its shielding effects, that his writings early and late might in fact be consistent with *The Birth of Tragedy*, equally compromised, equally questionable, and—if this can be imagined—equally uncharacteristic of "Nietzsche," if not of Nietzsche.

The underlying assumption of this study is that Nietzsche's first book does not mark a rupture with his prior philological undertakings but is in fact continuous with them and with his later writings as well. Not only had Nietzsche already stepped well beyond the philological paradigms even before he assumed his professorship at Basel in 1869. The argumentative and writerly strategies at Nietzsche's command in his first book are all reminiscent of his prior critical and quite radical philology, and they anticipate his later writings as well. These continuities are displayed above all in the entanglement of his surface narratives, in the self-consuming artifice of his writing, in the interplay of his voices, posturings, and ironies—in a word, in his *staging* of meaning rather than in his advocacy of this or that position. What is more, many of the substantive particulars of *The Birth of Tragedy* had already been anticipated in the earlier writings: the inversion of the Dionysian and Apollinian domains; the concessions made to metaphysical attitudes in the course of their critique; the ongoing, at times emblematic interest in the atomistic challenge to Platonism, which was one of Nietzsche's lifelong concerns; and the theory of the all-too-human subject that takes the form of a cultural anthropology—a haunting reminder of human pretensions and their limits, which is likewise a thread that runs through the whole of Nietzsche's corpus, critically undoing what his philosophy appears to erect. The coherence of Nietzsche's writings up to and including *The Birth of Tragedy* is incontestable: it points to a fact that needs to be turned to account in any reading of *The Birth of Tragedy*, namely that Nietzsche is a most unreliable witness to his own meaning. I hope to make the consequences of this last insight evident in the study that follows.

By far the harder case to make concerns the coherence of Nietzsche's writings, his style of argument in the broadest sense, from *The Birth of Tragedy* onward, and indeed across the entire span of his career. This claim has to rest on at least two subsidiary arguments that are bound to be hard to accept, given the status quo of Nietzsche studies today. One has to do with what is taken to be Nietzsche's later philosophy, although I would say that Nietzsche has no philosophy in the proper senses of "having" or "philosophy." This is an argument that can only be suggested here. The other concerns his thinking at the time of *The Birth of Tragedy*, which can be established here. To this end, the present study will begin by focusing on the broader comparison and by treating broader issues—for example, the relation of *The Birth of Tragedy* to the later writings; the problems involved in the metaphysics of appearances (as opposed to the identification of the metaphysical as a realm lurking behind appearances); and the appearance—the apparition—of metaphysics in both the early and late works. The latter parts of this study will focus more narrowly on the formal and thematic complications in the narrative of *The Birth of Tragedy*. *The Birth of Tragedy* is a self-standing, complexly organized, and (for the first time in Nietzsche's career) complete piece of imagining that needs to be examined on its own terms. And so, while connections to his prior and ongoing philology will be made as required, often they will be implicit. Of more immediate interest will be the surrounding philosophical reflections that Nietzsche made prior to and at the time of *The Birth of Tragedy*. But even these will be treated as needed and in passing, the primary interest being the self-presentation of the work itself.

That said, the principal claims about *The Birth of Tragedy* to be made below turn on a few problems that have not sufficiently been taken into account in previous readings of this work and that can be quickly stated. The first of these concerns Nietzsche's absorption of Friedrich Albert Lange's revisionist history and theory of materialism, which Nietzsche read and virtually adopted as his own at the time of its original publication in 1866. A few pages into his book, Lange shows himself to be singularly inhospitable to Schopenhauer and his followers, whose philosophy in Lange's eyes represents a "regression" from Kant into an older, uncritical metaphysics.[3] Materialism, with its resolute anti-idealism, is hard to square with Schopenhauerianism in any case, and Lange's version of materialism is no exception. How likely is it that, in the wake of his in-depth studies and his profound appreciation of both Lange and the ancient Greek atomists (a central focus of his philology from 1867–69), Nietzsche could ever innocently purvey a Schopenhauerian metaphysics of the will? And how are the brief but unexpectedly key allusions to atomistic physiology in *The Birth of Tragedy* to be squared with the metaphysical idealism of that work?

Second, Nietzsche's stinging critique of Plato and of Platonism in

The Birth of Tragedy, which follows, *inter alia*, from his sympathetic reading of Democritus, creates a difficulty for anyone who wants to see a positive reconstruction of Schopenhauer in Nietzsche's first book. Platonism provides one of the linchpins of Schopenhauer's metaphysics (the "*stages of the will's objectivations,*" he writes in *The World as Will and Representation* [1819], "are nothing other than *Plato's Ideas*").[4] As it turns out, although this is not a well-recognized feature of *The Birth of Tragedy*, Platonism performs the exact same office in Nietzsche's work as well. Noticing this tension not only sets the work squarely against Schopenhauer, it sets it abruptly against itself.

A third problem concerns Dionysianism. Dionysianism consists in features that, as will be shown, are legible only from a modern perspective. Worse still, Dionysianism seems in fact to be a recognizably modern phenomenon. What this means is that buried at the heart of Nietzsche's project is, in effect, a troubling anachronism. This last clue points us to the way in which Nietzsche's work asks itself to be read. What modern readers see in this work, purportedly about Greek antiquity, is ultimately an inverted reflection of their own desires. The question here is not simply how believable did Nietzsche want his work to be, but how ready to believe in the appearances of *The Birth of Tragedy* have its readers shown themselves to be?

Together these three problems, while not the only ones to be considered below, roughly delineate the overall progression of the present study, to which we may now turn.

The Problem of Periodization: Nietzsche's Appearances

Does *The Birth of Tragedy*, read closely, support the commonly held axiom of interpretation that it belongs to the (as it were) precritical writings in his oeuvre? Much, of course, depends on how we construe Nietzsche's assault on metaphysics in his later and critical (as opposed to his "precritical") phase. The vigorousness of that assault has never been doubted. But its scope and its effectiveness are open to a certain amount of disagreement. There are abundant signs that Nietzsche's early attitude to metaphysics, well before *The Birth of Tragedy*, is complex and enlightened. His philological explorations of Democritus (1867–69) suffice to show this by themselves. His philosophical sketches and notes on Kant and Schopenhauer, composed between 1867 and 1871, merely confirm the fact, and we will come back to his early critiques of Schopenhauer below.

The dates, if need be, can be pushed back into the early 1860s, by which time Nietzsche's antimetaphysical stance had already clearly formed:

> Once we recognize that *we are responsible to ourselves alone*, that we have only ourselves to blame and not any sort of higher powers for our failings in life, then we finally will strip the foundational ideas of Christianity of their outer covering and get at its core. [. . .] That God became man only indicates that man shouldn't search for blessedness in the infinite; rather, he should ground his heaven *on earth*. *The delusion of a world beyond* has cast human spirits and minds in a false relation to the earthly world: [That delusion] was the product of a childhood of peoples. (Letter to Krug and Pinder, 27 April 1862; emphasis added)

Here his position is constructivist: any *Jenseits*, or world beyond, is of our own making. As he would later put it in his preface to *On the Genealogy of Morals*, he had "learned early to cease to look for the origin of evil *behind* the world": the source lay closer to home.[1] The precocious instincts of the seventeen-year-old, doubtless already influenced by Kant, would be powerfully confirmed four years later by the neo-Kantian revisionist and author of *Geschichte des Materialismus und Kritik seiner Bedeutung in der Gegenwart* (1866), Friedrich Albert Lange. Adopting the perspective of a Kantian materialist, Nietzsche could affirm in 1866 that our inner and outer sensations alike are the "products of our organization" and that the concept of a thing in itself, divorced from its conceptual support in this organization (which is also its source), threatens to plummet into pure meaninglessness.[2]

Indices like these are exceedingly important records of Nietzsche's early, spirited attack on metaphysical assumptions—the postulates or hypostases of being, substance, the subject, reason, and so on—for which he had nothing but the greatest mistrust from early on. Consequently, such indices ought to have an indisputable bearing on his later writings. But they only hint at the complexity of his views. Metaphysics, Nietzsche recognizes early on, is a falsification; but at the same time it is a symptom of deeply seated needs (*Gemüthsbedürfnisse*). Metaphysics may be a mere construction that is valuable for purposes of edification (*Erbauung*) and it may be no more than a kind of conceptual poetry (*Begriffsdichtung*), but it is not for all that something that can be simply waved away.[3] Nor, for that matter, can the metaphysical residues in Nietzsche's thought be simply waved away, even in his final writings, if we rely on Nietzsche's own and in many respects compelling definitions of what these residues amount to. Dating Nietzsche's suspicion toward metaphysical assumptions is evidently not a problem. Locating the logic of his position and the inflections this logic takes in various contexts is a distinctly more challenging task.

The attempt to parcel out Nietzsche's career into periods or phases according to his supposed acceptance or rejection of metaphysical assumptions is doomed to fail. Putting Nietzsche's attitudes in this way misstates the problem, as though metaphysics lent itself to one kind of response or the other. The wish to periodize Nietzsche into neat breaks blinds readers to the complex and often self-contradictory gestures that run through all of his writings. Nietzsche continuously found himself in a dilemma when it came to the question of metaphysics. In 1867/68, in the course of a fascinating critique of Kant, he wrote despairingly, "We remain mired in metaphysics and must conjure forth a *Ding an sich*," whether in the form of objective reality or of the idea of a subject.[4] He would never veer from this judgment.

The significance of Lange's ideas for Nietzsche has never been fully appreciated, and that influence is again felt here. Lange offered Nietzsche a model for confronting materialism (which Lange viewed as an essential component of the history of philosophy) with Kantianism, the most powerful modern instrument in the critique of traditional metaphysics. This is known. But what Lange teaches Nietzsche, even if Lange may simply be confirming Nietzsche's own philosophical instincts, is not only that metaphysics is a fictional enterprise worthy of being shattered once and for all but also that its resurrection is an inescapable and constitutional need deeply implanted in human nature. A brief rehearsal of Lange's argument from the more radically conceived first edition of his *History of Materialism*, the version with which Nietzsche was familiar, will be necessary if we are to appreciate Lange's truest significance for Nietzsche. Lange provides a crucial background to Nietzsche's attitudes toward metaphysics.

Abyssal Metaphysical Surfaces: F. A. Lange

Lange's *History* traces the birth of philosophy out of the primordial antagonism between sensation and imagination: "The first attempts to get free of these contradictions, to conceive the world in a unitary way, and to rise above the common ground of sensory appearances, are already pathways into the field of philosophy" (p. 3). The "dualism" that comprises these contradictions—for instance, between materialism and idealism—is not owing to a fundamental division between nature and the mind; it is rooted in the very "natural perception of things," which for Lange is forever fundamentally at odds with itself.[1] Philosophy is an attempt to sort out these constitutive difficulties, and its history begins with the first attempts to free thought from the shackles of mythology and from the illusions of metaphysical thinking.

As promisingly antimetaphysical as they are, the concepts of matter and sensation, instead of providing a way out of the problem, simply lead back into it. Materialism, for all its demystifying and antimetaphysical attractions, is for Lange a disguised form of metaphysical thinking. Lange's narrative thus oscillates back and forth as it traces the repeated attempts and failures of philosophy to lift itself above the constraints of sensation, but especially above its own contradictions. The atomism of Leucippus and Democritus in the fifth century B.C.E. is the starting point of Lange's analysis; Kant is the climactic moment of his history. Lange, Kant's would-be successor, will not be satisfied with either materialism or idealism. What he wants is a critical blend of these two philosophical impulses, one that in any case will mirror their joint evolution. What he obtains is their critical antagonism. Nietzsche could not have found a more congenial influence.

Seen in one light, Kant's critical philosophy spells "the beginning of the end" of materialism. In Lange's pregnant phrase, Kantianism represents "the catastrophe of the tragedy," the fatal peripety of materialism (p. 241). With Kant, the objectively ascertainable reality of things in themselves is forever banned from our discourse as an unattainable fiction, but then reinstalled as a functional limit. In default of this reality, we are thrown back onto the forms of our perceptions and sensations, which can give only a subjective, or logical, insight into things. The naive faith in the objective and determinable basis of sensation, of space and time, is powerfully shaken; materialism has been dealt a hard blow; and Protagoras, the author of post-Democritean phenomenalism and relativism, is in a way vindicated. But whereas, Lange writes, Protagoras was just a short "leap" away from the concept of the thing in itself, which would have redeemed him from endless subjectivism (p. 15), Democritus' third-century B.C.E. successor Epicurus is for Kant "the most distinguished of the philosophers of the senses": he stayed safely within the bounds of experience, on the principle, to which Kant could give his assent, that "there is nothing to be sought behind the things of the phenomenal world" (pp. 69, 236). This sudden and favorable proximity of Kant and an atomist is striking. It is prompted by a passage from *The Critique of Pure Reason* (A471 n./B499 n.),[2] but, as Lange says, "Kant's position vis-à-vis materialism has to be put in an unaccustomed light." For despite his resistance to materialism, Kant was anything but one of materialism's most disparaging opponents (p. 239). In Kant, Lange rightly sees an avenue back to the science of natural phenomena, but (oddly) a possible reconciliation of sorts between two ancient philosophical rivals in the atomistic tradition.

Kant shows, on grounds in fact quite removed from those of Epicurus, that knowledge with pretensions to a *Jenseits* of experience is empty, and he thereby provides the most rigorous and damaging refutation of metaphysical speculation to date. More precisely, Kant gives "just a glimpse" into what Lange, on a number of occasions, calls the "abysses [*Abgründe*] of metaphysics" (p. 252). The phrase is significant, as it already suggests a divergence from Kant (who had himself famously used "abyss" in a quite different sense, in an essay on the proof of God dating from 1763). Lange's personal contribution to the history he maps out lies in his reapproximation of Kant's transcendental idealism to the main motives of materialism. In essence, Lange both radicalizes tendencies already present in Kant and reads him in a materialist light. Even here, Lange remains true to his prediction from the outset—namely, that all philosophy remains irretrievably divided within itself. His revisionist view of Kant is both brash and far-reaching; it is also interestingly Nietzschean. It can for present purposes be summed up in a few words.

Using Kant against Kant, Lange attacks the a priori status of the a priori in Kant. He shows (or asserts) that Kant had overstepped even his own guidelines for cognitive certainty in claiming to know the forms of judgment in some absolute sense, when they can at most be claimed as necessary forms of thought (pp. 249, 270). Kant falsely divided knowledge into reason and sensation, the one being a priori (known prescriptively) and the other a posteriori (known after the fact of experience). He did so on the wrong assumption that "that around which our sensation arranges itself"—which is to say, the conceptual apparatus taken by Kant to be formally constitutive of experience—"could not in turn be sensation" (p. 251).[3] In other words (and this is a remarkable finding by Lange), *the forms of sensation are themselves sensations or the product of sensations.* It is on the basis of this heretical "deduction" from within Kant (which must, for example, go against the explicit doctrine of *The Critique of Pure Reason* [e.g., A20/B34]) that Lange can make the shocking claim that "*the physiology of the sense organs is an evolved or corrected Kantianism*" (p. 482; emphasis added).

Finally, in the wake of Friedrich Ueberweg's refutation of Kant's logic of causation, Kant's much-venerated thing in itself is argued to be but a "hidden category," a projection of thought, and not a transcendental object or an empirical object materially independent of the mind (pp. 267–68).[4] With a shrewd sense for vulnerabilities, Lange heads straight for the constitutive limits of Kant's system. Judging by his wholesale appropriation of them, Nietzsche must have found the sequence of arguments dazzling to watch. They are worth retracing briefly.

First, Lange attacks the conceptual immunity of "limits." It is naive, he affirms, to believe that whatever holds true for a region demarcated by limits does not also touch those limits by way of their determination. Limits are subject to the same constraints and are every bit as much phenomena as the phenomena they define: they obey the same constraints but also arise from the same (subjective) origins. The crucial test case is causality, the laws of which hold true only within limits of the phenomenal world (causality defines those limits); therefore the category of causation itself is a phenomenal product, not their a priori condition. Pushed further, as it were to the limit, the contrast between the near and far side of phenomena must be "confessed" to be of our manufacture. The thing in itself, once exalted and venerable for lying safely beyond cognition, must fall.[5] The existence of things in themselves cannot be ruled out as a possibility or as conceivable in Kant's fashion. But their admittance into conceptual discourse comes at a high price: they can no longer ground a knowledge that is a priori valid. To speak with Kant and against him, things in themselves will enjoy only an a posteriori, belated, and "invented" existence. And "*herein our categories play the same role as our senses*" (p. 268). If it is the understanding that gives us categorical knowledge of the opposition between things as they appear and as they are in themselves, then it follows (Lange reasons) that it was the understanding that "*itself created this opposition*" (p. 268; emphasis added). Needless to say, for Lange (as for Kant), sensation is never purely a matter of objective constitution.

Pursuing this logic, Lange arrives at the truly astonishing conclusion, one that Nietzsche would quote with heady fervor in a letter to von Gersdorff at the end of August 1866 and then codify in practice. Ueberweg's objection that causality is but a concealed category is not only damaging. Adequately followed out to its last consequences, Lange writes, this insight "returns in a new and terrifying (*schrecklichen*) form": for it means that "the true nature of things, the ultimate cause (or "ground") of every appearance, is not only unknown to us, but the concept of it is no more and no less than the last, strange product (*die letzte Ausgeburt*) of an opposition that is conditioned by our [bodily and mental] organization; nor do we even know *whether this opposition has any meaning outside of our experience*" (p. 268).

"Last" here is pivotal, for it signifies not a determinable limit but only its *most recent* determination. "Everywhere we look we find nothing but the habitual empirical opposition between appearance and essence, which, as is known, reveals to the understanding infinite gradations." Here, Lange continues in a vein that is as remarkably daring as it is recognizably "Nietzschean": "*What is essence on this level of analysis shows itself on another, in relation to a still more deeply hidden essence, to be appearance again*" (p. 268; emphasis added). Lange's argument is that the concept of the "thing in itself" (or "essence") turns out to be a projection from within the phenomenal word. The implication, however, is that the thing in itself, once it is rehabilitated in this way, requires yet another projection, that of "a still more deeply hidden essence."

The process of projecting and recuperating ought to go on infinitely, just as the natural sciences continue to refine their hypothetical and heuristic frameworks without arriving at a stable endpoint of analysis: hence the "infinite gradations" that are interposed between appearance and essence in an endless fluxion of remodeled conceptuality (pp. 252, 268, 379). This was the core of Nietzsche's skeptical and critical philology, and I believe it is the core of his maturest philosophy as well.[6]

I take this last implication to be the radical finding in Lange: namely, that philosophy proceeds by way of an inevitable and repeated hypostasis of a metaphysical ground or cause. On the whole, Lange's attitude is constructive and constructivist. From a different perspective, and at its most thrilling, the consequence of Lange's reasoning is a dismissal of, or "indifference" toward, unconditional essences.[7] Either way, things in themselves are carried, by necessity and sooner or later, back over into the phenomenal world. And there may be nothing of any consequence left beyond this world's confines. Lange's "metaphysics" consistently makes provisions for both views. He admits, at the conclusion of this train of thought, that on his own showing metaphysics has been brought back into line in an "incomparably sharper" way than Kant ever intended it to be. Kant had "just glimpsed" into the abysses of metaphysics. But with this bit of analysis, Lange has taken the plunge—into its infinitely recessed *surfaces*.

Here is where the real significance of Lange's ideas for Nietzsche lies. At a stroke, Lange does away entirely with the contrast between appearances and things in themselves, while in the same breath he reinstates it as something entirely ineliminable from thought. The contrast is both demolished and preserved—demolished as a fact about the world, and preserved as a hypothesis essential to our construction and experience of the world. As we shall repeatedly have occasion to see below, it is not only the destruction of metaphysics but also its resurrection as an inescapable and constitutional need—reflecting what might be called a metaphysical recidivism—that reverberates through all of Nietzsche's writings as his most outstanding, if unspoken, homage to Lange.[8] Moreover, with his historical perspectives on materialism and idealism and their endless antagonism, Lange seems to have encouraged Nietzsche's way of thinking about the present in terms of reflexes and atavisms from the philosophical past: Lange's philosophical narrative is ghosted by the memory of the earliest historical struggles it retails, and it thereby suggests something about the incorrigibilities of the human mind (whose organization Lange anyway takes to be fundamentally given). By virtue of a transvaluation of metaphysics into a "critique of concepts" that is to be tied closely to a "historical critique," and by virtue of folding skepticism and materialism back into Kantianism, Lange could claim to have arrived at a critical method "more rigorous" than Kant's. Skepticism, made sober, could now serve the "revelations" of beauty and the good. Dogmatisms would wither away like weeds. Objective, empirical truths would vanish with them. And knowledge and creativity, *Erkennen und Schaffen*, would be granted equal, unrestricted rights.

It would therefore be a simplification to hold that Lange's stopping-point (and therefore Nietzsche's too, in his early, Lange-influenced phase) is the view that metaphysical entities, like things in themselves, are undemonstrable, unknowable, *and coherently real.*[9] What Lange in fact holds is that all these traits apply save the last. Things in themselves may be to some degree inevitable and even necessary products of our constitution, our sensory apparatus, our psychology, and by implication our history. But, Lange holds, dilating on Kant's own metaphors from "The Transcendental Dialectic" in the first *Critique*, metaphysical entities always remain products, creations, fictions, *fingierte Wesen*—mere abstractions and personifications (pp. 373–74, 489). Things in themselves, conceived of as real, are irretrievably indebted to their conception as real: really conceivable, they are (we might say) a real possibility, but impossibly real.

The real is always, therefore, an incoherency. Located on and not beyond the limits of thought, empirical and metaphysical entities are "best" described as the result of a process of "reciprocal determinations" and "blendings"—for instance, between sensation and conception, or between natural, biological processes and their anthropological (and anthropomorphizing) correlates. But they are this only if they also represent a "colossal paradox" to our understanding (as well as being its product), in the same way that the body, perhaps the least intelligible of all phenomena, is for us just a schema of reality, an optical product, and a representational image (p. 485). As the body goes, so goes the self: a "metaphorized" subject, matter is inscribed with subjective traits (p. 374). But at a deeper level, the subject is itself a "Thing" (in itself)—in Kant's terms, it is a substance without content, a pure noumenon (*CR*, A346/B404). In Lange's terms, it is the real of our "organization": "Our real organization remains just as unknown to us as the realities in the external world. We continually have only the product of both before us" (p. 493).[10] That our "physical-psychical" organization can enjoy so paradoxical a status is due to the lesson drawn by Lange above, one that tends to be partially obscured in the course of his lengthy exposition—namely, that bodies, selves, and metaphysical objects alike can exist only by virtue of the second lease of life that their critical *démontage* has booned them: crucially ineliminable, they remain doubtful, if not totally dubious, reconstructed things, never again in-themselves, and never simply "real." They are always vulnerable to a further unmasking and remaking.

The Appearance of Metaphysics in *The Birth of Tragedy* and Beyond

With Lange behind us, we can now return to Nietzsche. The idea, which is commonly held, that Nietzsche could have successfully defined a target in some region of conceptuality and then proceeded to dismantle it seems at first glance a bit quixotic. Metaphysics is a far broader and more insidious domain for Nietzsche than is commonly assumed. Nietzsche's problem, at any point in his crusade against metaphysical prejudices, was not determining what was a metaphysical object worthy of criticism but rather finding some safe ground from which to launch his critique, and this in a language that was not already in use to support some variety of metaphysical thinking. Targets were everywhere. There was simply no place to stand, and nothing decisive to say against them. That is precisely the problem. On Nietzsche's view, even in his later writings, metaphysical assumptions are operative in the very structures of thought, language, and perception by which day-to-day experience is articulated. The esoteric jargon of philosophy merely provides these assumptions with an elaborate justification. It might be thought that, because on Nietzsche's view reinterpretations of experience are possible and equally correct, it follows that for Nietzsche "language makes no commitments regarding the world."[1] Nietzsche's claim, on the contrary, is that language makes commitments so basic and so insidious that they are an indelible part of its unconscious structure and of our own—assuming that language and the unconscious may even be distinguished for Nietzsche (as I believe they cannot). This is what he calls "the metaphysics of language" (*TI*, III, "'Reason' in Philosophy," 5).[2] Inevitably, to reinterpret experience is not to break free of these commitments; it is to repeat and reinforce them, with no hope of complete disentanglement.

This is not only Lange's position; it is likewise the lesson of Nietzsche's early treatment of the Presocratics. Take for instance his never-finished essay "Philosophy in the Tragic Age of the Greeks" (1873), which is frequently understood to presage his later Zarathustran musings. What we learn in this early document is that Nietzsche's inquiries into ancient philosophy do not reveal in the Presocratics a premetaphysical thinking that points beyond metaphysics. The Presocratics point, instead, to the inescapability of metaphysical thinking. All of his Presocratics are exemplars of metaphysical thinking, not its opponents, despite their efforts to free themselves from inherited mythologies. As Nietzsche writes, speaking in the first person (here against Parmenides, but the critique is generalizable to Parmenides' peers): "It is absolutely impossible for a subject to want [viz., to be able] to see and know something beyond itself, so much so that knowledge and being are the most contradictory spheres there are."[3] The "subjective concept" is "eternal"; we can never accede to a region "beyond the wall of relations" by which we are conditioned; beyond lies merely "*a mythical primordial ground of things (fabelhafter Urgrund der Dinge)*."[4] One of these mythical grounds was Thales' "metaphysical assumption (*Annahme*)," his belief in the reducibility of all there is to water.[5] These phrases, "primordial ground" and "metaphysical assumption," are resonant, and they have obvious implications for *The Birth of Tragedy* which we will want to draw on below. The will to power, that great promise of a final liberation from metaphysics, is no exception, but only supplies a spectacular confirmation of Nietzsche's view about the limits and persistence of metaphysical thinking.[6]

There is a nightmarish quality to Nietzsche's embattled position. The analogy to dreams may be less fantastic than it seems. Nietzsche once wrote the following about dreams and their "misunderstanding" in a passage reminiscent of the letter to Krug and Pinder from sixteen years earlier: "In the ages of a cruder, more primordial culture, man believed that in his dreams he came to know a *second real world*; this is the origin of all metaphysics. In the absence of dreams, one would have found no reason to make a division in the world" (*HA*, I:5; trans. mod.). Here, Nietzsche purposefully locates the origins of metaphysics in an unreachable condition—in some remote, archaic epoch ("a childhood of peoples") that signifies a primary, if not primordial, condition, but also one that is situated within the cultural domain, indeed as its bedrock. The dilemma that Nietzsche constructs is oppressive. If we cannot grasp the origins of metaphysics because they lie so deeply embedded in our experience, neither can we grasp them as such because they are so massively diffused today. Because its origins are rooted in the preterit, metaphysics is all the more present and inescapable. Added considerations only enforce the presentness of the past depicted in the parable (which is in fact an ominous genealogy). In dreaming we repeat the past, inevitably and uncontrollably; and if dreams are the origins of metaphysics, culture (it is hinted) provides the ground of their persistent afterlife. Metaphysics is in the end as intangible and prevalent as culture and dreams.[7]

If metaphysical ideas are fixed by accidents of the body and of culture, they are also bound by affect and emotion. "All that has hitherto made metaphysical assumptions *valuable, terrible, delightful* to [men], all that has begotten these assumptions, is passion, error and self-deception," Nietzsche writes in another passage from the same work (*HA*, I:9). But the object of these emotions scarcely needs to be the contemplated starkness of a *Ding an sich*. Far more stirring is what such a contemplation puts into even starker relief—namely, that *things are not "in themselves" but just themselves.* Metaphysical alternatives may be suggested in dreams, but they are rendered indispensable by waking reality, against which they offer the greatest possible protection. This is one more, somewhat unexpected but no less paradoxical, aspect of Nietzsche's equally divided view of metaphysics: his utter antipathy toward it, and his acknowledgment of its utility and even necessity. Metaphysics, at times opening horrific prospects onto the universe, can itself disclose an even greater horror, a *horror vacui*—the prospect of its own impertinence, its absence, and its nullity. Here, metaphysics takes on the frightening image that it simultaneously suggests, the image of the void—here, of a world bereft of metaphysics, a world without consolation and devoid of redemption.[8]

Here Nietzsche is drawing a lesson from his contact with the atomists, particularly Democritus, whose physical system incorporates void into the very constitution of the world and thus juxtaposes, in a graphically shocking and simultaneous display, a vision of the world's "fullness" as something infinitesimally overdetermined (to the point of overfullness and surfeit, chance becoming proximate to necessity), with a vision of the world's disjunct character, its estranging emptiness. In Schopenhauer's words, atomism gives the uncheery prospect of a "physics without metaphysics."[9] Democritus, it could always be objected (even by Nietzsche himself, in the wake of Schopenhauer), was only availing himself of one more metaphysical postulate, the atom. But by the same token Democritus made void itself into a metaphysical component of reality, which was henceforth ineradicably built into a metaphysically conditioned image of a world that is abruptly physical but without any redemptive metaphysical value. Instead, the only prospect offered by atomism is that of a bleak series of contrasts: void and body, pitted against empty, phantasmal appearances. Atomism offers up the fragments of a metaphysical vision and a glimpse into the horrors of metaphysical thinking ("Metaphysics as vacuum"[10]). It is this complexity of horror—as a metaphysical constituent, and as the implied voiding of all metaphysical possibilities—that is the double inheritance of Democritean atomism.

Nietzsche would take all this to heart, and despair at the possibilities. This is one of the deepest dilemmas in his thought. For there is a profound paradox in having to register one's belief in the inescapable necessity of metaphysical assumptions that by themselves inspire absolutely no belief.[11] For Nietzsche at all stages of his career—including his late, simultaneous affirmation and denial of the will to power—metaphysical thinking is as necessary as it is pernicious, as pervasive as it is vapid. "We remain mired in metaphysics and must conjure forth a *Ding an sich*," owing to the painful limits of our intellect and to our cultural habits as well. Metaphysics, in Nietzsche's eyes, is the utterly banal predicament of modern culture. Woven seamlessly into culture's own mythologies and ideologies, metaphysics is for him not something that can be dispelled. It can only be disbelieved. This is perhaps not the conventional or received wisdom on Nietzsche (though it can be shown to be compatible with much of it).[12] But it is the view that will be adopted here, just as it will be argued that *The Birth of Tragedy*, far from being uncritically enthralled to a metaphysics that Nietzsche later abandoned, is a perfectly consistent example of his earliest and latest thinking on metaphysics. As such, it is a document that, one might say, should be read but not believed. It would be too simple a matter to take *The Birth of Tragedy* at its word and then dismiss it as philosophically naive. Nietzsche's best reply to this would be that all thinking is in many ways, and willy-nilly, naive (cf. *WP*, 522, 584), and that appearances, even Nietzsche's own, are always deceiving (*passim*).

Suspicions about *The Birth of Tragedy* are not entirely ungrounded, then. Nietzsche invites them himself in his "Attempt at a Self-Criticism," a preface added in 1886 to the reissue of his first book under a new title, *The Birth of Tragedy, Or: Hellenism and Pessimism, New Edition with an Attempt at a Self-Criticism*. This preface has universally been received in the way that Nietzsche seems to have intended it, as a retraction or mitigation of the book's most objectionable contents. But to take up Nietzsche's invitation in this manner is a curious way to read a gesture that is elaborately complex. It is doubtful that the tainted elements of *The Birth of Tragedy* could be counteracted by the antidote of self-rejection (or by dropping, as Nietzsche did, the original and fulsome "Foreword to Richard Wagner" of the first edition), when it is the very core of Nietzsche's earlier ideas—with its "artist's metaphysics" and its foundationalist scenarios—that is deemed to have been misbegotten (not merely misleading). A simpler, more effective means of expunging the harmful effects of his original misconception might have been to withdraw the book from circulation altogether, discarding it not just as a "first book" but as an utterly bad one, fit for the flames, but not to be read.

Nietzsche, however, does not call it a bad book. It is, just as he says, "an *impossible* book" ("Attempt," 2–3).[13] The simple addition of the second preface and the suppression of the first do little to relieve this sense of impossibility, and if anything they compound it. How do you read a book that is condemned but not quite disowned? Nor were Nietzsche's later opinions of his first book consistently or even damningly negative, as an abundance of passing allusions to it amply attest. The following passage in particular stands out, because it contains formulations that are strikingly close to *The Birth of Tragedy*, which, moreover, receives a resounding vindication here (a brief two years following the publication of the "Attempt at a Self-Criticism"):

> The psychology of the orgy as an overflowing feeling of life and energy within which even pain acts as a stimulus provided me with the key to the concept of the *tragic* feeling, which was misunderstood as much by Aristotle as it especially was by our pessimists.... Affirmation of life even in its strangest and sternest problems, the will to life rejoicing in its own inexhaustibility through the *sacrifice* of its highest types—*that* is what I called Dionysian. . . . *Not* so as to get rid of pity and terror, not so as to purify oneself of a dangerous emotion through its vehement discharge—it was thus Aristotle understood it—: but, beyond pity and terror, *to realize in oneself* the eternal joy of becoming—that joy which also encompasses *joy in destruction*. . . . And with that I again return to the place from which I set out—the *Birth of Tragedy* was my first revaluation of all values: with that I again plant myself in the soil out of which I draw all that I will and *can*—I, the last disciple of the philosopher Dionysus—I, the teacher of the eternal recurrence . . . (*TI*, "What I Owe to the Ancients," 5)

It is a simple matter to document the moments when Nietzsche continues to validate his breakthroughs made in *The Birth of Tragedy*; or the profusion of pages in which he restates and continues to explore the Dionysian/Apollinian thesis;[14] or those later texts that implicitly maintain the original distinction, despite Walter Kaufmann's assertion (which is repeated by Gilles Deleuze and others[15]) that the offices of Apollo are more or less obliterated by the figure of Dionysus, or rather absorbed into that god's greater and now greatly transfigured powers.[16] Nietzsche cannot hope, nor does he seem particularly eager, to evade the problems of self-reference that come with the bare mention of Dionysus, whose name inevitably conjures up his earliest attributes in Nietzsche's corpus. It is his commentators, but not Nietzsche, who assert that the distinction between the Bacchic god and Apollo is superseded in the later writings.

Whatever suspicions one may harbor about Nietzsche's inexhaustible capacity to enhance his past creatively through biographical imagining (giving himself, "a posteriori," a past—a possibility that he recognizes is "dangerous" but unavoidable, since that is, he believes, what any self-understanding ultimately amounts to),[17] there is in fact very little in the later Dionysian imagery that cannot be found in *The Birth of Tragedy*. Indeed, this holds for those very sections (§§16–25) which in the eyes of Kaufmann and others were lamentably appended, in the 1872 publication, to the first privately published version of 1871 ("Socrates and Greek Tragedy").[18] This is not to argue that Nietzsche's philosophical statements early and late are in all respects identical, but only that he found some of the primary components of his earlier conception of Dionysus and tragic representation sufficiently valuable to safeguard them throughout his career. Comparisons between such distant works are indeed misleading, but not because there are no overlaps between them. If anything, the interpretation of *The Birth of Tragedy* in *Twilight of the Idols* is too selective to give an undistorted reading of the earlier text, while the later passage is too impoverished to encompass the reach of Nietzsche's thought at the time of *Twilight* (which it purports to cover). The challenge with which the later commentary presents us is to find out what in the earlier work could possibly correspond to a "first" transvaluation of all values. It also asks that we reevaluate Nietzsche's second preface to *The Birth of Tragedy* from 1886, which no longer stands still or alone in the quavering light of its self-illumination.

Nor does it follow (and this is the more serious implication) that by subsuming two principles under one Nietzsche has stepped clear of the "dualistic metaphysics" toward which his early work "tended" (so Kaufmann). At most, if the claim about an eventual conflation of Dionysus and Apollo were right, Nietzsche would be guilty later on of having masked a dualism by concealing it with a monistic principle. But dualism is not by itself sufficient evidence of a straightforwardly dualistic metaphysics, and a monistic metaphysics might be as insidious as any other. The opposition between Apollo and Dionysus was never intended to be all-inclusive or of unlimited utility (nor does Nietzsche's thought at any time admit of totalizing disjunctions). If it happens that the opposition appears with sporadic frequency after *The Birth of Tragedy*, it is far more likely that Nietzsche has shifted the overt framework and strategy of his argumentation in the face of local considerations. The contrast between the two gods speaks to the specifically Greek portions of our cultural inheritances—and even then it is bound up with only one way of describing, or rather of construing, an aspect of Hellenism, which Nietzsche at times chooses to equate with the sources of Western metaphysical thinking. Compare a comment from his notebooks of 1872/73: "The opposition between truth and appearances was deeply seated in them." "[The Greeks] have in reality produced all types."[19] The opposition between Apollo and Dionysus is not "displaced" by the more recent pairing, "Dionysus versus the Crucified." Instead, the later contrast is best seen as reflecting another strategy, another polarity corresponding to a further cultural difference, and another set of vulnerabilities, at the same time that it overlaps with and conspicuously refers to Nietzsche's earlier, or simply other, contrast.[20]

A stronger argument for a volte-face is the renunciation of Schopenhauerian pessimism that Nietzsche seems to bequeath to himself after the fact in the later preface and to foreground in his changed title: "How differently Dionysus spoke to me! How far removed I was from all this resignationism!—" ("Attempt," 6). The problem is that pessimism continues to flourish, at least as a pose, in the later Nietzsche and even in the later preface, every bit as much as optimism is present in the early Nietzsche: "Is pessimism *necessarily* a sign of decline, decay, degeneration, weary and weak instincts [. . .]? Is there a pessimism of *strength*?" (ibid., 1).[21] It is slowly coming to be recognized that Nietzsche had overcome the pessimism of Schopenhauer by the time of *The Birth of Tragedy*.[22] That pessimism of this kind was a potential problem was already clear to the young philologist as he sought to distance himself from the "resignation" and "renunciation" of his professional peers.[23]

True, Nietzsche's emancipation from philology and Schopenhauer can be found overstated in Nietzsche himself. In a note from 1887 Nietzsche suggests that he came to realize only "around 1876" that he was imprisoned ("compromised") by philology, Wagner, and Schopenhauer.[24] Similar misgivings, we saw, appear in the second preface ("Attempt at a Self-Criticism") to *The Birth of Tragedy* (1886). It is indices like these that lead the unsuspecting astray. The "Attempt" is a plea for a closer and more careful reading of his first book, not a rejection of it, and the same is true of his judgment in *Ecce Homo*: "People have had ears only for a new formula for the art, the intention, the task of *Wagner*—what of value in the book was not listened to" (*EH*, V, "The Birth of Tragedy," 1). Ironically, what is of value in *The Birth of Tragedy* is Schopenhauer's recognition that the Greeks "stood decisively in favor of the affirmation of life" (*W*, 2.2, §46): "It is not unworthy of the greatest hero [sc., Achilles] to long for a continuation of life, even though he live as a day laborer" (*BT* §3)—such is the victory which the Greek will . . . obtains over suffering and the wisdom of suffering" (*BT* §18, ad fin.). Schopenhauer naturally disapproves of the Greeks for their decision and applauds them for being "nonetheless deeply affected by the misery of existence," to the extent that they were.[25] But this unexpected momentary agreement suffices to show that there is more to Nietzsche's polemics than easy rejection or acceptance. Here, Nietzsche is in fact siding with Schopenhauer against Schopenhauer's inferior instincts. But neither does optimism need to have been Nietzsche's only answer to Schopenhauer, for affirmation is not in itself a sign of either optimism or pessimism. Affirmation, whatever else it may be, is in any case a tricky category that exists in a pure form only as an impossible ideal.[26] As Nietzsche writes in a notebook from 1869/70, the life-affirming Greeks were "neither pessimists nor optimists": they were fascinated with "horror."[27] The conventional options are too confining: for the most part and at every stage, Nietzsche seems content to ironize the problem of pessimism and optimism rather than adopting either position.

The far more penetrating argument in favor of a fundamental shift in Nietzsche's philosophy after *The Birth of Tragedy* is the apparent identification in that text of the Dionysian realm with "the metaphysical comfort . . . that life is at the bottom of things, despite all the changes of appearances, indestructibly powerful and pleasurable" (§7; cf. §8[28])—that is, with "the real truth of nature," "the eternal core of things," and "the thing-in-itself" (all of which are contrastively juxtaposed with the realm of "appearances"). The shock that these concessions to metaphysics send to readers who are more at home in the balance of Nietzsche's critical output after 1872 may be gauged from the following concise formula by Alexander Nehamas in his recent and influential study: "In the later writings Nietzsche comes to deny the very contrast between things-in-themselves and appearance which was presupposed by his discussion of tragedy."[29]

This view has a long pedigree, and it has gradually hardened into an unquestioned truth about Nietzsche's thought. Walter Benjamin, in his essay on the German *Trauerspiel*, was visibly disappointed by Nietzsche's uncritical surrender to Schopenhauer and Wagner, whose metaphysical views "vitiated the best aspects of Nietzsche's work," which for Benjamin dissolves into self-defeating paradoxes (in the wake of its glimpse into "the abyss of aestheticism" and its attendant nihilism).[30] More recently than Benjamin, there has been a tendency to couch the metaphysical divide that periodizes Nietzsche's output in terms of a shift in allegiance in linguistic models (whereby proper meaning gives way to metaphor), or to view his early work as an instance of a kind of "logocentrism" (whether melocentric or phonocentric), in contrast to its later refutation or exposure. However one constructs one's conceptual enemy in the writings of a conceptual ally, weakness and error are located, to everyone's chagrin, in the early document, against the sounder, possibly just latent instincts of the more mature philosopher.[31] This approach founders crucially at both ends of the spectrum: it underestimates Nietzsche's concessions to the metaphysical structure of thought in his later period, and it overestimates his commitment to this structure in the earlier period.

It is questionable whether Nietzsche ever sought, even in his later writings, to cast the world in a new light that was bare of all opposition or unstructured by contrasts that are themselves plainly metaphysical equivalents of that between things in themselves and appearances. Nietzsche's "theory" of the will to power is a case in point. The spectacle it presents, of perspectival forces acting upon one another, is alienating indeed: "The 'apparent world,' therefore, is reduced to a specific mode of action on the world, emanating from a center" (*WP*, 567). In question, often (and here), are "force-centers," not quite beings or agents as we know them to be: they are more like "atomistic" intensities of power—"*Kraft-Atomen*" as he sometimes calls them. On the strength of this scenario, Nietzsche claims to have reduced metaphysical dualism to naught: "The antithesis between the apparent and the true world is reduced to the antithesis between 'world' and 'nothing'" (ibid.). The contrast between phenomena and metaphysical realities is supposed to have disappeared, but has it? Doubtfully.

Reducing reality to nothing, nothing with which we can identify, Nietzsche reinvents the world as its apparent negation. Far from eliminating appearances, he actually confirms them; they are simply given a new philosophical justification: the "apparent world" is "a world viewed according to values"; that is the premise and the conclusion of his reasoning. Indeed, Nietzsche's critique of Democritus for the latter's having populated a bare, physical reality with features borrowed from phenomenal experience can be made valid against Nietzsche himself: what, after all, is a "center"? Nietzsche has not so much eliminated the distinction between reality and appearances as he has brought out its horrific dimensions, simply by posing the question, What if the world is not as it really appears? Yet all the old dilemmas persist (starting with the question itself, which is philosophically suspect and ought to be illegitimate). There is a rhetorical force to all this alienation, but the force of Nietzsche's counterargument, or rather counterscenario, is strictly parasitical on the force of the distinctions that are being put into question. Is such thinking possibly metaphysical? Nietzsche's attack on metaphysics, by way of a radical dehumanization of reality, has a flip side to it, palpable in the claim, for instance, that "man . . . mirrors himself in things [and] has *humanized* the world" (*TI*, IX, "Expeditions of an Untimely Man," 19), which is plainly a metaphysical argument about the state of the world. So, rather than asking whether Nietzsche's thinking is metaphysical (it obviously is), the more relevant question is whether there is any thinking that is not. And here Nietzsche has a sobering lesson in store:

> That cloud there! What is "real" in that? Subtract the phantasm and every human *contribution* from it, my sober friends! If you *can*! If you can forget your descent, your past, your training. (*GS*, 57)

The point is that we cannot forget our descent, our past, our "training" in the habits of culture. The same aphorism incidentally goes on to describe the attempt to "subtract the phantasm" as a "will to transcend intoxication," a velleity that "is as respectable as your faith that you are altogether incapable of intoxication." Is there something intoxicating about metaphysics? If so, it is clearly a special kind of intoxication, which leaves its subjects with the illusion of their own sobriety. Plainly, metaphysical contrasts don't simply go away in the later period. The point is so obvious that it should hardly need to be stated at all.[32]

Elsewhere Nietzsche revives the contrast between reality and appearances by conjuring up not "nothing," but "chaos":

> The total character of the world, however, is in all eternity chaos—in the sense not of a lack of necessity but of a lack of order,

arrangement, form, beauty, wisdom, and whatever other names there are for our aesthetic anthropomorphisms. (*GS*, 109)

This admittedly runs up against the claim that it was Nietzsche's early (and later abandoned) view in *The Birth of Tragedy* that "the ultimate nature of the world is to have no orderly structure: in itself the world is chaos, with no laws, no reason, and no purpose."[33] As with the world construed as will to power, "chaos" has a positive, which is to say negating, value: it designates a lack, a denial of all that is familiar and dearly (or unreflectingly) cherished, and all that we will continue to project onto the resistant base of the world out of our inveterate and incurable rages for order, arrangement, form, and beauty. On the other hand, it is impossible to disentangle the "nothing" of Nietzsche's propositions from their rhetorical and polemical force or effects. He may have been out to construct an alternative metaphysical worldview, but it is far from clear that this was ever his primary aim, if it was ever his aim at all.[34] The main force of his alternative construction (of a world hostile to human purpose) is derived from, and is unthinkable apart from, its enormously destructive intention. After all, the site of his construction was in his reader's mind, and Nietzsche, from first to last, remained scrupulously attentive to that mind's possible capacities, contents, and limits.[35]

It might be possible to extract a positive philosophical teaching out of these late fragments, but as I hope is becoming increasingly apparent, it is not even a foregone conclusion that Nietzsche himself believed, or needed to believe, whatever he wrote. There is a sense in which his beliefs were experimental, or better yet, theatrical; he liked to try on a concept as one would an article of clothing, without giving oneself entirely over to it ("I favor any *skepsis* to which I may reply: 'Let us try it!' [*Versuchen wir's!*]" *GS*, 51). We might recall that his "Attempt at a Self-Criticism" was equally an experiment, a *Versuch*. Not truth and falsehood, but experiment and compulsion form the boundaries of the domain within which Nietzsche's thought roams restlessly—most often, by making vagabond incursions into the less daring, less aggressively self-reflective boundaries of his readership. It is, above all, a thinking without erasure.

This last point cannot be overstressed. Compare another entry from *The Gay Science*:

> *The consciousness of appearance.*—How wonderful and new and yet how gruesome and ironic I find my position vis-à-vis the whole of existence in the light of my insight! I have discovered for myself that the human and animal past, indeed the whole primal age and past of all sentient being, continues in me to invent, to love, to hate, and to infer. I suddenly woke up in the midst of this dream, but only to the consciousness that *I am dreaming and that I must go on dreaming* lest I perish—as a somnambulist must go on dreaming lest he fall. (*GS*, 54; emphasis added)

Much could be said about this passage, but only one point needs making here—namely, that appearance continues to function as a live and active category even once it has been discredited ("No shadow of a right remains to speak . . . of *appearance*" [*WP*, 567]; but cf. already *HA*, I:16–20). Appearances are the diet of our perceptions, whatever their actual status may be argued to be. Even when "appearance" is a nonfunctional contrast to "essence," whether in Nietzsche's putative rejection of the distinction or in dreams, it lingers and haunts, and we are enjoined to "go on dreaming" so that we may go on "prolonging the earthly dance."

It is because of our frailty that we can experience the world only as appearance. For the same reason, no amount of logic or rationality can dispel the peculiar sensation and grip of this experience: "Appearance is for me that which lives and is effective and goes so far in its self-mockery that it makes me feel that this is appearance and will-o'-the-wisp and a dance of spirits and nothing more" (*GS*, 55). So the lesson of the later writings is also a rule of thumb for their interpretation: talk of appearance is not necessarily a sign of a metaphysical stance in favor of or against appearance, nor is the framing of appearance within some contrast necessarily a sign that the contrasted item (chaos, nothing, primary urges) reflects a metaphysical commitment. Nietzsche acknowledges in us something like what I earlier called metaphysical recidivism: no conceptual models can be purged clean, because no ideas are free of prior associations and habits, while metaphysical habits are simply the habits of thought itself, for "humans have always been philosophers" (*WP*, 570).[36] And, as if to advertise this point, Nietzsche deploys his own thought in a highly wrought staging of scenarios, voices, and stylizations that are so multiply overdetermined as to produce a dialogical echo-effect and an internal dissonance within his writings. His style of philosophical exposition is best described as theatrical or ventriloquistic. It is an ongoing dramatization, an agon, a posing, and a posturing. What only adds to the fascination of Nietzsche's writings is his knowledge that he is not exempt from an identification with any of his appearances, and generally speaking he is identical with all of them.

This is why a reading like that of Maurice Blanchot, epitomizing an entire tradition of interpretations, misses out on the character of Nietzsche's style, by effacing its lines of force, as though Nietzsche were an indifferent, even innocent, spectator of his own constructions and, as is often the case, of his contradictions. Referring to Nietzsche's aphoristic style, Blanchot writes: "The language of the fragment ignores contradictions, even when it contradicts. Two fragmentary texts may be opposed, but they are only juxtaposed, one next to the other, one without relation to the other, one related to the other by this indeterminate blank space which does not separate them, does not join them, which brings them to the limit to which they point and which would be their meaning."[37] From his early essay "Homer's Contest" (1872) to his later writings, Nietzsche consistently advances the cause of self-contestatory thinking. What matters for Nietzsche is not "exclusivity" of difference (which matches the modern sense of opposition, and so too Blanchot's "neutral murmur of contradiction") but rather *inclusivity* of difference: that is the far more difficult form of internalizing opposition, because it is compromising, complicitous, and social.[38] Nietzsche, we might say, doesn't expound perspectivism, he dramatizes it. He not only critiques projections (of, say, anthropomorphic features onto the world), but practices them: his writings are their incorporated expression. Nietzsche inhabits his opposites.

Thus in *Ecce Homo* he can make the truly remarkable claim that, when all is said and done, is the only plausible claim he can make, that his description of Wagner and Wagnerism in *Wagner in Bayreuth* (though it might as well have been said of all his writings) is a complex amalgam of incompatibilities:

> The pathos of the first pages is world-historic; the *glance* which is spoken of [on the seventh page] is the actual glance of Zarathustra; Wagner, Bayreuth, the whole petty German wretchedness, is a cloud in which an endless *fata morgana* of the future is reflected. Even psychologically *all the decisive traits of my own nature are worked into that of Wagner*—the proximity to one another of the brightest and most fateful forces, the will to power as it has never been possessed by any man, the ruthless bravery in the things of the spirit, the boundless strength to learn without the will to action being thereby stifled. (*EH*, V, "The Birth of Tragedy," 4; emphasis added)

Retrospectively, Nietzsche can affirm that everything there was written in the mood of projection (of his own hopes and even character, onto Wagner) and anticipation (of his future creations, especially *Zarathustra*). "Wagner" (if not Wagner) is after all Nietzsche's creation: Nietzsche "found" Wagner, and in a sense negated him in the act of elevating him to the rank of Nietzsche's imagination (as a pedagogical "magnifying glass" [*EH*, I, "Why I Am So Wise," 7]). The result is nothing less than a crisis in proper names: "In all the psychologically decisive passages I am the only person referred to—one may ruthlessly insert my name or the word 'Zarathustra' wherever the text gives the word 'Wagner'" (*EH*, V:7; cf. ibid. III:4 for the same threat of reversibility). The massive substitution Nietzsche proposes is less absurd and less glazed with megalomania than it sounds. But it is also more complex. For the latency of critique directed against Wagner is ultimately directed as well against Nietzsche himself—not only, then, "*Contra* Wagner" but also "*Contra* Nietzsche." Nietzsche consumes everything around him, in an act of incorporation that at times resembles nothing so much as an act of martyrdom, though the gesture is destined to remain incomplete, not least of all because it is not something a reader can coherently follow. Nietzsche's "Attempt at a Self-Critique" is another such gesture that is rendered incomplete in part just because the act of incorporation with which his critique is coupled yearns to be so complete: there is nothing left to critique. This is but one aspect of Nietzsche's presentational style, *his* mode of appearance. Viewed against the ensemble of Nietzsche's critical styles, the "Attempt" is by no means Nietzsche's final word on his earlier, richly layered work.

The Complication of Appearances

Nietzsche is famously one who delights in masks (*GS*, 77). Masks are in ways a perfect metaphor for his style of philosophizing, which in turn, I would argue, is a mask for his presumed "philosophy"[1]—but what lies behind that? Masks are a surface, a disguise, they conceal, and they are easily discarded. What is more, and this is a much less well recognized feature of Nietzsche's masks, they can reveal their concealing, and even what they pretend to hide. Above all, masks promote the illusion of a hidden recess, a depth, a place "behind" or "beyond," a dimension of invisibility that cannot be rendered visible. Thus, masks give Nietzsche the opportunity to play a surface off against what it conceals, without ever betraying his passion for either the masking or the unmasking. In one sense a passionate game, in other respects the play of masks is in Nietzsche's eyes an essential ingredient in self-improvisation, self-examination, but also in self-deception. A feature of free spirits and decadent subjects alike, masks are a sign of a disavowed, all-too-human condition.

It is a basic law of optics: without masks, without the intervention of a redundant distance within oneself, so to speak, and without the benefit of a perspective on the ordinary field of view, vision risks being deficiently flat, myopic, and distortive. Appearance "appears" with deceptive simplicity, minus the complication that could potentially redeem it from itself. When it no longer appears as such, appearance begins to take on the aspect of a reality: "Without this art [of self-magnification] we would be nothing but foreground and live entirely in the spell of that perspective which makes what is closest at hand and most vulgar appear as if it were vast, and reality itself." But now thanks to this art, Nietzsche continues, we can perceive ourselves "as heroes, from a distance and, as it were, simplified and *transfigured*" (*GS*, 78; emphasis added). We will want to return to the idea of transfiguration. Clearly, appearance by itself is not sufficient to prevent its own "invariable" reduction to a metaphysical "essence" (cf. *GS*, 58). But then, what is? Nietzsche is in effect describing a double bind, through a rhetorical effort so slight that it can pass unnoticed: "unredeemed," appearances lead to naive metaphysical illusions (the disappearance of appearance into the real); "redeemed," they foster another illusion, one that is no less susceptible of being awarded metaphysical status (the disappearance of the real into appearance). At this point, the line demarcating the two kinds of illusion looks to be very fragile indeed. Nietzsche provides us with no means of distinguishing between them, although he has given us a first clue to this circular logic. Metaphysics is the "destruction" (invalidation) of appearances (*BT* §24).[2] But the generation of metaphysics takes place from within appearances themselves. This process, which Nietzsche considers both necessary and inevitable, is what I earlier called "the metaphysics of appearances."

One of the most potent destructions of appearance is thus the creative act of complicating appearance, by allowing appearance to "appear." This is what Nietzsche, in the same passage from *The Gay Science* in which he expounds the theory of self-enhancement through self-distancing, calls "the art of staging and watching ourselves" (*GS*, 78). At stake in this principle of complication is of course a theory of self-presentation; but it is also intimately bound up with the logic that governs representation generally. The compulsion "to go on dreaming" felt from within the dream is typecast in *The Birth of Tragedy* as an Apolline tendency; it is the characteristic condition of the "naive" artist: "Let us imagine the dreamer: in the midst of the illusion of the dream world and without disturbing it, he calls out to himself: 'It is a dream, I will dream on'" (§4). This bifurcation of the (artistic) self goes hand in hand with an exponentially altered potency of appearance, what Nietzsche describes as the "appearance of appearance" (as in the consciousness that I must go on dreaming): it is *der Schein des Scheins*, the moment when appearance appears as such.[3]

These creative enhancements of apparent reality in *The Birth of Tragedy* function analogously to the staging of apparent selves by way of the supplement of a distance in *The Gay Science*. Both obey the logic of "the metaphysics of appearances," which is to say that they point to the generation of metaphysics, of a perspectival distance, from within the apparitional domain. Dionysus appears, after all, only thanks to the Apollinian principle: "That he *appears* at all with such epic precision and clarity is the work of the dream-interpreter, Apollo" (§10). And the appearances of art, in the end, are "not merely [an] imitation of the reality of nature but rather *a metaphysical supplement* of the reality of nature, placed beside it for its overcoming" (§24; emphasis added). It is *appearances* that are metaphysical, while beyond them lies nothing—nothing but another appearance of something, of some metaphysical beyond, before which appearances efface themselves, like some transparent screen. Such is the "metaphysics of art" and of the "Dionysian *phenomenon [Phänomen]*," both of which are subject to the constraints of appearance and not independent of them (ibid.; emphasis added). And it is these constraints that furnish Nietzsche with his topic throughout *The Birth of Tragedy*. As I hope to show below, this complication of appearances is written into the form and structure of *The Birth of Tragedy*, into the very way in which this work appears. For now, however, it will suffice to explore in greater detail the thematic occurrence of appearances and reality there.

Anticipations: The Physiology of Dreams

We have already seen how *The Birth of Tragedy* is structured on the surface around a contrast between appearances and some underlying metaphysical reality and how this contrast is figured, respectively, by the two titular divinities of the treatise, Apollo and Dionysus. There is little point in rehearsing the well-known facts about the relationship of these two divinities, their division of roles and their corresponding art forms, and even states of mind (dream and intoxication). Suffice it to say that their separation is so complete that music and tragic myth can be said to derive, as Dionysian expressions, "from a sphere of art that lies beyond the Apollinian"; the primacy of the Dionysian is consequently claimed to be absolute, "the eternal and original artistic power that first calls the whole world of phenomena into existence" (§25). How well does this picture hold up?

On a first approach, we may begin by considering an allusion that stands out as conspicuously odd in the opening pages of *The Birth of Tragedy*, indeed in the second paragraph: namely, the appeal to a distinctively *Lucretian* and *atomistic* (which is to say eidolic and simulacral) interpretation of phenomena, whereby Nietzsche understands the whole of the apparitional domain (*Erscheinungen*), which is at the same time a "physiological" one:

> It was in dreams, says Lucretius, that the glorious divine figures first appeared to the souls of men. (§1)

Pivoting on a theory of images as atomic films (images as simulacra generated by atomic realities), this aetiology takes in its sweep the classical pantheon, and specifically the titular divinities of *The Birth of Tragedy*, Apollo and Dionysus: it names them both, quite simply, as *appearances*. The reference to the dreamy quality of divinity also exerts an undeniable pressure on the whole of the text's own appearances, which henceforth—from the very beginning of the work—stand in the unfamiliar and troubling light of a philosophical suspicion.

The natural way to allow the meanings of this passage to collude with one another also brings its overt system of contrasts into crisis. Are the text's principle referents, Apollo and Dionysus, no more than an illusion passed down from antiquity? How much credence are we to give to a Lucretian—which is to say, to an atomistic but also a fundamentally Democritean—reading of the "physiological phenomena" of "*dreams* and *intoxication*," two contrasting "art worlds" that "present a contrast analogous to that existing between the Apollinian and the Dionysian" (ibid.)? Atomistic "physiology" (the study of nature) is a critique of appearances (phenomena). On the atomistic view, Dionysus and Apollo would be just one more appearance, one more complex bundle of atomic films drawn from the limitless fund of "images" (*phantasmata*) that abound in the universe and that the mind itself generates and then shapes into idealized forms in accordance with subjective desires and acquired collective habits.

That is the picture drawn by all the atomists, starting with Democritus, who is followed with few deviations by Epicurus and then by Lucretius in the fifth book of his *De rerum natura* (early first c. B.C.E.), to which Nietzsche is alluding.[1] For Democritus, as Nietzsche is aware, inspired poets seem to be overwhelmed physiologically by the abundance of eidolic images with which their nature is gifted. What holds for uniquely gifted souls holds with even greater rigor for the common run of mankind, whose experience of divine visions in dreams is described in a handful of surviving Democritean texts.[2] These connections are made more explicitly in an aside that never found its way into the final draft of *The Birth of Tragedy*: "What might Democritus have been able to inform us about poetics, prophecy, and mysticism—he who, with his splendid Aristotelian keenness for observation and his lucidity [literally, "sobriety": *Nüchternheit*], lived in a more propitious age!" (*KSA*, 14, 54; originally from *BT* §16 and resuming notes to Nietzsche's earlier, and by now abandoned—or rather, transformed—project on Democritus).[3]

The relevant passage in Lucretius reads:

> Next, what cause spread abroad the divine powers of the gods among great nations, and filled cities with altars, and taught men to undertake sacred rites at yearly festivals, rites which are honoured to-day in great empires and at great places; whence even now there is implanted in mortals a shuddering dread, which raises new shrines of the gods over all the world, and constrains men to throng them on the holy days; of all this it is not hard to give account in words. *For indeed already the races of mortals used to perceive the glorious shapes of the gods with waking mind, and all the more in sleep with wondrous bulk of body.* To these then they would assign sense because they were seen to move their limbs, and to utter haughty sounds befitting their noble mien and ample strength. *And they gave them everlasting life* because their images came in constant stream and the form remained unchanged, and indeed above all because they thought that those endowed with such strength could not readily be vanquished by any force. They thought that they far excelled in happiness, because the fear of death never harassed any of them, and at the same time because in sleep they saw them accomplish many marvels, yet themselves not

undergo any toil. (*De rerum natura*, 5.1161–82; trans. Bailey; emphasis added)[4]

As the sequel to this passage confirms, and as Nietzsche remarks in one of his notebooks from 1867/68, Lucretius is drawing on a physiological account of religious superstition that stems from Democritus: "The gods are traced back to natural events (*Naturvorgänge*) by Democritus and *Lucretius*" (*BAW*, 4, 74).[5] Here as elsewhere, Democritus and Lucretius are for Nietzsche two closely proximate figures in the atomistic tradition, despite the distances that separate them. Both share "poetic" instincts (unlike Epicurus); they stand mutually in awe of Empedocles; and Lucretius' treatise is moreover filled with Democritus' views: "We come across Democritus' views at every moment in Lucretius. E.g., as concerns the *names of gods*."[6] One shared feature that is implicit but (so far as I know) not remarked upon by Nietzsche is the perishability of atomic images of divinity. Democritus held this view; Epicurus revised it, controversially making the gods immortal; and Lucretius defers to Epicurus on the question.[7] Still, simulacra are frail things, and of even frailer ontological status: their being perishable merely underlines this fact. A further feature they have is likewise written all over their face, as it were: they are an expression of an internal, all-too-human need. The anthropomorphism of the god-images is proof of this alone, and was taken as such in antiquity. But it is also further evidence of their perishability—just as, we might as well add, the very idea of the gods' being imperishable is a sure sign of their anthropomorphism. For the idea of the eternal is possibly the most anthropomorphic conception there is: it is the incarnation of disavowed mortality itself.[8] Needless to say, the reduction of divinity by way of atomistic natural inquiry (*physiologia*), the school position of all the major atomists (Lucretius, Epicurus, and Democritus), marks an "emancipation," not only from a shackling belief in the gods but also from an equally shackling "metaphysics" (*BAW*, 3, 334).

The core of this critique is contained in an ancient summary of Epicurus: "The idea of God's existence originated from appearances in dreams, or from the world's phenomena, but the idea of god's being everlasting and imperishable and perfect in happiness arose through a process of transition from men"—in other words, as a result of a transferential process whereby human properties were projected onto divinity.[9] How, then, can the reference to Lucretius and the allusion to atomism it contains square with a metaphysical reading of *The Birth of Tragedy*? Perhaps a better question to ask is how does the Lucretian strain subvert the metaphysically naive reading that the text also encourages?[10]

To approach an answer we must turn to the opening paragraphs of *The Birth of Tragedy*:

> We shall have gained much for the science of aesthetics, once we perceive not merely by logical inference, but with the immediate certainty of vision, that the continuous development of art is bound up with the *Apollinian* and *Dionysian* duality—just as procreation depends on the duality of the sexes, involving perpetual strife with only periodically intervening reconciliations. The terms Dionysian and Apollinian we borrow from the Greeks, who disclose to the discerning mind the profound mysteries of their view of art, not, to be sure, in concepts, but in the intensely clear figures of their gods. Through Apollo and Dionysus, the two art deities of the Greeks, we come to recognize that in the Greek world there existed a tremendous opposition. . . .

It is difficult to make straight sense of these statements, which brim over with paradox and impossibility. Some of these impossibilities have long been recognized, for instance the incongruence of the scholarly pretenses of the treatise and its attack on the limitations of scholarly knowledge—although this way of putting things leaves Nietzsche's "own" position, which may be one of exempted privilege or of undermined authority, still undiscussed. Nor is the contrast between the form and content of the writing by itself informative, in the light of so many of Nietzsche's early philological sketches and essays, which could be far more scholarly in form and as viciously hostile to the premises of scholarship as *The Birth of Tragedy*. Indeed, the attempt to discredit Nietzsche on scholarly grounds, the way Wilamowitz once tried, is a lot like knocking down an open door. Asked by a scholar for "*proof*, just a single piece of *ancient evidence*, that in reality the strange images on the *skēnē* ["stage"] were mirrored back from the magical dream of the ecstatic Dionysian chorus," Nietzsche soberly replied, as he only could: "Just how, then, should the evidence approximately read?. . . . Now the honorable reader demands that the whole problem should be disposed of with a single attestation, probably out of the mouth of Apollo himself: or would a passage from Athenaeus do just as well?"[11]

The argument from learning goes nowhere. But there are problems of a more immediate and pressing kind. In the first place, these opening lines demand that a "science of aesthetics [*aesthetische Wissenschaft*]" be perpetuated by supplementing logic with an unmediated certainty, one that comes straight from *Anschauung* ("perception," "intuition," "apprehension"). There is both a faint pleonasm to this formulation ("aesthetics" is itself already a kind of perception) and an affront to logic, but perhaps nothing that is any more disturbing than the threat posed to classical epistemology by any privileging of art, and the more so if aesthetic theory must be taken, as Nietzsche elsewhere insists that it should, as itself a form of natural science, to wit, "physiology": "Aesthetics makes sense only as natural science [*Naturwissenschaft*]: like the Apollinian and the Dionysian" (*KSA*, 7, 16[6]; 1871/72). If we seem to be going in circles, we are.

There is no point in belaboring the obvious. That Nietzsche has no intention of giving a straightforward, unmediated account of the "origins" of art, let alone a theory of aesthetics, emerges from his opening reminder that "the terms [literally, "the names"] Dionysian and

Apollinian we *borrow* from the Greeks" (§1; emphasis added) and in the ensuing chain of borrowings and the observations that are contingent upon these borrowings.[12] It is only "*through Apollo and Dionysus* [that] we come to recognize that in the Greek world there existed a tremendous opposition" between the two gods and the art-realms they oversaw (ibid.; emphasis added); hence, "our knowledge is tied to the Greeks' twin gods of art" (in a more literal rendering of this same sentence). Through a borrowed distinction and borrowed names we are to attain to a vision of the Greek world that is, evidently, illusion-free (not to say "immediate").

The perspective advertises its partiality. There is a "duplicity" (*Duplicität*) and not just "duality" to this founding opposition of Nietzsche's treatise. Soon we will be told, in a sort of commentary on the opening paragraphs, that what binds together these routes of access to a bygone vision is the "beautiful illusion [literally, the beautiful "appearance" of dream worlds [*Traumwelten*]" (§1)—dream worlds that give us the very clarity that aesthetic science requires to achieve its total perfection: "In our dreams we delight in the immediate understanding of figures; all forms speak to us; there is nothing unimportant or superfluous" (ibid.). It is this illusion that guarantees that we will penetrate not to "concepts, but [to] the intensely clear figures of their gods," or rather, "of the gods and the world they inhabit" (*Götterwelt*). If so, then what prohibits the world of the gods (*Götterwelt*) from being one such beautiful appearance (*Traumwelt*)—one more instance of "mere phantoms or dream images" (ibid.)? The answer clearly ought to be, Nothing.

The conclusion seems irresistible: Nietzsche's immediacy of vision and insight into the conditions of Greek culture and its aesthetics is controlled, indeed mediated, by those very same conditions—which are those of the dream (or appearance)—as channeled through transmitted "names" or "figures," which is to say through inherited simulacra of meaning and figuration. *The Birth of Tragedy* is itself an appearance of the birth of tragedy, glimpsed through a dreamwork and perpetuated as such, in the half-secret knowledge that to write on Greek art in this way is to indulge, knowingly, in appearances: "We still have, glimmering through [the experience of the dream], the sensation that it is an *appearance*" (ibid.). It is perhaps not quite comforting, although it is entirely within reason, to be reminded soon after that "we can speak of [the Greeks'] *dreams* only conjecturally" (§2). Nor is it assuring to know that "it was in order to be able to live that the Greeks had to create [their] gods from a most profound need" (§3). It is perfectly in keeping with Nietzsche's assumptions, however, that the Greeks, even as they dreamt their gods, should have had "an obscure feeling" that these latter were their own invention, and that as a consequence their myths contained within themselves their own ("skeptical") negation, one that expressed itself in the dark "intimation of a twilight of the gods" (§9). In a word, the Greeks knew very well that their gods were a fable, but they acted as though they believed in them just the same. Gods thus fall within the realm of disavowed knowledge, and the Greeks are exemplary in this regard. We will want to come back to this exemplification of disavowal and its significance for contemporary readers of *The Birth of Tragedy* at the end of the present study.

Nietzsche confronts us with a hard problem. We would like to make inferences about the past, but those inferences must now take on the doubtful status of a supposition, one that turns out to flirt with tautology. By what right do we infer from this well-advertised *appearance of an appearance* that it is underlain by something else that belongs not to the realm of appearance but only to reality? That reality will consist in historical fact (the actual state of affairs concerning the Greek mind), corresponding, whether in fact or by analogy, to a metaphysical substratum of some uncertain quality (which is yet to be discussed). And yet, the very cues that would authorize any such inference will also, just as persistently, render that inference no more plausible than an illusion or a dream. Is metaphysical apprehension reducible to a mere dream or illusion? In fact, metaphysics seems to result from a similar suspicion about apparent reality itself:

> Philosophical men even have a presentiment [*Vorgefühl*] that the reality in which we live and have our being is also an appearance, and that another, quite different reality lies beneath it. (§1)

Presentiments strike none too soon, however, for this presentiment is a late development in the history of mankind. This is one of the enduring themes of Nietzsche's thought. In *Beyond Good and Evil*, such presentiments are called the "prejudices of philosophers" ("at bottom it is an assumption, a hunch, a kind of 'inspiration' . . . that has been filtered and made abstract," and defended "after the fact"; *BGE*, 5). In a note from late 1872–early 1873, the habit of "striving after truth" is said to be acquired slowly over time; the inspiration, however, resides in fantasy: "Where one can know nothing true, lies are permitted. Every person lets himself be lied to continuously at night in dreams."[13]

Now, the two "drives" of the Apollinian and the Dionysian which course antagonistically throughout Hellenic prehistory "appear [*erscheinen*] coupled with each other" only at some "eventual" point in time, so as to give birth to Attic tragedy (§1). Their appearance and union is thanks to "a metaphysical miracle [*Wunderakt*] of the Hellenic 'will'" (ibid.). It would seem that it is metaphysics that eventually appears; and that the "metaphysical miracle" described is the birth of metaphysics itself. The appearance of metaphysics, pointing, profoundly, to the bottom layers of reality, the dark, sometimes vertiginous Dionysian mysteries of Nietzsche's text, would thus appear to be a myth, overwritten by a historically validating narrative. And yet, the metaphysical world only seems to exist—and seems, in order to exist—retrospectively, in the mode of "longing anticipation" (§10). This by itself should suffice to indicate how there exists a fatal tie between the historical, scientific horizons of *The Birth of Tragedy* and its metaphysical undertow. The truths that each domain can be held to contain are mutually implicated.

Nietzsche clutters his argument with telltale signs of his method, again advertising the partiality of his perspective and the patent illusoriness of his project. So, for instance: "It is the fate of every myth to creep by degrees into the narrow limits of some alleged historical reality, and to be treated by some later generation as a unique fact with historical claims" (ibid.). This reads like a sad commentary on any literal reading of *The Birth of Tragedy* that would unaccountably have to suppress this very statement, and many others like it, in order to establish an understanding of Nietzsche's project as a metaphysical and not a mythological one.[14] That Nietzsche can describe his own project as the analysis of "an elaborate historical example" (§16) not only creates a dissonance in Nietzsche's project but also reinforces its delusiveness: we are left with a project that consists in reading a succession of myths that are taken for history. To defend Nietzsche's evidence, we must rob it of its credibility. But then, "the true goal is veiled by a phantasm" (§3), and never more effectively than when the phantasm is the truth of the goal itself.

The myth that Nietzsche is citing in §10, the tale of Prometheus, is said to have been "taken over" by Dionysian truth, and it points fearsomely (but always mythically) to the potential undoing of Olympian mythology. Just as the Titans, once powerful, were overthrown by the regime of Zeus and Apollo, so too does the eventual overthrow of Olympus shine through the figure of the Titanic Prometheus: "Thus did the Delphic god interpret the Greek past" (which is to say, "the pre-Apollinian age" in which Titans were dominant) as well as the "extra-Apollinian world—that of the barbarians" (§4). What description of a "pre-" or "extra-" Apollinian world won't be controlled by Apolline exegesis? Evidently, the Dionysian is not in contradiction with Greek myth but a constitutive and essential ingredient of it: it is one way in which myth gestures toward its own evacuation and thus adds to its own urgency and vividness—always under the auspices of Apollinian appearances. And, as it happens, it is the (constitutive) revitalization of myth, when myth is on the verge of collapse, that awakens "a longing anticipation of a metaphysical world" (§10). One needn't rely on Lange's stinging (and Lucretian) critical review of classical mythology, religion, and beliefs in the opening pages of his *History of Materialism*, where it is argued that not even the Greeks beheld their Olympian gods with any genuine belief, to suspect that this "longing anticipation" of a "metaphysical world" takes on in Nietzsche's case a decidedly anthropological, if not physiological, hue.[15] The appearance of the metaphysical in Nietzsche's thinking at any moment of his career always arrives—appears—last in a sequence of events. It is the final crystallization of a delusion, the retroactive justification of a "presentment." Appearances can, indeed, be deceiving.[16]

The presentiment of a preexistent metaphysical domain is a sensation that comes belatedly: "late, very late" (*HA*, I:16). As the late Nietzsche would say,

> The metaphysical need is not the *origin* of religions, as Schopenhauer supposed, but merely a late offshoot. . . . What first led to the positing of "another world (behind, below, above)" in primeval times was not some impulse or need but an *error* in the interpretation of certain natural events and processes [*Naturvorgänge*], a failure of the intellect. (*GS*, 151)

Here, once again, Nietzsche is taking a physiological (or if you like, genealogical) approach to the question of religion and metaphysics and their derivation. Like Lucretius and Democritus, Nietzsche is addressing a dimension of reality beyond the natural world and its apparitions (*Naturvorgänge*—the very word he had used twenty years earlier in reference to the atomistic derivation of the gods and their names). This dimension, call it divinity or the sanctions of morality, is, however, plainly an invention that is modeled after false analogies to the nature of things—in other words, analogies drawn from a misreading of the nature of nature. This misreading can be ascribed, paradoxically, to an unnaturally acquired failure to be content with the nature of appearance, a failure to "stop courageously at the surface, the fold, the skin, to adore appearance, to *believe* in forms, tones, words, in the whole

Olympus of appearance" (*GS*, Pref. 4; emphasis added). But might not this later description of the Greeks, which is valid even within the frames of reference of *The Birth of Tragedy*, be even more valid still were we to concede now what Nietzsche would later ask us to concede—namely, that the depths concealed behind appearances, like the recesses within the Langean model of metaphysical appearances, are themselves just another fold of skin, a surface that is made to appear as a depth, fashioned "out" of forms, tones, and words?

If so, then it will be possible to make sense of the paradoxes of depth that can be generated out of surfaces and from an excess of surface, both here in *The Gay Science* and earlier in *The Birth of Tragedy*. "Those Greeks were superficial—*out of profundity*" (ibid.). It is odd that we might feel entitled to concede so much meaning to this much-quoted remark, as if the word "profundity" were written under erasure, tongue in cheek, half-committedly placed in italics—*and the word "superficial" were not*. Nietzsche's celebrated statement from *The Gay Science* holds with the same degree of rigor for *The Birth of Tragedy* as well, even and most especially whenever it pretends to acknowledge a dimension of depth "behind" and "beyond." Could it be that we fail to recognize its applicability out of a fashionable commitment to the superficial? Could the rules of obedience, the decorum for reading Nietzsche, be dictated by a fear of depths? Could it be that we are *superficially*—superficial?[17]

"Delicate Boundaries"

Let us begin again by considering the ways in which Nietzsche introduces the concept of a ground or region beyond appearance, which has been the source of so much suspicion among his readers. The first appearance of the metaphysical domain in *The Birth of Tragedy*, apart from those already discussed (in its appearance as a late "metaphysical miracle" of Greek culture and as a "presentiment" of an a priori condition), comes in the initial description of the tutelary god of appearance, Apollo, the "shining one," whose realm is depicted not as pure surface but as a surface in bas-relief: his is the "inner" world of fantasy and of phantasms that creates heights and depths of its own—"the *higher* truth, the perfection of these states in contrast to the incompletely intelligible everyday world, this *deep* consciousness of nature, healing and helping in sleep and dreams" (§1; emphasis added).[1] The presence of such contours within appearance suggests a fissure within it. Indeed, the complexity of Nietzsche's discourse of appearance, of phenomena that would otherwise spread out before us as a flat expanse and as literally unremarkable, is due solely to the conceptual play that occurs around this fissure or half-visible line within appearances themselves. That is the case here too, for as Nietzsche quickly interjects, "We must also include in our image of Apollo that delicate boundary [*die zarte Linie*] which the dream image must not overstep lest it have a pathological effect (in which case appearance would deceive us as if it were crude reality)" (§1).

The boundary that sets appearance off as appearance and thus constitutes it as such is a feature internal to appearance, which accordingly contains in itself that which it is "not" (assuming, of course, that appearances in some sense "are"). It is the movements across this line, the line that gives appearances their determination and releases them from it as well, that give rise to what will later be called "the Dionysian." The inclusion is necessary. Whence comes this necessity? The answer is again given by the logic of appearances. The imperative "must" of this feature of appearances marks the essence of Apollo's compulsory logic (he is likewise "imperative and mandatory," §4) and staves off, we are assured, "the wilder emotions" through "measured restraint" and restriction, by delimiting what it opposes, always from within its own domain. The line, thus drawn, contains its own excess, the excess that is internal to appearances themselves. To what extent do appearances enact this excess so as the better to be able to contain it? To what extent, in other words, is the Dionysian the invention *of the Apollinian*? The question is crucial, because it suggests something that cannot be countenanced on a reading of the Dionysian as the far extreme of any otherness, far beyond the banalities of the "crude reality [*plumpe Wirklichkeit*]" that the Apollinian principle staves off. The conditions of possibility of the Dionysian principle are located within the realm of appearances, possibly as one of their aspects (their appearances); they are not located somewhere else, in some autonomously and untouchably remote and metaphysically separable realm—for instance, in "a sphere which is beyond and prior to all appearances," as the official version of Dionysian metaphysics has it (§6; trans. mod.). I want to suggest that *The Birth of Tragedy* bears witness to the construction of such a beyond through the offices of Apollinian appearances. In other words, there is a pleat in the texture of appearance, and this pleat or fold in the skin of appearances is the constitutive factor of the metaphysical.

This is, however, but a first approximation. For what we need to trace is the route by which appearances themselves receive a metaphysical determination, out of which is born their contrast, the idea of an underlying metaphysical reality. The question toward which all of the following reflections will be tending is how the world can be conceived in the absence of any such metaphysical construction. As we shall see, this possibility, which is a purely abstract one, contains the real threat to the Apollinian/Dionysian scheme. Defending against this threat is what generates the scheme itself. As Nietzsche puts it in the passage from *Human, All Too Human* quoted earlier: "In the absence of dreams, one would have found no reason to make a division in the world." The question, though, is whether it is even possible to live without dreams. Could, in other words, the contrast between Apollo and Dionysus be a defense against the perception of the world shorn of metaphysical meaning? But this is getting ahead of ourselves.[2]

First, in order that we may have a better inkling into what it would mean to claim that the metaphysical is a pleat within the surface of appearances, we may recall what was said earlier about Lange concerning the endless recession of surfaces into a metaphysical vanishing point, and then compare a comment by Nietzsche from 1888 in which he claims that the impulse to project appearances, to generate appearance as such, qualifies as a "metaphysical" gesture in its own right—or rather as a "'metaphysical'" gesture: "The will to appearance, to illusion, to deception, to becoming and change is *deeper, more 'metaphysical,'* than the will to truth, to reality, to being" (1888; emphasis added).[3] By being all these things, appearance is at the same time and in some sense "prior" to truth, reality, and being (its "pleasures" give the premise, to which the latter's "pains" are just the "consequence"). In an adjacent note, the will to appearance is said to be "more primordial [*ursprünglicher*] and more 'metaphysical'" than the usual metaphysical suspects (viz., those just named).[4] "Metaphysics" is a site of origins; and origins under the sign of appearance are the source of appearance's complication as "'metaphysics.'" The very postulation of appearances is itself a metaphysical act. Thus, the origin of metaphysics may turn out to reside not in a primordial condition but, more trivially, in the mere thought of appearances as such. If so, the difference is not between two metaphysics but between two ways of appearing metaphysically. There is, we might say, one metaphysics, which appears to be (and in order to be) metaphysical, and another that deceptively conceals its metaphysical character as appearance in its near transparency to itself (appearance qua appearance). Their difference is illusory: each depends on the illusion of a difference from the other, which is to say their difference lies in their mode of appearance (their "*Erscheinungsweise*"),[5] in their construction and interpretation. Nietzsche is playing with the "fine line" that distinguishes these appearances of the metaphysical in *The Birth of Tragedy*. But let us follow out the logic of the entrance of the metaphysical there.

The moment of Dionysian "terror" arrives when, in Schopenhauerian terms, a cognitive failure or wandering occurs, when the principle of individuation, which is Apollo's, "collapses" (as "myth" nearly does) and gives way to another perception, to a contradiction of appearances and perhaps even to their defeasibility as such (their "exception"). It occurs "when [one] suddenly loses faith in [or "goes wrong," "goes mad," "is distracted by"] the cognitive form of phenomena" (§1; trans. mod.).[6] Just as dreams (appearance as appearance) satisfy profoundly "our innermost being, our common [deepest] ground [*der gemeinsame Untergrund*]," so too, symmetrically, do "terror" and "blissful ecstasy . . . well up from the innermost depths [*Grunde*] of man" once the strict controls of the Apollinian principle relax. Then "we steal a glimpse into the nature of the *Dionysian*" (ibid.). The Dionysian now becomes visible; it appears; and appearance disappears from view in the gap created within itself. "Depotentialized" (through a *Depotenziren*), appearance seems to be "the [mere] appearance of [mere] appearance [*Schein des Scheins*]"; it appears as such and is instantly demoted, pointing as it does to its own invalidation by "a hidden substratum," which is to say, by an untouchably remote metaphysical realm, the root of our being (§4). Primordial union and harmony are now attained: in the language of another metaphor nearby, it is "as if the veil of *māyā* had been torn aside and were now merely fluttering in tatters before the mysterious primordial unity" (§1).

And yet the phrase "as if" risks pertaining, with all its signs of rhetorical embarrassment and indulgence, not to the veil and its tatters but to the "mysterious primordial unity" that, in the present context (and indeed wherever it occurs), requires no small amount of explanation. Nietzsche nowhere explains what this unity is but merely dangles it before us as a promised return to wholeness and—what ought to set off further alarms—as a glimpse we cannot endure into a condition we can only fleetingly endure.[7] Note that the unity does not appear unless it is through the veil's intermittent fluttering: the principle of individuation may be broken, but it also persists, in the form of its tattered fragments. Nothing so far permits us to presume that such a unity could ever exist except as "glimpsed" in the way described—which is to say, in an imaginary form. Dionysus exists, after all, only as imagined in a "vision" (§8), and the same holds for his realm.[8]

No doubt the strangest feature in Nietzsche's accounts of the primal, mysterious "ground" of being (§4) is their vacillation. The "unity" of this ground (*das Ur-Eine*) is mysterious indeed: it is often described by Nietzsche as a primordial "contradiction," at times in an adjacent correcting gloss, as in "the primal unity, its pain and contradiction" (§5), or as in "the truly existent primal unity, eternally suffering and contradictory" (§4). At one point, the equation assumes depths of its own: "the primordial contradiction and primordial pain in the heart of the primordial unity" (§6). That the primordial *unity* of being should be the source of a tragic and not a joyous knowledge strains credulity by itself. That such knowledge should be knowledge of the "world-genius" (an alias for primal unity) and of his primordial pain, and that the symbolization of his pain is his "perpetual entertainment," amounting to "the comedy of art" (§5, ad fin.), brings us to the brink of some greater intrigue.[9]

Nietzsche could be broadcasting the difficulties of wrestling with a subject that passes all description and, indeed, all concepts. Difficulties, or absurdity? Presumably we are to understand that the ground of being stands in contradiction to what it grounds, but we are also to understand that it is itself in a state of "eternal contradiction."[10] Either the mysterium of being is forever and essentially riven in itself, or it is forever in contradiction with appearances and inconceivable independently of them. A third possibility, perhaps the most elusive of all, and which would seem to follow from either of the first two, is that the primordial ground just is the contradiction of appearances internal to them, that it is analogous to "that delicate boundary" which sets appearance off as appearance.[11] This manufacturing of a contradiction within appearances (eventually to be rebaptized as a metaphysical experience) would occur by means of a process of distantiation that Nietzsche calls the (naive) "demotion of appearance to appearance" (§4), the enjoyment, through a kind of relative "indifference," of appearance as pure positing, as pure appearance (appearance, as it were, for appearance's sake), and not yet as "symbol" ("as a sign of truth").[12]

Let us linger on this threshold for a moment, prior to the passage from, as it were, the naive to the sentimental. Nietzsche will want to claim that the naive condition of the artist is in reaction to a suppressed (pre)sentiment of a beyond. The question I want to press is to what extent the distantiation just described is sufficient to produce an effect of alienation that literally compels a subject to look for a metaphysical ("symbolical") dimension beyond them. Can one dream, in other words, the metaphysical redemption, or even hallucinate it? Once we've seen how far the delicate logic of appearances can take us by itself, we can turn to Nietzsche's account of what lies beyond them.

To "demote" appearance in the way described is to accentuate its character as appearance (it appears as such). It is to demarcate less a "ground" than a principle—that of individuation—that governs the behavior of appearances and describes their functional essence. This principle (or its actuation) is the source of their internal dissonance, which demarcates a boundary of awareness, "a fleeting sensation of illusion" (§1). It is the pure (if contradictory) sensation, we might say, of phenomenality itself that is felt whenever appearance appears as such. And this is productive of intoxication.

In defense of this last suggestion, it might be noted that in the essay "The Dionysian Worldview" (1870), written in one of the preliminary stages in the composition of *The Birth of Tragedy*, Nietzsche explicitly equates intoxication with the sensation of appearances as such: intoxication, as a condition, "is similar to what occurs when one dreams and simultaneously perceives the dream as dream. *So must the thrall to Dionysus be intoxicated, while simultaneously lurking behind himself as an observer*" ("DW," 555; emphasis added). That is to say, the condition of intoxication involves a double consciousness, or rather the doubling of consciousness, whereby one perception lurks "behind" the other, folded in the other. How ecstatic is the Dionysian reveler, in fact?

How much *disavowal* goes into the perception of oneself as a member of a satyr chorus (§8)?

Later in the same essay, Nietzsche makes a similar and even more striking conflation by referring to *Verklärungsrausch*, which is to say, intoxication that comes with the transfiguration of appearances (ibid., 558). Can transfiguration *produce* intoxication? We might compare a later set of notes (from 1888), in which the Apollinian characteristic is recognized to be itself a kind of *Rauschempfindung*: a tranquil, more or less classical intoxication and an enhanced feeling of power. Indeed it is the "highest" form of power. As such, intoxication can come with a perception of "extreme subtlety and splendor of color, clarity of line, nuances of tone: *distinctness*, where otherwise, under normal conditions, all distinctions are lacking."[13] The attributes of the Apollinian and Dionysian here do not so much blend together as they simply meet. In *The Birth of Tragedy* these attributes are at times polarized, but they are always mutually implicated. At any rate, appearances can be recognized as such only when we produce for ourselves the consciousness of an apparent appearance, in what we might term, after Nietzsche, a "superfoetation" (§13). A perceived incongruence results—the incongruity of perception itself.[14] Appearances are in this way made "metaphysical": they are transfigured, clarified, and idealized. The question is to what extent the metaphysical domain owes its appearance as such thanks to this fold within the surface of appearances.

To be transfigurative, appearance must first of all appear, in its constitutive excess. With its birth arrives, likewise full-born, the notion of something that underlies appearance, as its metaphysical ground (whatever lies "beyond" it): one assumption entails the other, and both are produced in an instant crisis of being. In Hegel's terms, "The supersensible is appearance qua appearance."[15] Nietzsche could easily agree, although this does not yet commit him to either a Hegelian or a Schopenhauerian position. On Nietzsche's account, the motivation to heighten appearances, virtually to *produce* them, is in part psychological, although he does not yet offer a clear model for this motivation, apart from what can be read out of the desires of the "primordial unity" ("a primordial desire for appearance"), or, more proximately and convincingly, out of the desires of the Greeks ("It was in order to be able to live that the Greeks had to create these gods from a most profound need" [§3]). However it does happen, the impulse to behold appearances accelerates the impulse to go behind them:

> For the more clearly I perceive in nature those omnipotent impulses [here: the impulses to dream and to waking reality], and in them an ardent *longing for illusion*, for redemption through illusion, the more I feel myself impelled to the metaphysical *assumption* [*Annahme*] that the truly existent primal unity, eternally suffering and contradictory, also needs the rapturous vision, the pleasurable appearance, for its continuous redemption. And we, completely wrapped up in this appearance and composed of it, are *compelled* to consider this appearance as the truly nonexistent—i.e., as a perpetual becoming in time, space, and causality—in other words, as empirical reality. *If*, for the moment, we do not consider the question of our own "reality," *if* we conceive of our empirical existence, and of that of the world in general, as a continuously manifested representation of the primal unity, we shall then have to look upon the dream *as* the appearance of appearance, hence *as* a still higher appeasement of the primordial desire for appearance. (§4; trans. mod.; emphases added)[16]

Earlier, we read how metaphysics (its presentiment) comes last in a sequence of developments (§1). Here, that same evolutionary structure is now put into a logical syntax. Metaphysics, being constitutionally iffy, is a matter of "assumption" (*Annahme*). It is a belated inference, drawn from a change in the potency of appearance (its "demotion" to appearance, when brought to its boundary conditions), and from an awakening to a second order of appearance (the appearance of appearance, a paradoxically enhanced appreciation of "depotentialized" appearances). Awakened is the assumption (as opposed to the perception) of an external source, as the logical conclusion to a series of hypotheses aimed at isolating even further, in a higher, rarefied locale, the conditions of appearance and its possibilities. As Nietzsche makes clear, direct access to this "beyond" is strictly forbidden, indeed by the very process that allows the "beyond" to appear at all:

> We looked at the drama and with penetrating eye reached its inner world of motives . . . [and] we wished to draw away [its meaning] like a curtain in order to behold the primordial image behind it. The brightest clarity of the image did not suffice us, for this seemed to wish just as much to reveal something as to conceal something. Its revelation, being like a parable, seemed to summon us to tear the veil and to uncover the mysterious background; but at the same time this all-illuminated total visibility cast a spell over the eyes and prevented them from penetrating deeper. (§24)

If we seem to be in the ambit of the celebrated contest between the two Greek painters, Zeuxis and Parrhasius, we are. Let us recall the setting. Parrhasius, having learnt that Zeuxis had painted grapes so lifelike as to attract birds to the canvass, responded in kind by drawing a picture of a curtain. When Zeuxis requested that Parrhasius draw back the curtain to reveal the painting behind it, he perceived his error and declared Parrhasius the victor: for whereas Zeuxis had only deceived birds, Parrhasius had deceived an artist.[17] The veil of *māyā* is another such curtain. "We wished to draw away [the meaning of the drama] like a curtain in order to behold the primordial image behind it"; but what draws us to the image arrests us at the surface: we are "prevented from penetrating deeper."

My account raises the question concerning the source of this movement from appearance to its appearance as such. Nietzsche's claim is that the source is the primordial contradiction of a primordial unity. Eventually, we shall see that what is contradictory is likely to be not the world but merely ourselves. But first we can pinpoint a little more plausibly the source of Nietzsche's equivocations regarding the metaphysical fundament of appearances: it is his backhanded critique of Schopenhauer.

"On Schopenhauer"

It is evident, and known, that Nietzsche not only models his metaphysics in *The Birth of Tragedy* after Schopenhauer but also significantly modifies the philosophy of his predecessor. Schopenhauer's view can be quickly sketched. He imagines a world sundered into reality (will) and appearances (representation), whereby the will, a mobile, agitated thing in itself (a "dark" and unintelligible "drive"), objectifies itself in the realm of appearances, greedy for representations and driven by its "will to life." The will's conquests over appearances are a Pyrrhic victory at best. The higher the will ascends along the scale of appearances, the more constrained by them and their contradictoriness does it feel itself to be. Casting forth illusions and ripping them open again, the will torments itself, literally "lacerating" its own substance, torn apart by its predicament, by the principle of individuation to which it must submit, and by its relentless, ever unslaked urge to life. What lies exposed, at the end of all this carnage, is a life not worth living. Hence, the pessimistic conclusion of Schopenhauerianism, its "resignationism" (in Nietzsche's term), which opens a view onto the "horror" of existence in both of its forms (as appearances and as will). The only hope for a subject is to still its desires through quietism (what Nietzsche will call a "Buddhism of the will"). But even this possibility remains a hope, a mere representation, and so too another pained expression of the indomitable and unsatisfied will.

The similarities with *The Birth of Tragedy* are obvious. But there are interesting and problematic differences. The will for Nietzsche is no longer the uncontested metaphysical foundation of the universe. In the contemporary notebooks, as we shall see in a moment, the will is generally made into an appearance, and in the place of the will Nietzsche now substitutes what he calls, departing from Schopenhauer, "the primordial unity." In *The Birth of Tragedy*, the situation is muddied even further. There, he retains both the Schopenhauerian concept and his own modifications. The will is sometimes officially Schopenhauerian (and opposed to appearances), sometimes replaced by "the primordial unity"; sometimes it is an appearance; and on one occasion it is virtually identified with "the primordial unity." Thus Nietzsche can maintain that "the 'will' longs so vehemently for . . . existence" (§3) alongside the claim that music "*appears* as will" but "cannot" be will (§6). What is most disturbing in all of this is Nietzsche's vacillating proximity to Schopenhauer: is he following Schopenhauer or revising him? When Nietzsche is not making reference to the will, he reverts to his neologisms, while the "will" drops out of view, an illusion of itself or else troublingly other than the "primordial unity" (ibid., ad fin.). In the beginning of §17 he switches terminology once again, now invoking, in close proximity, "primordial being" and "world-will." The fluctuation of this terminology in *The Birth of Tragedy* is astonishing and confusing. This might in itself be a sign that trouble is afoot with the Schopenhauerian scheme. Possibly, Nietzsche is naming the vague tendency in Schopenhauer that points mystically to "the essence [*Wesen*] of things beyond the will," but more likely he is naming Schopenhauer's own confusions about the exact location and determination of his "will."[1]

These vacillations aside, there is as I mentioned the even more troubling and regular association of "primordial unity" with "primordial contradiction" and "primordial pain," sometimes in the form of a clarifying gloss, but once clearly designating the essence of this unity ("the primordial contradiction and primordial pain *in the heart of* the primal unity," §6; emphasis added). Here, there can be no question of a contamination from Schopenhauer. By introducing "contradiction" into the heart of the Schopenhauerian conception, Nietzsche is freely embroidering on the latter's account. In all of this terminological wandering, Nietzsche is carrying over the habits of his contemporary notebook speculations in a Schopenhauerian vein. And if there Nietzsche is exploring the difficulties of expressing an ineffable metaphysical content, it seems evident that those difficulties are not so much his own as they are Schopenhauer's. Nietzsche's firm positioning of the will on the side of appearance, becoming, and representation marks in fact a breach with Schopenhauer. But the breach dates back to 1867/68, when Nietzsche wrote a short disquisition entitled "On Schopenhauer." The essay is a devastating deconstruction of the master's general doctrine, and absolutely central to Nietzsche's evolving position vis-à-vis traditional metaphysical thinking. Its conclusions are worth encapsulating briefly, especially since they are so rarely taken into account.

In this document, a mere ten printed pages, Schopenhauer's "will" is attacked for concealing its ultimate dependence on Kant's concept of the thing in itself—that is, for its pretense of absolute, and absolutely sundered, objective existence. For Schopenhauer and Kant alike, the thing in itself is, Nietzsche says, "'just a hidden category'" (p. 354). In this comment, he is leaning hard on Friedrich Ueberweg's critique of Kant (whence the quotation), but also on Lange. The thing in itself on this interpretation of it is not a metaphysical entity that lies beyond the categories of thought and representation; instead, it marks the secret reimportation of those categories back into the transcendental conditions that are supposed to exceed them. Schopenhauer's failure is double: he does not go beyond Kantianism as he boasts to have done and as "it was necessary to do"; and his will remains hopelessly entangled in the subjective categories of experience with which the will, as "thing in itself," purportedly stands in an absolute contrast. The result is "an *apparent* objectivity," clothed in subjective predicates that have been "borrowed" and "translated" from the phenomenal world and its construction ("OS," 357; emphasis added; cf. pp. 354 and 358). Nietzsche had previously raised similar objections to Democritus: the concept of the atom is an importation from the phenomenal world and a violation of the atom's presumed prephenomenal status.[2] This critique of Schopenhauer should incidentally lay to rest any doubts one might have about Nietzsche's early commitment to the concept of things in themselves.[3] But we have not yet exhausted the essay on Schopenhauer.

Chief among the predicates that Schopenhauer unwarrantedly applies to the will are not, as one might expect, time, space, and causality (the Kantian forms of subjectivity), but more deeply and devastatingly "possibility, . . . unity, eternity (i.e., timelessness), freedom (i.e., groundlessness)" (pp. 355, 358). These predicates have all been generated out of a contrast to the world of representation; indeed, the "concept of opposition," as applied to the presumed gap separating the thing in itself and its appearances, is completely "meaningless" (p. 354).[4] The will is in fact something that "never can be an object," can never be objectively free of phenomenal categories, because it requires the positing of two phenomenal worlds, the one in excess of the other: "*On such a view, a phenomenal world is placed* [or "posited," *gesetzt*] *before the phenomenal world*" (p. 359; emphasis added). This damning verdict, which may well play off a trope that is found in Lange, is strikingly reminiscent of Nietzsche's later and more familiar phrase: "The 'real world' however one has hitherto conceived it—it has always been the apparent world *once again*" (*WP*, 566).

Schopenhauer ought to have "gone beyond Kant" and beyond the concept of a thing in itself (p. 354). What Nietzsche significantly does not do in his essay is reprimand Schopenhauer for not having gone far enough in the direction of a metaphysical realm beyond—into a region of "being" that lies most rigorously beyond all opposition and all appearances, for instance into the reality of some "primordial unity" or "primordial contradiction." Rather, Nietzsche gives up on the notion of any such beyond and that of all metaphysical oppositionality too. In their place he introduces some unsettling substitutes: impossibility—of all metaphysical oppositions, of any successful metaphysics (this, as we shall see, is the fatality that Nietzsche ascribes to all conceptualizations)—and the darkness of contradiction and of self-contradiction. "Schopenhauer's system" is "perforated with contradictions" (p. 355). Once brought to the surface, these factors are driven back by Nietzsche into their source; they are made immanent to the system of Schopenhauer's philosophy and its objects, like a shadow cast by metaphysics' own self-illumination. There is a "dark contradictoriness in the region where individuation leaves off" in Schopenhauer's system, which is to say that his system exhibits a "dark drive" toward impossibility, negation, and conceptual (and even metaphysical) paralysis (p. 352). Schopenhauer failed to acknowledge this. He failed, in other words, to allow this "dark drive," which "reveals itself as world when it is brought under the apparatus of representation," to "enter into" the *principium individuationis*—that is, as an explicit feature of his causal principle.[5] But this is just what Nietzsche, in revenge, will do, as he brings Schopenhauer's philosophy, the most advanced statement on metaphysics at the time, as it were up to date, in the light of its most radical implications.

At the end of his essay, Nietzsche argues powerfully for the complete immanence of individuating intellect—the last rung of the ladder leading upward to appearances on Schopenhauer's view—to the thing in itself; these are "eternally" and indissolubly conjoined, in a virtual identity (Nietzsche writes that intellect is the thing in itself and is the will, p. 360).[6] The principle of individuation is thus *constitutive* of the contradictoriness and impossibility that the principle was designed to represent, or, in Schopenhauer's language, to "symbolize." And by the individuating intellect Nietzsche has in mind not some shadowy appearance but the human mind: the metaphysical predicates named above are "inseparably linked to our organization" (p. 358; the turn of phrase and the argument are plainly Langean). The immanence of individuation to the now rephrased Schopenhauerian system is cast, moreover, as an emphatically this-worldly, not *jenseitig*, conception, one that shows the world to exceed our grasp as much as any transcendental condition, for the simple reason that the world conceived in itself is a radical contradiction: the very idea of "the world in itself" is incoherent.

Nietzsche's final conclusion, borrowing all the rhetorical bluster and "dictatorial" poses that he so harshly criticized in Schopenhauer (cf. ibid., 356), is resoundingly firm and original. On the arguments so far presented, "the Schopenhauerian thing in itself would simultaneously be the *principium individuationis* and the ground of necessitation: in other words, the existing world," the world before our eyes (*die vorhandene Welt*) (p. 360).[7] So stated, the thing in itself *just is its* appearances, not their remote or distinct ground. It is the contradiction of the world before us as it exists, not beyond us. Better yet, the thing in itself is simply the contradiction of any attempt to construe this world. And finally, the thing in itself represents the impossibility of any transcendental metaphysics as well as "the dark drive" that impels subjects to metaphysical speculation, what elsewhere in Schopenhauer is called a "metaphysical need."[8] Nietzsche is not professing his faith in Schopenhauer's philosophical system. He is merely (if shrewdly) conjuring forth its truth—the only truth it can possibly contain. The will, so defined, can function only *per impossibilitatem*, as a negative metaphysical and transcendental possibility (p. 355). Indeed, its ultimate grounding appears to lie in its mere conceivability and (what amounts to the same thing) in its incoherence.[9]

This is the starting position of the notebook entries from two years later, in which Nietzsche appears again to be trying out Lange on Schopenhauer. But he also now adds Democritus into the mix, with remarkable results. Aggrandizing the will into a passionate primordial being (*Ur-Eines*) and deflating this in turn to the level of an atom (which is the sign of its incorporated "objectivity"), Nietzsche reveals, in a dramatic and trivializing way, the concealed subjective features of Schopenhauer's conception, such as were critiqued in the essay "On Schopenhauer." He thus paves the way for the eventual invalidation and evacuation of Schopenhauer's philosophy.[10]

Compare the following entry from 1870/71, where the thought about "a phenomenal world placed before the phenomenal world" is transposed into an atomistic reflection. Here, Schopenhauerian will is reduced to an atomistic moment of representation; the locus of the will is now literally an atom:

> The unity between intellect and the empirical world is the pre-established harmony, born in every moment and repeating itself in every smallest atom. There is no interior that doesn't correspond to some exterior.
>
> Thus, for each atom there is a corresponding *soul*. That is, everything before us is *twice* a *representation*: first as *image*, then as *image* of the *image*.[11]

Now compare Lange:

> The natural disposition of our reason induces us to make the assumption [*anzunehmen*] of an imaginary world above and beyond the world that we take in with our senses. Insofar as we make any representations of this imaginary world to ourselves whatsoever, it is a world of illusion [*eine Welt des Scheines*], a phantasm. But insofar as we see in it only the concept of the nature of things lying beyond our experience, it is more than a phantasm; for, precisely because the phenomenal world [*Erscheinungswelt*] is a product of our organization, and precisely because we can discover this fact, we must also be able to assume a world independent of the ingre-

> dients of our perceptions and categories, viz., the "intelligible world."[12]

The nature of any such reality beyond our constructions of it is heuristically available to us—that is, available to us only as an assumption. But our knowledge of it, too, is "a product of our organization," as it only can be. As we saw earlier, essences are for Lange infinitely convertible with appearances; every metaphysical depth reveals itself to be a surface ("what is essence on this level of analysis shows itself on another, in relation to a still more deeply hidden essence, to be appearance again"). Such is the natural rhythm of thought as it is driven onward, projecting and discovering for itself ever new limits, which turn out to be ever so familiar again, mere reflections of itself. Thus, as Nietzsche writes in his essay, "On Schopenhauer," "an opposition between the thing in itself and appearance cannot be demonstrated." Indeed, "the concept of opposites here is entirely meaningless"; but this doesn't prevent the concept's being "thought," or imagined, just the same (pp. 354, 355), as it inevitably will be: we are condemned to think in terms of opposites, for we can think in no other way. That is the lesson of Lange, of the earlier essay, and of the notebooks from 1870/71: in both sets of reflections by Nietzsche, Lange's system, overlaid on Schopenhauer, essentially converts Schopenhauerian depths into further surfaces, further reflections of our subjective organization.

It is this same position that startlingly underlies *The Birth of Tragedy*. And in a draft of a preface to the new edition of the work (1886), Nietzsche's position remains fundamentally unchanged:

> The opposition between a true and an apparent world is lacking here [in *The Birth of Tragedy*]: there is only One World, and this is false, cruel, contradictory, seductive, devoid of meaning. . . . A so constituted world is the true world. . . . *We have need of lies* in order to conquer this reality, this "truth," that is, in order to *live*. . . .

> The very fact that lies are necessary in order to live is itself part of the terrible and questionable character of existence. . . . (*WP*, 853, I = *KSA*, 13:11[415]; trans. mod.)[13]

In all three cases, and in Nietzsche generally, the world exists in a state of utter contradictoriness, of impure dissonance, and of resistance to any and all reductions. The world is very like the will, which now has been made to embody its opposites and thus to enjoy the uncomfortable, overcharged status of thing in itself *and* appearance. So reformed, the will is the world as representation. And there does not seem to be anything left over to occupy its former place. But of course there is a leftover that needs to be taken into account, and that leftover is the forgotten premise of this construction of the world: the (missing) subject, of which Schopenhauer and his "metaphysical need" are the first instance.

Nietzsche nowhere claims that the world just "is" in some nonmetaphysical sense. That is a judgment that is beyond his or anyone's purview to make. Undoubtedly one of the greatest sources of contradiction in "the existing world" is, however, its proneness to metaphysicalization, the fact that it cannot be faced without the shelter of metaphysical illusions (which notably include the "will" itself),[14] and that it somehow fosters these illusions, in a sweeping succession of incessant and momentary rebirths, of "worlds":

> *The projection of appearance is the artistic primordial process.*
>
> Everything that lives lives on appearances [or "illusion," *Schein*].
>
> The will belongs to appearances [*Schein*].
>
> Are we simultaneously a primordial being? . . .
>
> Pain as appearance—difficult problem! . . .
>
> The Genius is the summit, the enjoyment of the one primordial being: appearance compels the Genius into *becoming*, i.e., into the world. Every world that is born has its summit somewhere: a world is born in every moment, a world of appearances with its

> self-enjoyment in the Genius. The succession of these worlds is called causality. (*KSA*, 7:7[167])

The will is metaphysical because it is a projection, a *Vorgestelltes*, like a phantom pain:

> Is pain a representation? . . . The will is something metaphysical, it is *our representation* of the autonomous activity of the primordial gaze [lit., "visions"] (*KSA*, 7:7[148]; emphasis added)

And yet, how odd that just when Nietzsche seems to be reducing metaphysics to its representational apparatus ("our representation") he reintroduces another metaphysical instance ("the primordial gaze"). The instance of this autonomous gazing agency, whose mention is puzzling, is not, however, prior to the will or to its representation by us. Nietzsche's claim implicates in us some kind of imaginary reflection: representation is acted out before the mirror of its own projection. This imaginary other, whose presence is virtual, exceeds representation simply by occupying the point of its limit, a limit that is not metaphysically grounded but is rather implicitly at work and ineliminable in every act of representation.[15] It is in this sense, and this sense only, that representation is indelibly and inescapably "metaphysical." As Nietzsche writes later in the same notes: "Contradiction as the nature of things mirrors itself in tragic action once more. It [sc., this contradiction] produces out of itself a *metaphysical illusion*, which is what tragedy takes as its object."[16] Nietzsche is not, however, primarily describing a condition of the world. What he is describing, first and foremost, is the contradiction of the human world, the birthright and tendency of the subject to be a being that produces metaphysics out of itself—a subject that is never just human but only "all too human."

Schopenhauer's metaphysical will is another "all too human" projection and a symptom of the subject. Nietzsche's argument in "On Schopenhauer," as we saw, is directed against the coherence of the

Schopenhauerian (and by implication, Kantian) thing in itself. There, Nietzsche showed that Schopenhauer's will, "his" thing in itself, cannot be postulated without recourse to predicates drawn from the phenomenal world and from our psycho-physical "organization." Most damagingly of all, unity, eternality, and freedom (groundlessness), three of the most absolute imaginable characteristics of the will, also happen to be most embarrassingly "bound up with our organization." As a consequence, "it is utterly doubtful," Nietzsche writes (in a faithful paraphrase of Lange), "whether they have any meaning at all outside of the human sphere of cognition" ("OS," 358). This line of argument is nothing new; it signals no advance over the position that Nietzsche had assumed in his encounter with Democritus or with Kant from around the same time.[17] What gives the argument its extraordinary significance is its explicit and uninhibited application to Schopenhauer.

Nietzsche might have rested his case here with his logical refutation of the will's apriority. Instead he goes on to make a secondary argument that has interesting implications for any reading of his notebook materials from 1869 to the time of *The Birth of Tragedy*, and so too for any reading of *The Birth of Tragedy* itself. It is this second set of implications that will preoccupy us in what immediately follows.

Proof of the will's essential attachment to humanly conditioned "needs" is to be found, Nietzsche says, in the way in which Schopenhauer's will "is constantly *compelled* to make borrowings from the phenomenal world, i.e., to transfer over to itself the concepts of plurality, temporality and causality," viz., the very contraries of its alleged properties (ibid.; emphasis added). Nietzsche is not inventing here. He is partly just restating Schopenhauer, whom he earlier quotes: the will, "'this thing in itself . . . , had to *borrow the name and concept* of an object *if it was nonetheless to be conceived objectively*'" (p. 356 = *W*, 1.1, §22; Nietzsche's emphasis). The "compulsion" of the will, its blind strugglings into the world of appearances, is greater than any logical necessity and is equal only to the compulsion to metaphysics which these borrowings invariably mask. Such is the "ruse" of metaphysical philosophizing, which "secretly removes from view" its own transcendental premises and hands over to the subject only phenomenal ones in the guise of their opposite (p. 357). Nietzsche's point is not just that the will would not avail itself of phenomenal properties were it to hold true to the nonphenomenal and a priori conditions of its being. The point is not that these borrowings are illicit or illegitimate (or, as it were, mere metaphors), or that they vitiate the will: the will is *eo ipso* incoherent, Nietzsche finds, just on its (illegitimate) definition as a priori eternal, uncaused, one, etc. But what Nietzsche is driving at is far more insidious than a mere refutation. His point is that Schopenhauer's descriptive account of the will's day-to-day activities is in effect a dramatization of the ways in which the very concept of the will as an objective reality is incoherent: describing the will's habitual phenomenal borrowings, Schopenhauer is tacitly, and willy-nilly, "naming" the fatal flaw in his conception, which is to say, the role played by the idea and the language of appearances in the initial, baptismal definition of the will. The will is already contaminated by such borrowings, even before it begins to stir; its activities are merely exemplifications of this primary contradiction (pp. 356–58). In Schopenhauer, the will's activities function only to "conceal" the logical misstep that enables the will's constitution and that loans it—in Nietzsche's caustic language—its "*apparent* objectivity" (p. 357; emphasis added). In Nietzsche's hands, this concealment turns into an ongoing revelation.

What this means is that for Nietzsche the "narrative" dimension of the will, the retailing of its evolution through successive stages of objectivation, can be read differently, as containing and exhibiting the logical structure of the will's definition, or rather the logical flaws of that structure, its utter "failure" ("Der Versuch ist mißlungen," p. 352). And the possibility of such a reading obeys a necessity that Schopenhauer is powerless to control: his "contradictions" are "scarcely avoidable" (p. 356). Spotting the logical "gaps" that "riddle" Schopenhauer's philosophical system, Nietzsche turns the entire issue around by reconceiving the narrative of the will as a narrative, virtually an allegory, of Schopenhauer's system and its flaws. He notices and complains, for instance, that in the will's coursings, its "earliest, primordial determinations as a thing in itself are all but lost to memory" (p. 359). The will behaves like a thing in this world, and "forgets" that it is at bottom not of this world, but only something that exists in itself, in a realm apart. Consequently, "wherever this memory intervenes again, it only serves to bring to the harsh light of day this utter contradiction" between the will's putative origins and its only discernible activities—including its primary activity, existence (ibid.). On Nietzsche's reading, Schopenhauer's system knows and denies its own flaws, and it occasionally betrays itself, as it were against its own best intentions. With "On Schopenhauer," Nietzsche has done more than carry out a philosophical refutation. He has sketched the unconscious memory of a philosophical system.

Attacking the logical structure of the will and the "history" of its evolution (its structure of "forgetting"), Nietzsche can take on Schopenhauer from several sides at once. His critique is more than a philosophical one; it is an imaginative rendering, in *dramatic* form, of Schopenhauer's philosophy and its immanent critical weaknesses. This move is of capital importance. I believe it will prove to be Nietzsche's hallmark maneuver in all of his philosophizing to come. And as we shall see, it is inscribed into his narrative of the birth of tragedy as well. All the faculties of Schopenhauer's system and their histories thus start their life in an original contradiction of logic, which their subsequent activity (to Nietzsche's mind) only serves to make vivid. The will, as constructed by Schopenhauer, is in itself an absurd contradiction in terms. Nietzsche's supplement, both here and in the notebooks from 1870/71, makes Schopenhauer's logical preconditions coeval with their later history; their points of departure are merely hypothetical back-projections, as unreachable in the "past" as they are unfathomable in the "present." In the immediate sequel, Nietzsche goes on to illustrate this insight with a critique of a Schopenhauerian thought-experiment about prehistory (*Urzeiten*). The argument is worth turning to briefly, because it forecasts Nietzsche's model of genealogy to come.

At one point in his *Paralipomena and Parerga*, Schopenhauer raises a teasing question about the existence of the world in a hypothetical geological age prior to consciousness and intellect, a thought that leaves the status of the will somewhat uncertain: its existence must be assumed (for without the will there is no world), but in the absence of consciousness and intellect how could the will express itself (p. 359)?[18] Nietzsche takes the bottom out of the question by following it up with another: how can the will even have existed in some *Urzeit*, let alone have expressed itself, if there was no intellect and hence nothing to provide the conditions of space, time, and causality by which such an *Urzeit* might be triangulated? In Nietzsche's hands, the hypothetical geological *Urzeit* is transformed into the hypothetical preconditions of the will's logical definition, its "primordial determinations," and both can be simultaneously exposed as a myth that ignores its own internal contradictions. "*Either* intellect must be added as a new predicate and as eternally conjoined with the thing in itself," Nietzsche concludes, "*or there can be no intellect, because no intellect could ever come into existence*" (p. 360; emphasis added). The disjunction is misleading. Nietzsche holds both positions, because he regards Schopenhauer's system as a vast and shaky hypothesis, one that is literally "riddled" with logical gaps, out of which both possibilities flow as inescapable consequences. The intellect posited by Schopenhauer has at most a "hypothetical" existence. For the system to be consistent, intellect must be part of the substance of the will's definition. But that definition is thereby reduced not only to a hypothesis but also to an absurd contradiction. Here we have a first instance of Nietzsche's so-called genealogical method, which, as can be seen, is directed not toward the ends it is usually taken to serve (the scandals of historical revelation) but toward quite different ones—namely, the scandals of logical paradox and self-refutation. *The Birth of Tragedy* is another such genealogy, as I hope will soon become apparent.

Before returning to the metaphysical narratives of that work, there is a final point that needs to be made about Schopenhauer's conception. Nietzsche, we saw, criticizes Schopenhauer for importing phenomenal features illegitimately into his definition of the will. One of these importations is the very notion of "unity," and here Nietzsche's criticism goes to the very heart of Schopenhauer's contribution to philosophy. For as Nietzsche makes plain from the first pages of this early essay, if you subtract the Kantian inheritance from Schopenhauer, all that remains is "the one word 'will' together with its predicates" (p. 353).[19] The phrase "the one word 'will'" is in fact Schopenhauer's. It is occasioned by his boastful claim to have solved "the riddle of the world" by introducing his novel concept—indeed by uttering this single, "magical" word (p. 355).[20] Nietzsche replies, in revenge, that the will is one only *as* a word, while in every other respect it is riddled with contradictions. Its monistic pretensions, the desire to capture an essential unity of being and representation, burst the seams of the theory, which remains both monistic and dualistic and therefore essentially flawed. Not even the aesthetic construction of the will—for Schopenhauer was able to conceive of the will "only with the aid of a poetic intuition" (p. 354)—can salvage the integrity of the will. By "poetic intuition" Nietzsche intends the very garbing of the transcendental will with the categories and features of experience that involve the will in self-contradiction.

It is likely that in coining the terms "primordial unity" and "primordial being" in his notes from two years later and as resumed in *The Birth of Tragedy*, Nietzsche is advertising his difference from Schopenhauer, in line with his critique from "On Schopenhauer." Nietzsche isn't claiming to have achieved, impossibly, what no human intellect could achieve and thus to be offering a coherent glimpse into reality beyond appearances. Nor is he (equally impossibly) simply erasing the effects of his damaging critique from two years earlier. On the contrary, he is continuing that critique in a new form. In all three cases, Nietzsche is exposing the difficulties of the Schopenhauerian conception, and especially of the isolation of a will or a thing in itself on the opposite side of representation. The very *need* for appearances that the primordial unity has points *all by itself* to the absurdity of trying to indicate a nonphenomenal entity like primordial unity. This is evident in the will's objective need for self-contradiction ("When the primordial unity needs appearance, the essence of that unity is contradiction," *KSA*, 7:7[152]). Such is the will's un-Schopenhauerian need to "redeem" itself "eternally" in appearances (*BT*, §4).[21] The very vacillation of Nietzsche's vocabulary, between primordial "unity," "pain," "contradiction," "will," and "thing in itself," points to the contradictoriness at the heart of Schopenhauer's conception—as do the suggestions, witnessed in *The Birth of Tragedy* above, that the Apollinian principle of individuation is lodged at the heart of the Dionysian metaphysical fundament of reality.

"The will appears; how could it appear? Otherwise put: *whence comes the representational apparatus in which the will appears?*" ("OS," 358; emphasis added). The same question besets the notebooks two years later: "*But whence comes representation? That is the enigma.*"[22] The will is saturated with representation in Nietzsche's early critiques of Schopenhauer; and it is accordingly saturated with contradiction. Isn't "the primordial *One*" itself a product and instance—the self-contradictory hypostasis—of the principle of *individuation*? That was Nietzsche's earliest position in "On Schopenhauer." It is also the position around which he generates his philosophical puzzles in the notebooks from two years later. The note on the "enigma of representation" above ("*But whence comes representation?*") replies to its own question, "Naturally, [representation exists] *likewise from the very beginning*; *for it can never have come into being*" (emphasis added).[23] In his study on temporal atomism from 1873, Nietzsche writes, "A representing agency cannot 'not represent' itself, cannot represent itself away," while in his lectures on Democritus and Leucippus he states that if we "think away" the subject, the world vanishes too.[24]

What these reflections show is something about the inescapability not just of the subject but also of its idealism, which is always bound up, for Nietzsche, with the subject's infinite capacity for delusion. And that is, I believe, his position in *The Birth of Tragedy* as well. Similarly, with the equivalent, and sometimes essence-defining, description of "primordial unity" as "primordial contradiction," Nietzsche is naming the contradiction not of the world but of Schopenhauer's conception of the world, and all the painful consequences that follow from that conception. Nietzsche's rewriting of Schopenhauer, which makes of the will both a thing in itself and "simultaneously" the *principium individuationis*, merely brings to the surface this original, "primordial" contradiction in Schopenhauer's conception (its "*prōton pseudos*," p. 356).[25] What is more, beyond putting on display the faultlines of Schopenhauer's conception, Nietzsche at the same time effectively names Schopenhauer's disavowal of them as well. Schopenhauer knows perfectly well that his system overreaches itself: "Our entire cognition and understanding is bound up with the forms [of our intellect]," viz., the logic of temporality, of cause and effect, in short, with "the principle of sufficient reason" and the laws of representation; "consequently, . . . we cannot get outside of this sphere, wherein all the possibilities of our knowledge reside" (*W* 2.2, §50). Yet he carries on as if these limits posed no obstacle to philosophy just the same. Disavowal here is, for once, perfectly *consistent* with metaphysical idealism: it is, after all, the defining feature of this form of illusion.

Hence, no doubt, Nietzsche's remark to Deussen from early 1870 that he had glimpsed "more deeply into the abysses of [Schopenhauer's] idealistic *Weltanschauung*."[26] Dionysian contradiction *is* unspeakably abysmal in nature. It is not grounded in some metaphysical beyond; it is ungrounded in the metaphysical tendencies of the human mind that Schopenhauer's will so grandiosely exemplifies. Nietzsche's earliest writings around the time of *The Birth of Tragedy*, and that work as well, have to be read as indices of a sophisticated and tactical deployment of ideas the truth of which Nietzsche simply cannot believe.

Transfiguration

The difference between appearance and its (metaphysicalized) appearance as such is entirely perspectival.[1] The name for such a transference in Nietzsche's lectures on rhetoric from 1874 would be a "metonymy" (a substitution and reversal of an effect for a cause, which yields not the effect of a cause but the effect of an effect).[2] The name he gives to it in *The Birth of Tragedy* is "transfiguration," using the example of Raphael—a favorite paradigm of Nietzsche's throughout his career, and indeed a classic example of consummate art at least since Winckelmann. Here, Nietzsche takes up Raphael's painting "The Transfiguration of Christ," a work that is said by Nietzsche to illustrate—by embodying as well as picturing—the problems we have been discussing. Let us consider his account briefly.

On its surface, through its pigment (Nietzsche claims), we can read and experience in this canvas the "demotion [lit., the "depotentializing," *das Depotenziren*] of appearance to appearance." Occupying the lower half of the frame, appropriately enough, are the despairing, the dispossessed, the bewildered and terrified disciples of Christ, who show us "the reflection of suffering, primal and eternal, the sole ground of the world." "'Appearance' [*Der 'Schein'*] here is the reflection [*Widerschein*] of eternal contradiction, the father of things" (§4). One could try to make sense of Nietzsche's analysis of the image as an illustration, or allegorization, of the genesis of Apollinian appearance: out of the depths of suffering (which are depicted) emerges a serene contemplation of the appearance of suffering (which is just the outward phenomenalization of pain). The movement is to a halo-wrapped protection from suffering, the refraction of a reflection, which in its way is incidental, because it is but the appearance of suffering as such, its mere phenomenality: "From this appearance arises, like ambrosial vapor, a new visionary world of appearances, invisible to those wrapped in the first appearance"—that is, to the bearers of suffering, whether painted on the canvas, like the soldiers unconscious of their painted battle, as described toward the end of §5, or whether to observers like ourselves, caught up in the immediacy of the reflection. This second world of appearances involves, or simply is, "a radiant floating in purest bliss, a serene contemplation beaming from wide-open eyes."

Aesthetic pleasure can thus be complex: a sublimation of phenomenal pain and pleasure, it is distinct from both. Alternatively, Nietzsche's analysis shows the mysterious generation of ambrosial appearance not out of the depths of suffering but out of the surface of appearances: "*From this appearance arises . . . a new visionary world of appearances*" (emphasis added). This is the apprehension of another painting imaged within the painting (as it were, a world within a world),[3] only this other painting is now one without objects, because it is but the imaginary investment of paint with an inner aura (hence, it is "invisible to those wrapped in the first appearance"). The surface signifies its own aesthetic transfiguration, the transfiguring of phenomena into their pure phenomenality: a "sublime artistic symbolism," indeed. Released in the apprehension of this work is *signifiance*, the work of signifiers bathed in their own self-illumination. Their light (the painting's "light") is itself one more signifier at play, unmooring objects from their customary seat, taking light away from "light" and freeing both to groundless apparition. The resulting product is a kind of *jouissance* ("a radiant floating in purest bliss") that hovers indecisively between two kinds of phenomenality, between the appearance of appearance and the disappearance of the apparent. Paint, not pain, is the ground of the perception, before it is appropriated as an inner sensation.

It is this unbearable lightness (and lightlessness) that paves the way for a projection onto the painting of another contrast, between the phenomena and their "prephenomenal" cause. The reasons for this projection are not explicitly given, but (Nietzsche's metaphysical directives aside) they can easily be rendered as a feature within the logic of appearances and of representation itself. Out of the contradictoriness of the phenomenality of phenomena—their senseless extrapolation from appearance—the scene gives over to the imagining (transfiguring) of higher and lower realms: the "Apollinian world of beauty and its substratum, the terrible wisdom of Silenus." This giving over may have no other source than the sudden illumination of the invisible "delicate line" between appearances and their phenomenality, that excess of appearance in the light of which a shadow is thrown onto appearances and beneath them, which makes of them a *bas-relief*: this is the "wisdom" they contain, and their negation. Appearances thus entail a distortion, a disfiguration, namely their own.[4] "With his sublime gestures, [Apollo] *shows us how necessary* is the entire world of suffering, that by means of it the individual may be impelled to *produce* the redeeming vision" (ibid., emphasis added), which is precisely the sublime, Apollinian vision with which Apollo compels individuals to engender the vision that he represents, circularly.[5] Such is the logic of "aesthetic justification."

The "necessity" of suffering (its metaphysical fundament) and indeed the suffering itself are as much a product of Apollinian appearance as is the appearance of what we learn to call phenomenality: it is a lesson learned and not something disclosed in the mere transparent "reflection" of suffering. It is not mere pain but metaphysical pain, the pain that results from the effort to achieve a metaphysical truth, that Nietzsche is describing. The impulse to produce a ground or an appearance and their mutual necessity comes less from within the realm of appearances than from their complication, which is to say from a representational dilemma. The metaphysical cannot be a domain that underlies appearances because appearances are already in themselves infected with metaphysical qualities in Nietzsche's account. Nor is it evident how metaphysics could come from any other sphere than that of appearance, illusion, and dreams ("in the dream world of a Dionysian intoxication," §15). When the "Dionysian-artist" "feels himself a god, he himself now walks about enchanted, in ecstasy, like the gods he saw walking in his *dreams*" (§1; emphasis added). The pathological step is taken; the fine line that defines appearance as appearance is transgressed; but the transgression takes place within the phenomenal limits of appearance. And yet, this is just what a "metaphysical" reading, a reading that posits an absolute independency for the ground of appearances, even in their groundlessness, will not permit. Nietzsche, however, disappoints all attempts to locate any such realm except in the mode of a relation, which complicates either half of any purported metaphysical divide so as to render both halves problematic: appearances are rendered "'metaphysical,'" while Dionysus, as Nietzsche would later put it in his "Attempt at a Self-Criticism," is rendered "one more *question mark*."[6]

Beyond Metaphysics—To Its Banality

Nietzsche continually invites us to see "the eternal core of things, the thing-in-itself" in what Dionysus reveals, in contrast to the world of appearances. But each time, the contrast turns out to be difficult to sustain and it is replaced by what more closely resembles a "duplicity" than a stark opposition, a complicitous relation (the "primordial *relationship* between the thing-in-itself and appearance," §8), which Nietzsche habitually figures as a contradiction (the "primordial *contradiction* that is concealed *in things*," §9; emphasis added). Might not the basic contradiction lie in the representation of contradiction as metaphysically primordial? So viewed, the fabric of Nietzsche's assertions subtly dissolves.[1] It may be that music and myth can be said to derive, as Dionysian expressions, "from a sphere of art that lies beyond the Apollinian." Consequently, the primacy of the Dionysian is claimed to be absolute, "the eternal and original artistic power that first calls the whole world of phenomena into existence" (§25). But the temporalities of this story are betrayed by another, according to which neither "drive" can exist in the other's absence, and so too, oddly but crucially, it has to be conceded that "where the Dionysian powers rise up as impetuously as we experience them now [which is to say, wherever they rise up at all], Apollo, too, must *already* have descended among us, wrapped in a cloud" (ibid.; emphasis added). But more accurately, perhaps, it is Dionysus who appears in the "frame" of the Apollinian "cloud formation" (§8). Such is the transparent "architecture" of appearances: "The form of the Greek theater recalls a lonely valley in the mountains: the architecture of the scene appears like a luminous cloud formation that the Bacchants swarming over the mountains behold from a height—like the splendid frame in which the image of Dionysus is revealed to them" (§8).

Dionysianism, when it is elevated to a position of primacy and depth, is evidently an "assumption" (*Annahme*), one that, to be sure, may bring comfort, specifically the "metaphysical comfort . . . that life is at the bottom of things, despite all the changes of appearance, indestructibly powerful and pleasurable" (§7)—to the extent that a supposition like this can be said to provide any comfort at all.

Section 18 opens with a description of the illusory comforts that such an assumption brings. It is a remarkable statement that, like so many of the examples cited previously, obstructs a straightforward reading of *The Birth of Tragedy*:

> *It is an eternal phenomenon*: the insatiable Will always finds a way to detain its creatures in life and compel them to live on, *by means of an illusion spread over things*. One is chained by the Socratic love of knowledge and the delusion of being able thereby to heal the eternal wound of existence; another is ensnared by art's seductive veil of beauty fluttering before his eyes; *still another by the metaphysical comfort that beneath the whirl of phenomena eternal life flows on indestructibly*—to say nothing of the more vulgar and almost more powerful illusions which the Will always has at hand. *These three stages of illusion* [*Illusionsstufen*] are actually designed only for the more nobly formed natures, who actually feel profoundly the weight and burden of existence, and must be *deluded* by exquisite stimulants into forgetfulness of their displeasure. *All that we call*

> *culture is made up of these stimulants*; and, according to the proportion of the ingredients, we have either a dominantly *Socratic* or *artistic* or *tragic* culture; or, if historical exemplifications are permitted, there is either an Alexandrian or a Hellenic or a Buddhistic culture. (§18; trans. mod.; all but last three emphases added)

The ideas underlying this passage are damaging to the surface assumptions of *The Birth of Tragedy*. And yet the passage is rarely looked at by readers, and then only in passing.[2] Commenting briefly on it, Paul de Man appreciates the "semantic dissonance" that it imparts to *The Birth of Tragedy* as a whole, a dissonance that is so deep that it takes the reader "beyond the text's own logic" into an endless deconstruction of the text's meanings.[3] But the passage is no departure from the text's own logic; rather, the passage is, as I hope is becoming evident, perfectly consistent with the text's self-disrupting logic. Surely there is nothing in this passage that cannot be found in Nietzsche's previous statement from §7 cited above, and to which the passage here directly alludes. And the same holds for another, still earlier statement concerning "the metaphysical assumption [*Annahme*] that the truly existent primal unity, eternally suffering and contradictory, also needs the rapturous vision, the pleasurable illusion, for its continuous redemption" (§4). The assumption covers both halves of the proposition—the postulation of a primal unity and of its redemption in appearances. Our redemption, upon glimpsing into the "eternal joy of existence" (§17), lies in the mere thought of primordial unity and its redemption. The comfort is that of metaphysics itself. Metaphysics here has the nature and structure of a belief.

It should also be apparent that the ideas underlying these passages could have been expressed at any point in Nietzsche's career. Compare a draft of the preface to the new edition, dating either from late 1887 or early 1888: "Metaphysics, morality, religion, science—in this book these things merit consideration only as various forms of lies: with their help one can have *faith* in life" (*KSA*, 13:11[415]; 193 = *WP*, 853). Metaphysics is just one more lie, one more "stimulus to life

[*Stimulans zum Leben*]." Here, there can be no question: Nietzsche is accurately rendering the contents of his earlier work, with no additions—and no intervening changes of heart either. On both occasions, his stance toward the "lie" of metaphysics is provocatively, and deliciously, equivocal. In the later text Nietzsche can claim to have pierced through the "antithesis of a real and an apparent world" (it "is lacking here: there is only *one* world, and this is false, cruel, contradictory, seductive, without meaning"). He is, however, simply restating the terrible wisdom of Silenus, with its glimpse into the reality of the "primordial unity" and its contradiction and suffering. When in another later note Nietzsche claims that beyond the agonies of individuation and "the profoundest conception of suffering" there is the deeper comfort afforded by the wisdom that "in reality, something flows on *underneath* individuals," he is repeating the metaphysical consolations of his youthful work (*KSA*, 11:26[231] = *WP*, 686; trans. mod. [1884]). These are only two further indices that Nietzsche's later thinking is more beholden to the metaphysical structures of thought than is generally acknowledged. But by the same token, at no point in his career is Nietzsche simply to be believed.[4]

Nor is the disruption caused by this text reducible to the mere formal "rhetorical" properties of Nietzsche's genetic narrative or of "literary language" (the focus of de Man's attentions), as distinct from "historical and cultural" questions. One reason is that those properties are themselves historically and culturally conditioned in Nietzsche's eyes. Indeed, it is this very conditioning that Nietzsche is putting on display in his text, through the unfolding of false narrations, misnamings, and equivocal structures of meaning that exhibit in their very performance (as in the essay "On Schopenhauer") the ineluctability of "all that we call culture." In a way strictly parallel to Raphael's *Transfiguration* (as read above), phenomenalities at different levels are played off against one another in Nietzsche's text like so many surfaces, resulting in illusory depths (*Illusionsstufen*). Here, Nietzsche poses two distinct puzzles: how can we order the three levels of illusion named above, and how can we imagine a world devoid of them? Nietzsche's answer will be that both questions are badly formed.

The "eternal phenomenon" that he sets out to describe stands superficially in contrast to the "eternal wound of existence" or to the "eternal life" flowing beneath the phenomenal "whirl." These latter ought, one should think, to be the illusions draped over "things" by a will that preexists phenomena or else protects us against a prior reality (including its own). That is what a Dionysian nature or ground of appearances ("the eternal contradiction, the father of things," §4) might be thought to be, and that is, in fact, what Nietzsche says here too. But in the phrase "it is an eternal phenomenon," "phenomenon" has an all-inclusive meaning. It refers to the repetition of appearances that include within their folds the illusory, "eternal," and prephenomenal realm, with all its wounds, contradictions, and uninterrupted flowings. And it includes the will itself, which can be said either to instigate these repetitions—or to be identical with them. However we look at it, there seems to be no getting past the phenomena, past the "weight and burden of existence," to something that exists independently of them and not as some response to them.[5] This is to say, in Nietzsche's terms, that there is no getting beyond culture and its determinations, for *culture is what the phenomena of existence are*. All distinctions within them, be they Socratic, artistic, or tragic, or (as a variant of the proofs reads) be they "theoretical," "artistic," or "metaphysical," are equally part of a cultural refraction, which is to say, of "the lie of culture" and its "illusions" (§8).[6] The "metaphysical" repetition of phenomena, which comes into view whenever appearance itself is made to appear, is just one of the phenomena of cultural repetition. The illusion of a metaphysically vital undercurrent that they create (disclose and conceal) is merely a version of the Socratic hope, but delusive in its own way, to "*correct*" phenomena. Their very apparent separation (as a world apart from appearances) is a token of this correction of phenomena. Finally, any imagined world devoid of these illusions would itself have to be the product of one of these same illusions.

It is an intriguing, if understated, aspect of Nietzsche's discussion in the passage before us that he refuses an exclusive status to any one of what we may now more readily refer to as the three instances of "cultural phenomena": culture is at bottom indifferently constituted out of all three types of "stimulus" to forgetfulness and illusion; all three are constants within all cultural formations in the West and are continuously present, even when their proportions vary. This is part of Nietzsche's fluid, if not quite continuist, view of cultural shifts: Socratic (theoretical), artistic (Apollinian), and tragic (metaphysical) formations are not incommensurable; they are simply different redistributions of elements that are present in all three states, and they are possibly just versions of each other. It is not yet clear, however, that this picture of cultural transformation is Nietzsche's final word. A tantalizing question suggests itself: what further overlaps or homologies might one expect to find between, say, the Socratic and the tragic, which elsewhere in the treatise are represented as absolute and mutually destructive polar contrasts? We will have more to add to this consideration below. But first we need to consider what it is about "the weight and burden of existence" that impels subjects to escape into the illusions of a realm beyond.

The rule of proportionality announced here, which implies a fine individuation, is less strict than might be assumed, far less precise than even Nietzsche's own remark from §25 that the "two art drives must unfold their powers in a strict proportion, according to the law of eternal justice." By "justice" we should perhaps understand a kind of "justification" and recall not only Nietzsche's famous dictum that existence is eternally justified as an aesthetic phenomenon (§5; cf. §24) but also his version of an Aeschylean "conceptual formula" that is said to be equally Apollinian and Dionysian in nature: "All that exists is just and unjust and equally justified in both" (§9, ad fin.). If Nietzsche's dictum about eternal justification seems to suggest that all three stages of illusion from above are merely aesthetic versions of each other, this claim about equal justification suggests something more. For at the bottom of the phenomenal world, which is to say prior to its interpretation by us, may lie neither an Apollinian artistry nor a Dionysian unity or contradiction, but something that is indifferently all or none of these things: not so much a Schopenhauerian indeterminacy (a Will in itself) as an underdetermined condition that may be at bottom blank and indifferent, a surd quantity or quality that is also absurd—or else simply one that is too mundane to warrant even a thought, let alone to imagine. It is one of the great unsuspected and partially hidden ironies of Nietzsche's text that the "metaphysical comfort" that cries out for a romantic interpretation ("only a romantic age could believe this," §3) is in fact a device for warding off whatever sensation most approximates to a perception of life-*un*justified, in all its blank indifference and—shall we add?—utter banality. What it defends against is not a metaphysical horror (the terrible wisdom of Silenus) but a *horror vacui*, the horror felt before the consciousness of everyday existence and its cruder, clumsier truth (*die plumpe Wirklichkeit*). This is a highly resistible assertion, to be sure. On Nietzsche's own logic, it is an assertion that no one can, in fact, accept.[7]

Nietzsche gives strong hints, for instance, that it is not in the apprehension of a Dionysian "reality" by itself that metaphysical absorption is experienced, but in the "return" from some displacement of consciousness to a normal state, in a deflationary equilibration. Such a displacement needn't be glamorized with the trappings of official *ekstasis*: it could result from the experience of dreams, from any physiological alteration, or from the sheer fact of conceptually isolating experience or appearance "as such." This is what Nietzsche would no doubt include within the category of forcing nature's secrets by resisting it unnaturally (§9), by which he means installing a contrast where there was none before, whether through incest, wisdom, or just by seeking some difference in the experience of sensation itself. Let us assume, for a moment, the existence of what later, belatedly, comes to be called a state of Dionysian rapture, "with its annihilation of the ordinary bounds and limits of existence" (§7). It is a lethal moment, literally "lethargic," because it is flooded with forgetfulness. A gulf intervenes between two realities, two states of mind, the everyday and the Dionysian: "This chasm of oblivion separates the worlds of everyday reality and of Dionysian reality" (ibid.). Eventually the felt difference, which intoxication produced, subsides. And "as soon as this everyday reality re-enters consciousness, it is experienced as such, *with nausea*" (emphasis added).

Nietzsche's subsequent description presents a picture of a pained Dionysian man, frozen, like Hamlet, into inaction by the paralyzing knowledge that day-to-day experience is inert, that action is ineffectual, "for . . . action could not change anything in the eternal nature of things." But the passage is dripping with irony, and it is increasingly impossible to separate "the *horrible* truth" that emerges from a glimpse into the Dionysian from the truth, the nauseating horror, that emerges upon the return to drab, gray-as-slate consciousness:

> Now no comfort avails any more; longing transcends a world after death, even the gods; existence is negated. . . . Conscious of the truth he has once seen, man *now* sees everywhere only the *horror* or absurdity of existence . . . ; *now* he understands the wisdom of the sylvan god, Silenus: he is *nauseated*. (§7)

Art intervenes, pours its balm on the wounds, comfort and healing are restored, and—here Nietzsche runs together the two kinds of response—"these nauseous thoughts about the horror or absurdity of existence" are converted "into notions with which one can live," whether through tragic or comic sublimation, which the satyr chorus, both primordial and obscene, can impersonate ambidextrously. The redemption here is not from an existence belied by a deeper possibility, nor is it from a world drained of all meaning, but merely from *oneself*.[8] Thus, "the Apollinian state of dreams" is a condition "in which *the world of the day* becomes veiled, and a new world, clearer, more understandable, more moving than that everyday world and yet more shadowy, presents itself to our eyes in continual rebirths" (§8, ad fin.; emphasis added). The dream-state is the state through which the world of metaphysics appears and is beheld.

Clearly, "metaphysics" is whatever stands between man and the disturbing banality of his existence. It is this banality, and not its transfiguration, that is most deserving of the epithet of metaphysical horror and that we should endeavor to read back into every account of the metaphysical offered by Nietzsche in *The Birth of Tragedy*. Metaphysical horror is the horrible presentiment that metaphysical ways out might be void of meaning and that existence without a metaphysical overlay would be insufferable; it is the intuition, which can never be direct, that the sublime sensations of art have no grounding, that redemption can never be absolute, but only partial and delusive.[9] In the face of such a prospect, "existence is negated along with its glittering *reflection* in the gods or in an immortal beyond" (§7, ad fin.; emphasis added). Isn't the Dionysian precisely the consummate form of escapism and the cleverest seduction to aesthetic illusion, in the guise of the absence of all such illusion?

An indication that it is, and a precedent for Nietzsche's *Birth of Tragedy* that has strangely been overlooked in the past, is to be found in Lange himself, whose first edition of the *History of Materialism* opens with a discussion of atomism and closes with a reflection on Dionysus:

> And when I look the changes between life and death, between swelling fullness and abrupt decline, in the face, in this way I arrive at the origin of the cult of Dionysus; and when I throw a single glance at the contrast between the highest ideal and all that is alive, I find myself in utter need of redemption. (p. 544)

Lange's irony, which brings him into such close proximity to Nietzsche, is that the very perception of fullness and decline in life is itself a metaphysical one:

> It is up to me whether I see mainly imperfection or perfection in nature, whether I project my ideas of beauty onto nature and then receive them back again in a thousandfold ways or whether I see the traces of decay, of diminution, of a struggle to the death everywhere I look. (ibid.)

Nietzsche's irony, which completes Lange's logic, is that the need for redemption is not a response to life's vicissitudes but to its barrenness, to the prospect of a life without any metaphysical redemption. And because this is not a prospect anyone can endure, it is not a prospect anyone can ever genuinely have.

This is Nietzsche's cruelest moment in *The Birth of Tragedy*, his sharpest comment on cultural intoxication: the recognition of its utter requirement, its "necessity," and the concomitant acknowledgment of its total bankruptcy. The perception of a world bereft of metaphysics is the fruit of an imaginary isolation strictly symmetrical to that of "appearance as appearance." Only here, what is imagined is the foundation of existence ungraced by the accessories of appearance or ground, which so glimpsed wavers, desperately and unfounded, in the consciousness that it, too, is a foundation without foundation, a mere appearance. Indeed, such a view of things gives a view onto "a metaphysical supplement"—the supplement, namely, *of* metaphysics ("assuming that art is not merely imitation of the reality of nature but rather a metaphysical supplement of the reality of nature, placed beside it for its overcoming," §24). To look upon this process and its voiding as a mere appearance is to look upon the transgressive "line" within appearances, their definitional crack or flaw, which in turn opens onto the greatest void of all: life without justification.

"That is your world! A world indeed!" (§9)[10]

Narrative Appearances

The generation of a deeper metaphysical meaning from within the apparitional domain has a striking parallel in the organization of Nietzsche's text and its meanings. His stance toward the banality of metaphysics and the dubieties of a tragic "birth" that always proves to be a repetition, a "rebirth," or, better yet, a "superfoetation" (§13) can be read out of the narrative structure of *The Birth of Tragedy* itself.

That structure is deceptive, inasmuch as its ostensible contents (the dogma about the reality underlying appearances) mask those contents' most obvious and hence most easily misrecognized form: their status, in turn, as illusory appearance. As I hope to show, the figure of Socrates, with his "one great Cyclops eye" (§14, ad init.) resembling in its own way "the pure, great eye of the world" (Nietzsche's name for the "primordial artist"),[1] is not only one of the elements of Nietzsche's narration but also a figure for its form, while the metaphysics that this narration purveys is unexpectedly Platonic.

How does Nietzsche's *Birth of Tragedy* appear? The model for his text, with its elaborate stagings and recessions of meaning, is not only Apollinian. It is also profoundly Socratic, as a note from 1885 wonderfully illustrates:

> I believe that the magic of Socrates was this: that he had one soul, and behind that another, and behind that another. Xenophon lay down to sleep in the foremost one, Plato in the second and then again in the third, only here Plato lay down to sleep with his own second soul. Plato is himself somebody with many recesses and foregrounds. (*KSA*, 11:34[66])

This description of Socrates or one very like it was, I believe, vividly present to Nietzsche when he wrote *The Birth of Tragedy*. Its image of structural involvement describes perhaps better than any other the pattern after which Nietzsche fashioned his argument in that text, which unfolds not in a forward progression but by involutions, within itself. The logic of Socrates' self-involutions gives, as we shall see, the logic of the contrast between the Apollinian and the Dionysian. Being bound up with the very nature of representation as it is, this logic not only furnishes Nietzsche with his theme but governs his own presentation of it as well. It is the texture of Nietzsche's self-staged artistry in his first book that needs to be put into relief if this work is to be appreciated in any of its elusive subtlety.

The remainder of this study will be a deliberately selective and partial reading of the narrative dimensions of *The Birth of Tragedy*, the goal of which will be to trace some of the ways in which Nietzsche's "impossible book" complicates its own appearances. My aim is to unravel some of the ways in which Nietzsche's strands of narrative and logic were never intended to "work" or cohere, and in this way to determine some of the "impossibility" of what remains Nietzsche's most underread and underinterpreted text. Only so can we appreciate how the work's appearances mimic and challenge—through a mixture of parody, irony, implausibility, and logical circularity—the metaphysical banalities that the work superficially conveys. *The Birth of Tragedy* may "appear" to us, but it does so groundlessly, without ever having recourse to a "metaphysical assumption" of a unity or essence that does not itself prove upon inspection to be just one more surface, a recess, a difference within appearances. This is not to deny the presence of metaphysical presuppositions in *The Birth of Tragedy*. It simply mobilizes them.

"Raving Socrates"

Poor Socrates only had a prohibiting demon; mine is a great affirmer, a demon of action, a demon of combat.

—BAUDELAIRE, "ASSOMMONS LES PAUVRES!"

The story of the death of tragedy is well known and quickly summarized. It is the account of how Euripides, under the spiritual tutelage of Socrates, himself just a magnification of forces of decline already prevalent in fifth-century Athens, infected tragedy with dialectical abstraction and inartistic pathos. The delicate cooperation of Apollinian and Dionysian forces present in high tragedy is thereby shattered. Art is escorted to the brink of the modern age (henceforth dubbed "Alexandrianism"), which, for the purposes of Nietzsche's treatise, stretches unbrokenly into the nineteenth century. The earlier contemplative ecstasy is replaced by deliberate, rational, and modern passion; and art, afflicted by scientism and withering on the vine, is in dire need of a Dionysian transfusion. Hence the call for a rebirth of tragedy out of the spirit of Greek music, whereby Wagner's *Gesamtkunstwerk* is proclaimed as awakening the hopes for a future regeneration of culture.

The terms of Nietzsche's analysis are not meant to be intuitively clear, but they strike a familiar chord in German aesthetic-cultural interpretation, whether they call to mind, from a distance, the Hellenism of Winckelmann and Humboldt (which is invoked in §20), Hölderlin's famous engagement of the ancient and modern *querelle*, or more relevantly Nietzsche's own study of ancient and modern rhythm (the "struggles" between ancient quantitative measures and the modern dynamic accent). The Dionysian, being the natural assumption of the modern sensibility and its pathological bent ("We presuppose [*setzen . . . voraus*] the Dionysian understanding"), is the only available access to the clarity of the Apollinian "image," the myth of the naive; the function of the Dionysian is to be a mere hermeneutic and symbolic—and not passional—mode, just as the Greeks used the "image" to explicate (symbolically) what was most inaccessible to themselves, Dionysian pathology: "The wisdom of Dionysus is [of the two] the more intimately familiar form for us"; it is "clear"; "the Apollinian is *what is difficult for us to understand*."[1]

Dionysus is the sign and symbol of passion, not the thing itself. He exists at the level of a representative ideal. In the two gods of Greek tragedy, accordingly, we have two faulty translations by symbols, based on two false assumptions and two idealizations. Nietzsche's logic is devastating: "*At first, both elements are not at all present* [*gar nicht vorhanden*]" (*KSA*, 7:9[10]; emphasis added; cf. *BT*, §8: "*Dionysus* was . . . not actually present at first [*nicht wahrhaft vorhanden*]"; trans. mod.). When do they appear? And could their very opposition itself be the product of a back-projection from modernity? Whatever the case may be (and we will come back to these questions), passions are for Nietzsche cultural phenomena and interpretive devices: symbolic forms of exegesis, they are aimed at cultural understanding (at the production of myth) but derived from cultural blindness (from incomprehension before the qualities of a culture's own myths).

Socrates (himself a myth) plays a pivotal and overdetermined role in this scenario, at the two ends of its spectrum. Prototypically responsible for the decay of tragedy in the fifth century, he is also the source of its imminent regeneration in the mid-nineteenth century. The "dying Socrates" at the forefront of a debased "aesthetic Socratism" is to be contrasted with a "music-practicing Socrates," the harbinger of a new cultural form (§15). He is the master of dialectical speculation, who can also be transformed through a slight shift in perspective into a "raving" and "demonic" Socrates.[2] These are the most immediate reasons why Socrates singularly stands for "the one turning point and vortex of so-called world history" (§15). No longer a person but a sequence of masks, Socrates acts as a structural hinge in Nietzsche's narrative. He is the breaking-point at which logic coils back on itself, reverses direction, or rather loses all sense of direction and narrative flow, only to be stalled in a vertiginous whirl. Socrates, we might say, is less a point of repetition than that point to which repetition can repeatedly refer itself. The greatest threat of Socrates' Socratism is in fact its endless capacity to "divert" a plot from its course (like the course of tragedy, or the unfolding of *The Birth of Tragedy*). The mask of Socrates is a principle of unmasking that can never be completely unmasked. He defies explanation, even as he embodies the impulse to intelligibility (which has its own kind of beauty) and to rational explanation. Such is Socrates' peculiar indeterminacy, which as we shall see comes from a certain overexposure of his figure as image.

Some of these complexities are contained in a brief but pithy parable in which the tragic artist and the "optimism" of Socrates are contrasted almost to the point of mutual unintelligibility and defiant illogicality:

> Whenever the truth is uncovered, the artist will always cling with rapt gaze to what still remains covering [*Hülle*] even after such uncovering; but the theoretical man enjoys and finds satisfaction

> in the discarded covering [*Hülle*] and finds the highest object of his pleasure in the process of an ever happy uncovering that succeeds through his own efforts. (§15)

It is instructive to linger over such passages, which otherwise can be deceptively transparent.[3] How well distinguished are the two types who are described here? The point is not that the artist celebrates the surface while the theoretician relishes the prospect of what lies hidden beneath. Both cling to the husk, distracted, in point of fact (whatever they may imagine themselves to be doing), from the pursuit of truth. The artist clings to the husk as concealing—thus promising, and vouchsafing—a depth ("what still remains covering"), and therefore out of allegiance to what lies or is imagined to lie below its surface. The theoretician, lost in the whirlwind of refutations that he produces, clings to the husk only insofar as it reveals further surfaces (in "an ever happy uncovering"). The two figures are joined together by default, more through an exasperation of their logical distinctness than through any essential identity. They are joined superficially, at the level of the husk, but also uncertainly. Is one the mask of the other?

This, I take it, is comparable to the deceptively simple logic of Socrates' position within the general narrative argument of *The Birth of Tragedy*, which the parable in some sense describes. There is a temptation to see realized in the figure of "Socrates"—Socrates the mythical assemblage, the mask—at times the theoretical man (which he plainly does evoke), at times the artist (the "music-practicing Socrates," which he strangely evokes, on the verge of death and in his extinction). But Socrates cannot embody the fusion of these radically opposed impulses, and neither would it suit Nietzsche's purposes to allow their differences simply to collapse into a convenient (if still troubling) identity. What Socrates can only embody is, rather, the impossibility of keeping these two stories straight, and indeed the story line(s) of *The Birth of Tragedy* itself. Always the gadfly and nuisance, Socrates becomes, in Nietzsche's hands, "Socrates," a difficult hinge and a narrative aporia—a Socratic question elevated to the level of a narrative crisis.

What makes this "Socrates" so infuriatingly difficult is that he is what *The Birth of Tragedy* increasingly comes to see itself as being about. The crisis this entails is one of identities that are perpetually folding in upon themselves, as in the parable of the cave-like souls cited earlier ("with many recesses and foregrounds"). Socrates, then, is not merely, as Nietzsche says, the "annihilation" of myth (§17). He is myth-*abîmé*, a destruction of myth by myth—which is to say, of myth's "ideality" (ibid.), which is what had always defined myth's reality from time immemorial. With Socrates' identity thus splintered into fragments and rendered an abyss (a "vortex"), tragedy's death could easily have occurred long before Socrates came on the scene to witness it. Tragedy had always exerted a fastidious fascination with being in control of death. Being prone to mythical forms of violence (and above all, to a controlled violence against myth) was the condition of its "unconscious metaphysics" (§23). Socrates is the emblem for the surfacing of this metaphysics again, only now in a *conscious* form. But even this account is partial, as it falls all too easily within the clear outlines of the myth of Socrates' irreplaceable individuality.

We have yet to penetrate to the heart of the Socratic myth. Amidst his several guises in Nietzsche's fiction, and perhaps preeminent among them, Socrates is conspicuously a Platonic character in a hybrid poetic form, the Platonic dialogue. Thus, to arrive at the terminus that Socrates is from within Plato means unpacking the multiple layerings of artistic creation that compose him, the narrative frames that radiate out in levels of embedded discourse, and the inset temporal recesses concealing, somewhere beneath all the folds and the husks, the historical Socrates, like some marvelous fruit.[4] A good instance of this embeddedness is Plato's *Symposium*, a dialogue that exhibits all of these formally distantiating features in a paradigmatic way.[5] We will want to come back to the details of this dialogue shortly, but there are additional considerations of a more general kind. Take the very hybrid nature of the Platonic dialogue-form itself, which, being "a mixture of all extant styles and forms, hovers midway between narrative, lyric, and drama, between prose and poetry, and so has also broken the strict old law of the unity of linguistic form" (§14). The Platonic Socrates is himself a hybrid, a centauric form, and as such he is at home in those anonymous genres that baffled literary classification even in Aristotle's day. In the *Poetics*, which is in so many respects the classical model for Nietzsche's treatise on tragedy, Aristotle with some deviousness arrays the "Socratic dialogues" alongside the mimes of Sophron as examples of generic literature without generic classification. Shortly afterward, Chaeremon's *Centaur*, a drama in mixed meters, is adduced as another instance of the same (*Poetics*, ch. 1). It is difficult not to imagine that Nietzsche had this portion of the *Poetics* in mind when he described the birth pangs associated with "Socrates and Greek Tragedy" (a precursor to *The Birth of Tragedy*): "Art and philosophy are growing together in me to such an extent that I will inevitably give birth to centaurs some day" (letter to Rohde, 15 February 1870).[6]

Socrates is evidently a symptom of literary indecision—and of a literary kind of criticism. His condition is purely symptomatic. So conceived, he is also the sign of the heterogeneity that all classical materials from Homer onward exhibit and of the philology that strives to encompass them in their essential classicalness. It is thus no coincidence that Nietzsche had deployed the image of the centaur to capture the multiple and divided essence of the discipline of philology in 1869 in his essay "Homer and Classical Philology." In particular, philology is "centauric" by virtue of its peculiar mix of "basic drives," which are part artistic, part scientific, and part historical.[7] Thus too, Nietzsche could write, anticipating his later work, "Science [e.g., scholarship] has in common with art that the most day-to-day affairs appear to it completely new and attractive, as if through the power of a spell they were just born and experienced now for the first time. *Life is worth being lived, says art, the most beautiful seducer; life is worth being understood, says science*."[8]

It is out of these strictly speaking poetic considerations that Nietzsche makes so great a fuss about the careful positioning of Socrates in his work, Socrates who is never Socrates alone but always "the Socratic tendency," and as such inseparable from his role as "dialectical hero" of the Platonic dialogues. It is significant that Nietzsche takes no pains to distinguish this Socrates from Socrates as portrayed through other hybridizations of fiction and reality, whether in Aristophanes, in the anecdotal literature from antiquity (as in Diogenes Laertius), or in his persistence in the Cynic traditions as another sort of "literary image" (§14).[9] Far from offering a competing "image" of Socrates, Plato provides us with its archetype. Nietzsche compresses this complex amalgam into a striking image of his own (although the basis of the conceit is to be found in the Romantic philosopher Friedrich Schlegel), which gives Plato's dialogues as the "barge on which the shipwrecked ancient poetry saved herself with all her children . . . crowded into a narrow space and timidly submitting to the single pilot, Socrates" (§14).[10] Socrates' position at the helm is not an expression of a Romantic aesthetics, nor is it an expression of self-effacing humility on the part of Plato. The image is far more involved than either of these alternatives. Nietzsche means for *Socrates* to be steering Plato's dialogues (and the *disiecta membra* of Greek literature), because there is a driving compulsion within him that masters Plato, even as Plato "writes" Socrates, "under the pressure of the *demonic* Socrates" (ibid.; emphasis added). Plato, too, submits to an image of Socrates, compelled by it to utter obedience, only to become *Socrates'* "work of art": "Plato," Nietzsche writes in a contemporary notebook, "is a Socratic work of art."[11] Just what this compulsion amounts to is given a page earlier: it is "the enormous driving-wheel of logical Socratism" that is "in motion, as it were, *behind* Socrates" and that "must be viewed through Socrates as through a shadow" (§13).

The Platonism of *The Birth of Tragedy*

We might rest content with having located, finally, the "key" to Socrates' character, his *daimonion*, or critical instinct, which, apparently driven *to* reason, nonetheless is driven *by* an urge that "in its unbridled flood . . . displays a natural power such as we encounter to our awed amazement only in the very greatest instinctive forces" (§13). It may be suspected, on the grounds of this quotation alone, that Socrates, to whom all irrational impulses are denied, is in fact being swept up by some greater force of irrationality. But here Nietzsche reverses our formula and makes it more precise: Socrates, while driven *by* reason, and perhaps *because* he is so driven by it, is compelled *to* irrationality.

This begins to explain the irony of Plato's project, which, dismissing art (and its metaphysics), ends up reinventing "by a detour" what he had set out to dismiss, through a transcendence of reality and an attempt "to represent the idea which underlies this pseudo-reality" (§14) by means of myth, dialogue, and dramatic forms (including tragedy itself). The thought of this association of philosophy and art, announced here in §14, is at once compelling and disturbing. In condemning art, Plato falls back on his wealth of artistic resources. An infection sets in. The formal return to art, the detour, takes place deeply within the very conception of Platonic Ideas (Forms): "Thus, Plato, *the thinker*, arrived by a detour where he had always been at home *as a poet* [prior to destroying his poems in a pious act of submission to Socrates]—at the point from which Sophocles and the older art protested solemnly against that objection [to art's validity of purpose]" (§14; emphasis added). The detour and return to art, as we shall see, is also a return to a prior, Dionysian metaphysics, or rather it constitutes a rejoining of that metaphysics, but now in a Platonic form. Is Plato's metaphysics secretly, or even openly, a *prolongation* of the Dionysian artist's metaphysics? Has Nietzsche been giving a *Platonic* interpretation of the Dionysian all along?

Platonism is, of course, hardly what Nietzsche himself can be expected to recommend when he advances the notion of a metaphysical, Dionysian *Jenseits*—or rather, we should say, the pre-Platonic "Platonism" of Socrates, since it is Socrates who propels Plato to the limits of reason. But consider the early part of §10, now in the light of

§14. Described are the repeated apparitions ("masks") of the "original" (in the metaphysical sense of originary, *ursprünglich*) god Dionysus, who can be seen glimmering through the Greek tragic heroes (Prometheus, Oedipus, etc.). The language is familiar from above: Dionysus, we might say, wells up through the mediating power of Apollinian appearances; his essential being is individuated, particularized, just by taking on a palpable, spectacular presence; and this "presencing" of godhead is by itself "tragic" (with the pain of individuation being enacted before the eyes of the audience). "It would follow that the Greeks simply *could* not suffer individuals on the tragic stage." So far, Nietzsche appears to be subscribing to Schopenhauerian pessimism, by retailing the story of the will's painful self-objectification through representation, individuation, and phenomenalization ("the Apollinian appearances in which Dionysus objectifies himself," §8, ad fin.). Dramatizing this process, and especially locating its drama in tragedy, also happens to fall in line with Schopenhauer's aesthetic preferences (favoring the *Trauerspiel* for its occupying the "zenith" of poetic artistry).[1] But now Nietzsche gives a slightly different, less Schopenhauerian (one might also have called it Hegelian),[2] analysis of the same process; and in general, Nietzsche's attitude to Schopenhauer is most accurately captured by his own explicit statement about him in *The Birth of Tragedy*: "I cannot follow him," (§5):

> Behind all these masks there is a deity; that is one essential reason for the *typical* "*ideality*" of these famous figures which has caused so much astonishment. (§10; emphasis added)

Such "ideality" ought to continue to cause us astonishment, because now Nietzsche is arguing for the essentially (and rootedly) *Platonic* character of Greek tragic drama and its "Dionysian" metaphysics. Further:

> The Platonic distinction and evaluation of the 'Idea' [sc., Form] in contrast to the 'idol,' the mere copy [*Abbild*], is very deeply

> grounded in the Hellenic character [*im hellenischen Wesen*]. (ibid.; trans. mod.)

For a moment Nietzsche continues in the same vein, before picking up again the abandoned language of agony and individuation:

> *Using Plato's terminology* we should have to speak of the tragic figures of the Hellenic stage somewhat as follows: the one truly real [*der eine wahrhaft reale*] Dionysus appears in a variety of forms. . . . (ibid.; trans. mod.; emphasis added)

Quite apart from the question of Schopenhauer and his relevance, the upshot of these passages ought to be plain: *Dionysus is nothing less than a Platonic form* (audible in "the one truly real" is the Greek *to ontōs on*), manifesting itself in the phenomenal world of particulars; and this Platonism is "very deeply" imbued in the Hellenic character, stamping it and all its cultural expressions indelibly. But even here Nietzsche is capitalizing on a characteristic trait of Schopenhauer's philosophy, which in fact brings together, in an obscure and incoherent fashion, Kant's "thing in itself" with "the eternal ideas" of Plato. The latter crucially mediate, by "stages," the former, thereby furnishing the "immediate and therefore adequate objectivity [*Objektität*]" of the will, viz., of the thing in itself (*W*, 1.1., §§31–32).[3] This ought to bear on the puzzling claims about the mediated character of "immediacy" raised at the outset of *The Birth of Tragedy*—concerning, that is, the vision by which we may be said today to grasp, "with the immediate certainty of vision," the phenomena and especially the "nonimagistic" Dionysianism of ancient Greece (§1). But it raises even greater difficulties for Nietzsche's alleged Schopenhauerianism, given the out and out critique of Platonism, and a fortiori (one should expect) the critique of any Platonizing interpretation of Greek culture, which we now can see lies at the heart of Nietzsche's text. How can Nietzsche both underwrite Schopenhauer's Platonism *and* undermine the Platonic Ideas—and especially their single greatest embodiment, Socrates? But the question is misphrased: Nietzsche does not actually refute Platonic metaphysics; he merely turns it on its head.[4] "My philosophy," he famously proclaims in a notebook, "[is] *inverted Platonism*: the further away from the truly existent [we stand], the purer, the more beautiful, and the better. Life in appearance as goal" (1870/71).[5] To what extent is Nietzsche's analysis of Greek culture, *qua* "Hellenic *Wesen*," itself an idealizing reduction of that culture, and to that extent *Platonic*?

These questions have strangely been elided or simply gone unasked in the literature on Nietzsche, but prima facie there is no easy way to contain the damage of their implications. Draping his arguments with a Schopenhauerian veneer, Nietzsche appears at the very same time to be demolishing, less by argument than by fatal association, the logical linchpin linking (and separating) *Wille* and *Vorstellung*—namely, the formal category of the Platonic "Idea." It would be all too convenient to try to salvage Plato's Ideas (and Schopenhauer's too) and to throw Plato away on the pretext that Plato is but a misguided instance of Platonism.[6] As we shall see shortly, Nietzsche has other, more unpalatable lessons in mind. For the very dissolution of the tragic form will testify to the untenability not of tragedy but of Platonism itself, while the resurgence of the tragic spirit in modernity, or rather the mere presence in modernity of this myth about antiquity and its "rebirth" today, attests to the urgency and the necessity of metaphysics, which is to say, to its unhinderable recidivism.

As for the association of Platonism with Greek culture, or more accurately, with the *idea* of Greek culture, what Nietzsche in his contemporary notes refers to as "the deepest affinity of Socrates with the Platonic Idea of the Hellenic" and what in his notebooks from 1885 he refers to again as a collection of "ghostly Forms,"[7] this is a problem that remains to be explored in Nietzsche's text. Plato, after all, is "the *typical* Hellenic youth," as Nietzsche himself says, with a teasing, paradoxical pun on the Platonic vocabulary for Forms (§14; emphasis added), recalling an earlier play on words, "typical 'ideality'" (§10).[8] Given Nietzsche's description of Hellenic culture as indelibly Platonic, Plato's "detour" has in fact to be seen a "return" to the same in the sense that it was a return *of* the same; and it is difficult in fact to see how Plato ever represented a genuine departure from essential Greekness. That is one problem of a peculiar narrative kind. But there are others.

In the light of the above, we might well be wondering about the precise roles of Apollo and Dionysus in all of this. Nietzsche's answer is again Platonic. Apollo, as the principle of appearance and of individuation, is that which grants appearance to the Dionysian Form: "That [Dionysus] *appears* at all with such epic precision and clarity is the work of the dream-interpreter, Apollo" (ibid.). His appearances are at best instances of "typical 'ideality,'" epiphanies of the "'idea'" or "'idol,'" mere masks and after-images (*Abbild*[*er*]). To "appear" Dionysus must take on a form. His epiphany is in fact but the form ("variety") of a form. Being one, he becomes "many" (a *Vielheit*). And the form he takes on is given by yet another form—the very *form of appearance*, that of Apollo. The question that remains is whether Dionysus is anything other than the idea of his appearance. The answer would seem to be an emphatic No.

A sentence from a fair-copy ms. from 1871, apparently edited out in the final stage, confirms what the text already suggests. In essence, "the Apollinian is nothing other than *the Idea of appearance* itself"; Dionysus, for his part, is "*the Idea that alone has true reality* [sc., "that is, in the Platonic sense," Nietzsche adds a little later in the same excerpt] and attains appearance only in the masks [of tragedy]" (emphasis added). So intent was Nietzsche on showing the underlying compatibility between Platonic and tragic metaphysics, or rather the applicability of the one to the other, that in the excised passage he actually worked out a complicated and far-reaching, if not far-fetched, scenario—confessedly translated into Platonese ("*nach der platonischen Terminologie*")—in which two Platonic Ideas, the Idea of reality (Dionysus) and that of appearance (Apollo), conjointly give rise to a common "form-copy" (*Abbild*), in the form of the tragic mask and protagonist.[9] Following the same logic, tragedy (the fusion of the Apollinian and the Dionysian) gives the presentiment of Platonic philosophy: together, both express "a longing anticipation of a metaphysical world" (§10). So, we might say, tragedy is the anticipation of Platonism, and even of the Platonism of Socrates. For who else is brought to mind by the picture of the prostrate tragic hero, who is no individual but rather *Myth* itself, hypostasized now as a protagonist in its own right (§10), "wounded" and "dying," taken over by Dionysianism yet teeming with expectation of an afterlife, "with the philosophic calm of the dying" burning brightly in its eyes?

> This dying myth [which is to say, this dying of Myth in general] was now seized by the newborn genius of Dionysian music; and in these hands it flourished once more with colors such as it had never yet displayed, with a fragrance that awakened a longing anticipation of a metaphysical world. After this final effulgence it collapses, its leaves wither. . . . Through tragedy the myth attains its most profound content, its most expressive form; it rises once more like a wounded hero, and its whole excess of strength, together with the philosophic calm of the dying, burns in its eyes with a last powerful gleam. (§10)

Awakening a yearning for and anticipation of a metaphysical world beyond, the myth portrayed here is none other than Socrates, who in the *Phaedo*, the dialogue that narrates his death, expounds and then illustrates how one must make a profession of dying. That profession is Platonic philosophy. It is only odd that tragedy should so anticipate, with an ardent longing, its own destruction—what Nietzsche calls its "suicide"—and that this suicide should consist in its approximation to Platonism.[10]

Let us pursue this mutual anticipation (it is certainly more than a parallel). Socrates/Dionysus: the two admittedly form an unlikely conjunction. Is not Socrates the signal "opponent" of Dionysus (§12)? But the improbabilities of their conjunction are mitigated, purposefully, by the reminder that an "anti-Dionysian tendency," a "Socratic impulse," indeed a kind of "Socratism" (as Nietzsche writes in his lecture from 1870, "Socrates and Tragedy"), preexisted even Socrates (§14).[11] In his introductory lectures to the history of Greek tragedy, focused around Sophocles (1870), the same thought is expressed quite vigorously: "Greek antiquity in its higher form had the same belief in the Idea—not conceptually, but instinctively—as later became conceptualized in Plato." Greece prior to Plato was "metaphysically idealist" *avant la lettre*, or rather in a purer (if less conceptually refined) form: "here everything was referred to a higher, transcendental order of things: life no longer seemed worth living. . . . Ideality of misfortune."[12] The very notion of "tragedy" is thus itself a Platonic one ("The *tragic idea* is that of the cult of Dionysus: the dissolution of the individual into another order of things").[13] This is perhaps not a fact. Within Nietzsche's increasingly unwieldy set of framing devices, it is an assumption that must be made for reasons that are no more compelling than those that force the anticipation of a metaphysical beyond. Nonetheless, once made, the assumption dictates a logical pattern that is rigorous and unswerving, and virtually fatal to itself.

As it happens, the sources of anti-Dionysianism are to be located in Dionysiac tragedy itself. And while this holds equally for all of tragedy, it will be simplest to illustrate the point with the example of Sophocles, the tragedian who inspires Nietzsche's most memorable account of tragic knowledge: the description of Oedipus' bright blinding (§9), prior to his healing apotheosis at Colonus, a moment that itself is charged with "the terrible wisdom of Silenus," the insight into the futility of existence (§3), but also bathed in "metaphysical comfort" (§17). In a later section (§14), Sophocles is rather differently remembered, namely as an innovator in tragic form. It was Sophocles who introduced a third actor onto the stage, thus inaugurating an "un-Dionysian" trend toward character delineation (§17). Nietzsche adds in passing that Sophocles even appears to have written a theoretical "treatise" (!) to complement his praxis—out of a basic "perplexity in regard to the chorus" (whose importance Sophocles' changes would only diminish). All this goes to suggest that even in Sophocles, the pinnacle of tragic achievement and of "'Greek cheerfulness,'" "*the Dionysian basis of tragedy is beginning to break down*" (§14; emphasis added). Indeed, Nietzsche goes further and claims that with the introduction of this (Sophoclean) feature, the "character" of the chorus, now leveled to a status approaching that of the actors—which is to say, now conceived as a part of the action (and in the service, moreover, of "*dialectical solutions*" [§9]; emphasis added)—is "completely destroyed" (§14).

This is damaging testimony indeed, which shows Sophocles, the brilliant example of the tragic effect, to have been a substantial cause of its decline. (The same features of Sophocles are equally pronounced in the public lecture "Socrates and Tragedy," given in Basel in early 1870, and they are hinted at as early as 1868/69).[14] We should, however, be careful not to confuse causes with effects. The chorus is historically the emphatic "*cause*" of tragedy and of the tragic, Nietzsche holds; and Sophocles, in another inversion, "no longer dares to entrust to the chorus the main share of the effect (*Wirkung*)" (§14). If it would seem difficult to keep causes and effects separate here, it is not just because a cause can at the same time be an effect. Nietzsche's account here is parallel to that of his contemporary lectures, *Encyclopedia of Philology*. In the lectures, he observes that starting with Sophocles there is a marked turn inwards in Greek religious culture: there is a search for a "metaphysical solution" to the mysteries of life (or else to the insolubility of the rational conception of justice itself); a Beyond (*Jenseits*) looms into view for the first time; philosophical speculation surpasses religion, it is deeper; the divinities suffer "an ethical degeneracy"; "the whole of mythology becomes a phantasm and a farce, because all deeper natures satisfy their metaphysical need in the mysteries [viz., mystery cults]. The only rehabilitation available to the gods is through a general symbolization and allegorization," and so on. The passage warrants fuller quotation:

> In the midst of this religious development stand Aeschylus and Sophocles, the one looking back, the other turned towards the end to come. It is the way from the sublime to the beautiful and, finally, to the symbolic. A strong yearning for justice is in evidence in Aeschylus. . . .
>
> Aeschylus discovers sublimity in the severity of the Olympian administration of justice. Sophocles, in its *inscrutability*. He brings back the popular perspective. The enigmatic apparent unreason of fate is his tragic premise. Suffering is understood here as something that sanctifies. The gap between the divine and the human is immeasurable: pious resignation is the most appropriate response. . . . Aeschylus continuously struggles to discover justice in every appearance: Sophocles considers this region [viz., appearances] unilluminable. *Life* does not solve the riddle; he presupposes a metaphysical solution; and Oedipus, shrouded in mystery at the moment of his vanishing, gives us a hint of the only place where the solution lies. Already here we see for the first time the looming into view of a Beyond [*Jenseits*], of which the older periods down to Aeschylus knew nothing. We see how the gods of beauty and justice cannot withstand the philosophical spirit as it gains ground. The deeper conceptions go over their heads; an ethical degeneration of the divinities sets in, the whole of mythology becomes a phantasm and a pose, because all deeper natures [can] satisfy their metaphys[ical] need in the mysteries. The only rehabilitation available to the gods is through a general symbolization and allegorization. ("ECP," 415–16 n. 37)

Appearances notwithstanding, Sophocles is not especially unique: the decline of tragedy inheres in its essence. Both tragedians, Aeschylus and Sophocles alike, are caught "in the midst" of a grand "development" and represent stages in its self-realization; Euripides merely brings everything to a final fruition. With this enlarged conception of tragedy, Nietzsche is going well beyond the commonplaces of the nineteenth-century *damnatio* of Euripides, a tradition that originates with the Schlegels' revival of an Aristophanic conceit.[15] In Nietzsche's hands, this commonplace is turned inside out even as it is superficially perpetuated. The paradox for Nietzsche is that as tragedy progresses and becomes purer, it becomes more purely decadent: "Sophocles *purifies* the dramatic poem by separating off the element of reflection from action," thereby freeing up "the conceptual element" for an independent development: formerly pervading the whole tetralogy form (as in Aeschylus), reflection is now concentrated in the lyrical and musical portions of the chorus.[16] Nietzsche's account (from his lectures on Sophocles from 1870) is intricate but in keeping with the premises of *The Birth of Tragedy*: conceptuality inheres in tragedy, reflection inheres in music. Not for nothing did the Greeks honor two of the tragedians with the tradition (Nietzsche says) that Socrates, Euripides, and Sophocles were proclaimed the three "wisest of men," in that order (*BT*, §13).[17] If there seems to be no room left for unmotivated irrationality in Greek tragedy, that is right: there isn't.

Euripides, instead of subverting the art form, brings it to its logical conclusion: he performs, as it were consciously, what prior tragedy performed unawares (§12; "IST," 37). Even Aeschylus is capable of posing "philosophical problem[s]" in his tragedies (§9), while both Aeschylus' Prometheus and Sophocles' Oedipus are different masks of Dionysus (§10). The problem lies in the masking itself. To observe the essence of tragedy, we have to go back to the origins of the chorus, which in any case was never anything else than the effect of an elaborate projection—of a reveling band that projected a vision onto itself, of themselves *as satyrs* who were empowered in turn with a vision of Dionysus (§8).[18] Dionysus "was not actually present at first"; "he was merely imagined as present," although the play revolved around him exclusively, which is to say, around the present vision of an absent Dionysus (ibid.). As tragedy evolved, its essence never altered; hence the multiple, phenomenal masks of the one god, the Idea of Dionysus, as described through the Platonic terminology witnessed earlier. But the Idea of the God may turn out to be nothing other than an imaginary projection, a mere idea.[19]

Tragedy, at its core and in its "historical" foundations, is the expression of an idealism. Thus the satyr chorus is no less an expression and an effect of this idealism than is its later, tragic descendant. One need only compare the "'ideal' domain . . . in which the Greek satyr chorus was wont to dwell" (§7); or its "archetypal" satyrs, genetically tied, as a "womb," to the tragic "dialogue" (§8), which in turn forecast the Socratic dialogues; or else, quite plainly, the "idealism"of Greek culture itself: "Dionysus-cult and Apollo (idealism of the Greeks)."[20] To look upon tragic spectacle with the eyes of a satyr chorus is in a profound and idealizing way to "overlook"—in both senses of the word—"the whole world of culture" before oneself (§8). So, Sophocles' innovation is not a cause of the decline of tragedy so much as an effect of the tragic form and its ambivalently admired constitution. Euripides' final glorification of Dionysus in *The Bacchae*, fatally betraying his lifelong opposition to him, should be no less shocking a paradox (§12). The Platonism of Socrates is just another of these same manifestations, a return, by way of a detour, to the origins of tragedy. Socrates, after all, "is simultaneously Prometheus and Oedipus," prior to their tragic undoing, which is to say, he is their tragic precondition.[21]

"The Goal of the Antipodes"

These complications, deep within the historical essence of tragedy (as presented by Nietzsche), put elements of §15 in a clearer light. We are reminded of Nietzsche's revaluation of Socrates, which may now be considered in a fuller context: "If we must thus assume an anti-Dionysian tendency operating even prior to Socrates, which merely received in him an unprecedentedly magnificent expression, we must not draw back before the *question* of what such a phenomenon as that of Socrates indicates" (§14; emphasis added). Probing this question further, Nietzsche slowly comes round to the same possibility that we just saw, namely that Dionysianism and its antithesis have historically conspired together, and indeed are so inseparable that moments of "evolution" prove impossible to distinguish from moments of "decline" or "corruption." The question, then, is not when did decline set in, but, *when was there ever no declining*? Even the Homeric Achilles is pictured as already "mourning [!] the decline of the heroic age" (§3). There is a circularity implied by Nietzsche's exposition of the Dionysian realm, whose decline and decay is guaranteed not by its evolution but by the very first appearance of that realm. This deepens rather than contests the meaning of Socrates' "anti-Dionysianism," which Nietzsche puts once more in question form, asking "whether there is *necessarily* only an antipodal relation between Socratism and art, and whether the birth of an 'artistic Socrates' is altogether a contradiction in terms" (§14).

In posing this kind of option, *The Birth of Tragedy* confronts its own structural "vortex." Nietzsche has been teaching us throughout how difficult it is to arrive at a sound conception of opposites or "antipodes." Doesn't *The Birth of Tragedy* show how "the opposition between Apollo and Dionysus became *more hazardous and even impossible*" (§2; emphasis added)? Nietzsche is not challenging, still less is he defying, his readers to try to arrive at neat opposites again here. He is holding out, without completely destroying it, one last shred of hope that some distinctions might still be maintained and that meaning, direction, and purpose might be salvaged. For "suppose someone proved convincingly that the goal of the antipodes [*Antipodenziel*] cannot be reached in this direct manner [viz., in a linear fashion; here, by boring a hole straight through the earth, in the name of concealed "depths"]: who would still wish to go on working in these old depths, unless he had learned meanwhile to be satisfied with finding precious stones or discovering laws of nature?" (§15)—that is, with interim solutions of the sort that both art and science must content themselves with. The repetition of the word "antipodes" is clearly meant to throw light back on the Socratic question posed above from §14; it also asks that we rethink the logic of opposites and of contradiction. Paradoxically, the hope for a *Zukunftsmusik* or *Zukunftsphilosophie* is wrapped up in the necessary dissolution of clear-cut contrasts (like those that give birth to tragedy itself, or as instanced by the idea of an "artistic Socrates"). Individuation must surrender to a condition, that of a kind of deindividuation, to which the very idea of individuation can no longer even be opposed.

Nietzsche is quite straightforward in his insistence that Socratism leads, sooner or later, to art, not because art and science are related in the way that antipodes are related to one another, but because in its essence science is art. Constituting itself in terms of its limits (the limits of knowledge, reason, understanding), science always stands in an essential relation to what exceeds it. This excess, its defining goal, is what Nietzsche deftly labels "the sublime metaphysical delusion" (§15). The phrase brings about an identity of metaphysics with delusion without determining the arrow of implication that would help us decide their exact relation (is metaphysics, *qua* metaphysics, delusory, or is delusion, qua delusion, metaphysical?). Driven on by its instincts for a realm beyond appearances, by the "driving wheel of logical Socratism behind Socrates," science is led to its consummating negation, "to its limits, at which point it must turn into *art* (*in* Kunst *umschlagen muss*)—*which really is the aim of this mechanism*" (ibid.). The translation misleads. Science does not "turn into art"; it undergoes instantaneous recharacterization. Its perceived character is what changes, not its essence. But even this does not tell the full story. The thirst for theoretical knowledge is in itself artistic (and tragic) because tragic art was driven by the same unquenchable impulse, by its pursuit of dialectical solutions to the tragic knot, by its metaphysical idealism, its Oedipal lust for uncovering nature's secrets beyond the veil of the apparent.[1] Hence, the following description could be predicated of tragedy or of science, although it is "the tragic myth" that is the subject: "[It] leads the world of phenomena to its limits where it denies itself and seeks to flee back again into the womb of the true and only reality, where it then seems to commence its metaphysical swansong, like Isolde . . . " (§22).

The notebooks only confirm these conflationary trends, through which the distinctness of theory and tragedy, of optimism and pessimism, of affirmation and negation, can no longer be said to hold. Both art and science have in common that *they deny life in order to reaffirm it.*[2] Art, too, is a form of "correction" of reality (*Weltcorrektion*),[3] or if you like, a "justification"; and the Dionysian drive compels both musical drama and philosophy.[4] The seduction of both art and knowledge (the knowledge of the "theoretical man") is double in nature: the enticement is in part to life (even Dionysian intoxication can be reckoned a "frightful" *Trieb zum Dasein* ["DW," 562], a joyous affirmation of existence [§17, init.]), and in part to the negation of life (both art and philosophy involve the refutation of appearance). Finally, the mythological impulse is present in both. Both are forms of "profound *illusion*" and of idealism, just as is Dionysianism itself.[5] To reject or embrace the "doctrine" of Dionysianism is beside the point: Dionysianism seems destined to locate the reader in a performative contradiction, in the very attempt to make sense of Nietzsche's meanings.

As if to illustrate the paradoxical nature of theory (the impulse, in the desire to know, to visualize the nonvisualizable), Nietzsche offers an image of the activity and "conversional" moment of theory that resembles nothing so much as a tragic theater (§15): standing on the periphery of an infinite circle—"the circle of science" which defines the territory of knowledge—at its "boundary points," theoretical man gains a view of "what defies illumination." The gaze gives way to horror before the sight of logic "coil[ing] up at these points and biting its own tail," at which point "tragic insight" is attained, and (more) art is needed to protect the gaze from this spectacle. Crucial to making sense of this image is knowing whether the horror comes from gazing within the circle of science or past its limits. What is the cause of the horror—what we know, or what exceeds it? The latter would suggest a metaphysical vision, and intuitively this gives Nietzsche's obvious meaning (with good Platonic precedents, e.g., *Phaedrus* 247c–d, where a subject stands on the rim of the world and looks out intently "beyond the heavens"). The former, describing the reach of the known, would be a banal knowledge (a repetition of the known), and this, one should think, could hardly be a source of horror—until one thinks of Hamlet and the painfully untransfigured realities of the day-to-day experienced as such, without the benefit of metaphysical solace on the horizon.

Two voids, each infinite, stare back from either side of the line. Which side contains the genuine horror? It is futile, perhaps, to pin down the image, but then, futility can be a useful exercise too. Nothing in the image suggests that Nietzsche would have us read it in either direction or exclusively in terms of the alternatives it presents. After all, it is the border, located between the two domains of the metaphysically sublime and the nauseatingly banal, which is in fact composed of "an infinite number of points" and which reproduces within itself the conditions of unknowability that either alternative, by virtue of their excessiveness (whether in their exorbitancy or in the extremity of what they lack), might be imagined to sustain alone. Here, too, we are left by Nietzsche on a limb and at a limit that points to the unpalatable conclusion that the metaphysical and its opposite are intimately, and inextricably, bound up with each other; that they are mutually conditioning factors, mutual "images" of each other; and—here we have the genuine horror—that they are mutually *indistinguishable*. Again, *the limits of phenomena are the phenomena* (which was, after all, the thrust of Lange's criticism of the *Ding an sich*, viz., that "what is essence on [one] level of analysis shows itself on another, in relation to a still more deeply hidden essence, to be appearance again"). The flight back into the womb of the true and only reality is a return to the false but equally necessary distinction (contradiction) between phenomena and their limits. Just to set down a limit is to create a reality that exceeds it, the way a line invokes its transgression, a surface "its" depth, a mask its concealment, and knowledge its skeptical or metaphysical alternative. There is no escaping this circle, which is perhaps best understood not in spatial but in hermeneutic terms, the spatial metaphors of "beyond" and "below" being the results, not the source, of a process of repeated projection and of self-sensation.

The Socratic Fallacy

Limits in Nietzsche's *Birth of Tragedy* are radically open boundaries, such as those that can be penciled in between art and science, or between tragedy and philosophy—but also between the Dionysian and the Apollinian, or finally (perish the thought) between Dionysianism and Socratism. It is easy to see how, to borrow a phrase from Nietzsche, the most "nauseating" and horrific moment for anyone habitually trained in the ways of the *Birth of Tragedy* would coincide not with a glimpse into the vortices of primordial being, as Nietzsche suggests early on in his treatise (§7), but with catching the reflection, within that abyss, of the image of Socrates sparkling back at you. The thought of putting these two "archetypes" side by side and on an equal footing, or even of allowing the one to contain the other, is, strictly speaking, unimaginable. Who would think to compare Socrates with Dionysus or with one of his votaries, say that "fantastic and seemingly so offensive figure of the wise and rapturous satyr" who, we are told, "is at the same time 'the simple man' as opposed to the god"—that bearded, goatlike creature, that wholly imaginary and "made-up" being (*fingiertes Wesen*; the phrase is Langean[1])—in short, that mythic projection if not product of a self-imagining, loaded, like Silenus, with negative wisdom (*BT*, §§8, 7). And yet this is, I believe, just what *The Birth of Tragedy* requires us to do: to read in Socrates the image of Dionysus, and vice versa. Isn't that the import of the "music-practicing Socrates"? The thought, horrific as it is, is contemplated in the contemporary notebooks, which turn out a series of associations that point in the same direction: "The tragic being.—The music-practicing Socrates"—"Shakespeare . . . consummates Sophocles, he is the *music-making Socrates*"—Shakespeare is the "consummation of Sophocles" and "*entirely Dionysian*."[2]

The way to the antipodes in Nietzsche is never direct, because these can be reached only by way of a return. And the way to Dionysus is not exactly from Socrates, but *without* Socrates, from *within* him. Dionysus, we might say, "must be viewed through Socrates as through a shadow" (§13)—although we need to invert the optical metaphor in order to realize that Socrates is the shadow cast by the illumination, from without, of Dionysus—the way a Platonic form might be imagined to make itself visible in its retreat from phenomena. It is this shadowy but still cheerful Socrates, dying, philosophizing, ever desirable and even erotic, thanks to his proximity to death and to his extinction in image and myth, who evokes the image of Dionysus in Nietzsche, following the hints of Plato: "He went to his death with the calm with which, according to Plato's description, he leaves the symposium at dawn, the last of the revelers, to begin a new day . . . ," while they, the revelers, dream on about him, in their drunken stupor (§13). Socrates is the name for this intermittent appearance, at daybreak. *He is the Platonic Idea.*[3]

Nietzsche's allusion, at the close of §13, is a literary one, recalling the last pages of the Platonic dialogue, *The Symposium*, in which Socrates has bested his fellow symposiasts, literally having drunk them under the table. The dialogue was Nietzsche's self-professed favorite, his "*Lieblingsdichtung*," as early as his school days at Pforta (1864).[4] The contents and even form of the dialogue provide *The Birth of Tragedy* and the surrounding notes with a virtual leitmotif, one which to my knowledge oddly has never been explored. Let us consider it briefly. The context of the dialogue, which is symposiastic, is explicitly

Dionysian. The dialogue's inset narrative is framed by the anticipation of a "judgment" to be cast on the claims to wisdom made by Agathon and Socrates (*Symp.* 175e), which we expect to see fulfilled, perhaps repeatedly fulfilled, in the course of the action to come. The final scene, allegorically stylized, is emblematic of that judgment: flanked on either side by the tragic poet Agathon and the comic poet Aristophanes, the philosopher is laboring to persuade both his interlocutors that the consummate maker of tragedies should be an equally consummate maker of comic dramas. In practice, tragic poets were also comic artists: it was the convention for tragic trilogies to close with a satyr play (a burlesque), thus rendering the sequence a tetralogy, but with effects that are still difficult to gauge.[5] It is no doubt a reflection of this practice that it was natural for Aristotle to believe that Homer had foreshadowed both the tragic and the comic genres. Homer was the author of the two great epics whose dimensions were so large that, as Aristotle notes, they contained countless tragedies within them; but Aristotle's Homer was also the author of a "dramatized" mock epic called the "*Madman*" (*Margites*).[6]

Plato's dialogue is an ambivalent expression of the same literary critical assumption. Formally, the dialogue replicates this impossible containment by literally bursting, Aristophanes-fashion, at its seams. A tableau, the closing scene graphically illustrates an impossible union, and indeed the impossible theme of the dialogue "entire" (namely, "the pursuit of wholeness," 192e). Its dilemma, to which Socrates is blind because he in fact embodies it in his person, can be put in the form of a question slightly different from the one Socrates asks: Is the union of tragedy and comedy (both officially presided over by Dionysus) something that is divided or effectuated by philosophy? Socrates is "about to clinch his argument" when his interlocutors, already stupefied by too much talk and wine, and so unable "to follow the train of his reasoning," drift listlessly off to sleep. The elenctic dialogue is exhausted, the question is left dangling. The judgment of Dionysus is suspended.

Perhaps one of the least expected and most overlooked features of *The Birth of Tragedy* is the way it tacitly draws the comic and the tragic dimensions into the closest, if frustrating, proximity. The incongruousness of the satyr-figure—his comic, libidinal wantonness, his mixed centauric form, and his tragic wisdom—is only the most persistent reminder of a larger incongruence in Nietzsche's text, one that reiterates the "conclusions" of the *Symposium*. The phenomenon that *The Birth of Tragedy* describes, the "artist's metaphysics" at its core, expressly shows itself from one perspective to be *tragedy*, and from another to be "this *comedy* of art" (§5; emphasis added). Each in its own way involves the production of a subject for an impossible other, not unlike the Aristophanic image of mankind's being faced—*by Apollo*—toward its own wounds (*Symp.* 190e). Only, on Nietzsche's version the wound is produced, as it were, by the act of straining to view it. *The Birth of Tragedy* describes an impossibly autopsical and dissonant vision ("like the weird image of the fairy tale which can turn its eyes at will and behold itself" [§5]), a transfiguration that can assume one of two forms, by taking a turn either to the sublime or to the comic (provided these can be distinguished), although both of these are in fact associated by Nietzsche with the "satyr chorus of the dithyramb," just as they were in antiquity.[7] Compare the following:

> Here, when the danger to [the] will is greatest, *art* approaches as a saving sorceress, expert at healing. She alone knows how to turn these nauseous thoughts about the horror or absurdity of existence into notions with which one can live: these are the *sublime* as the artistic taming of the horrible, and the *comic* as the discharge of the nausea of absurdity.

Nietzsche then directly adds a remark that installs a further crisis of identities in his work:

> The satyr chorus of the dithyramb is the saving deed of Greek art; faced with the intermediary world of these Dionysian com-

> panions, the feelings described here *exhausted themselves*. (§7; last emphasis added)

The tragic sublime and the hideous comic are directly embodied, indeed exhausted, by the satyr chorus, which points to the necessary conflation of banal nausea and metaphysical horror. It is impossible to separate "the horrible truth" that emerges from a glimpse into the Dionysian from the truth that (as we saw earlier) emerges upon the return to drab, gray-as-slate consciousness: "As soon as this everyday reality re-enters consciousness, it is experienced as such, *with nausea*," and so too, "now [the Dionysian man] understands the wisdom of the sylvan god, Silenus: he is *nauseated*" (ibid.; emphasis added). The glimpse into metaphysical truth, I want to suggest, is uniquely a glimpse into the banality of its "assumption" (§4).

How odd that this deflationary parodic and satirical feature of *The Birth of Tragedy*, flagrantly lodged at its center, should have been so successfully ignored, or rather left so half-concealed. How do you tell apart a comic satyr from a tragic satyr? The question has the same unsolved status in Nietzsche's text as it had in Plato's *Symposium*, to which we will return in a moment. Finally, it should be acknowledged that there is something self-defeating, or at least incongruous if not entirely comic, about the fact that the characterization of tragedy's zenith and decline (or rather "death") in *The Birth of Tragedy* should stem largely from the insight of a comic poet, Aristophanes (in his satirical play, *The Frogs*). Nietzsche advertises, obliquely, this oddity, "without here defending the profound instinct of Aristophanes against . . . attacks" by the moderns upon his credibility as a witness to an ancient view (§13, init.). In his unpublished lecture, "Socrates and Tragedy," in which this ancient perspective is endorsed, he writes that Aristophanes had, "like no other genius," a deep, elective affinity with Aeschylus; they are closely "*wahlverwandt*." "*Equals*," Nietzsche goes on, "*are recognized only by equals*."[8]

The proximity of the tragic and the comic around a shared incommensurability is striking. "In both concepts there is a palpable contradiction" ("DW," 567).[9] Plato's *Symposium* has its own ways of naming this incommensurability deep within the essence of art. One of the many complications of this theme from Plato, which is essential to any reading of *The Birth of Tragedy*, is a feature that Nietzsche all but draws out on the surface through his closely placed reminders, at the tail end of §13, a passage that concerns the wheels in motion "*behind*" Socrates and the specific dramatic setting of the *Symposium*. These, too, fall within the labile frames of a Dionysian scene, to which we must now turn.

When Alcibiades—drunk and uproarious, his temples wreathed with violets and ivy—bursts onto the scene of conversation at Agathon's celebration party, disrupting the orderly sequence with his physical presence (he seats himself between Socrates and Agathon, like a Dionysus sitting in judgment), he takes up the challenge to produce an encomium of Socrates. Here is how he begins:

> I'll try to praise Socrates, my friends, but I'll have to use an image. And though he may think I'm trying to make fun of him, I assure you my image is no joke: it aims at the truth. Look at him! Isn't he just like a statue of Silenus? You know the kind of statue I mean; you'll find them in any shop in town. It's a Silenus sitting, his flute or his pipes in his hands, and it's hollow. It's split right down the middle, and inside it's full of tiny statues of the gods. Now look at him again! Isn't he also just like the satyr Marsyas? Nobody, not even you, Socrates, can deny that you *look* like them. But the resemblance goes beyond appearance, as you're about to hear. (*Symposium* 215a–b; trans. Nehamas and Woodruff)

The identification of Socrates with Silenus is striking, if disconcerting. What takes the Silenus image beyond the pale of mere appearances for Alcibiades is, first of all, Socrates' ability to inspire Bacchic frenzy in his interlocutors, the utter disturbance he produces in their lives with his negative wisdom, his "*satyr's music*":

> The only difference between you and Marsyas [the mythical Phrygian flute-player, producer of ecstasy, and competitor of Apollo] is that you need no instruments; you do exactly what he does, but with words alone. . . . We are all transported, completely possessed. . . . You might actually suspect that I'm drunk! Still, I swear to you, the moment he starts to speak, I am beside myself: my heart starts leaping in my chest, the tears come streaming down my face, even the frenzied Corybantes seem sane compared to me—and, let me tell you, I am not alone. (215c–e)

But there is a second factor that causes Socrates to resemble, on the surface and deep down, a Silenus statue: his profession of ignorance, which (Alcibiades is convinced) is only skin-deep. "All this is just on the surface, like the outsides of those statues of Silenus," whereas beneath the skin and within, Socrates conceals a temperance and a virtuosity and a seriousness that is divine:

> I don't know if any of you have seen him when he's really serious. But I once caught him when he was open like Silenus' statues, and I had a glimpse of the figures he keeps hidden within: they were so godlike—so bright and beautiful, so utterly amazing—that I no longer had a choice—I just had to do whatever he told me. (216e)

Socrates' (at least outward) resemblance to a satyr became a commonplace in antiquity (as in Xenophon's *Symposium*), although the comparison always contained a whiff of paradox.[10] We do not know what the images of the gods within the Silenus statue are meant to resemble. We don't know, for instance, whether they include gods in whose name satyrs make a music that can either bewitch onlookers like Alcibiades (who, not insignificantly, has troubles of his own locating with any precision the place of interiority upon which his image so crucially rests; ibid., 218a),[11] or else dazzle them out of their will to existence ("*He makes it seem that my life isn't worth living*!"; 216a). But we do know that Socrates, so cast, cannot easily be extricated from his identification with the Dionysian, whether on the swollen, drunken lips of a Platonic character, or in Nietzsche's *Birth of Tragedy*, in which the likeness is allowed to flash through the intermittent flutterings of the veil of the text's appearances. Socrates, with his "*Silenus-like exterior*, his eyes of a crab, bulging lips and paunch," as Nietzsche describes him in his essay "The Dionysian Worldview,"[12] is for Nietzsche a quintessential "tragic being"—part satyr, part philosopher—who signifies both the tragic genre and the tragedy that the genre will undergo (its "swansong" melody [cf. *Phaedo*, 85a–b; and *BT*, §25], which was its first note as well). Indeed, as another fragment from an earlier essay-draft reads, "Socrates of the *Symposium* [is] the pure form of the artist [*der reine Künstler*]"—and, we might add, that art's fatality: its comic distortion.[13] "How could even Plato have endured life—a Greek life he repudiated—without an Aristophanes?" (*BGE*, 28).

The association, indeed the shared identity, of "the tragic being," Dionysianism, philosophy, and a Socrates who "practices music," which is no less prominent or explicit in Nietzsche's notebooks from the time, is as crucial to understanding *The Birth of Tragedy* as is the problematic blurring of the boundaries between the sublime and the comic. It installs a decadence at the conceptual center and mainspring of *The Birth of Tragedy*, and not merely on its periphery. And finally, true to Nietzsche's revisionist strategy in his "Attempt at a Self-Criticism," the association renders Dionysus into the genuine "question mark" that he always was. If in 1886 Nietzsche could write of *The Birth of Tragedy* that it was "an impossible book," indeed a "strange and almost inaccessible book" ("Attempt," 1), already in February of 1870 he could proudly write to his friend Paul Deussen that one of its predecessors, the lecture "Socrates and Tragedy," was "received like a chain of paradoxes."[14] The intimate connection between Socrates and Dionysus, their undecidable or perhaps just perspectival difference, is surely one of the important links in that chain, its most unspeakable paradox. Teasingly, Nietzsche hints in his "Attempt" that there is more to his earlier work than meets the eye: "O Socrates, Socrates, was that perhaps your *secret*? O enigmatic ironist, was that perhaps your—irony?"[15] But like so much else about this second preface, the comment merely points us toward the enigmatic nature of his earlier work, resolving nothing.

We might note in passing that Nietzsche's "reading" of the figure of Socrates from the *Symposium* merely accentuates the uncertain structure that Plato had already installed in his dialogue. A dialogue that mimes its subject matter, it is always, formally speaking, "in pursuit of wholeness." Its intricate form is that of a flawed circle; tragedy and comedy are fused, their "two natures blent into a sphere," so to speak, but only in the person of Socrates, an ambivalent locus to be sure. Like the Silenus toy of Socrates, the dialogue is "split right down the middle," while "inside it's full of tiny statues." More impressively, the form of the dialogue is built out of receding interiors, which recall Aristophanes' famous parable of mortal division; this latter, in turn, anticipates the incomplete but striving form of the dialogue entire, of which the parable is but a fragment and "symbol" (*Symp.* 189d–93b).

We would appear to be on the verge of yet one more self-discrepant *mis en abîme*, on the threshold of a cave within a cave. Perhaps this is what prompted Nietzsche's closing comment in his youthful essay from 1864 on his *Lieblingsdichtung*, the Platonic *Symposium* ("On the Relationship of the Speech of Alcibiades to the Remaining Speeches of the Platonic *Symposium*"), in which he begs permission for risking a "simile" that might illuminate the final (and apparently his favorite) speech by Alcibiades. For Nietzsche, this scene "marks the turning point [*Wendepunkt*] of the artistically elaborate drama and of philosophy too, both of which take a turn toward reality": "Thus did Plato bind together all parts of his dialogue in this one knot [*Knotenpunkt*], not unlike the way Zeus tied together the various sides and surfaces [*Häute*, lit., "skins"] of man with an umbilical cord, tying them into a knot" at the navel.[16] The simile, of course, is Aristophanic, and it is taken from the dialogue itself (*Symp.* 190e). Nietzsche's unabashed preference for the Aristophanic spirit that infects the dialogue might be inferred from his essay, were it not that Nietzsche says as much himself, arguing from Plato's artistry, but against what he takes to be Plato's judgment: of the two poets, Agathon and Aristophanes, "the intellectually greater man by far is Aristophanes" (ibid., 421). Socrates merely happens to occupy their point of comparison, their common juncture, and their shared "wound." The "reality" so admired by Nietzsche might in the end be nothing other than this radical confrontation with incompleteness.

The untenable distinction, in *The Birth of Tragedy*, between Socrates and Dionysus/Silenus follows from any elaboration of the image of Socrates as artist and musician, possibly from that of a "cynical" Socrates as well.[17] Its later follow-throughs are evident both in Nietzsche's proclamation of "the philosopher Dionysus" in *Twilight of the Idols* ("What I Owe to the Ancients," 5) and in the image of Socrates as *buffo* in "The Problem of Socrates" from that same work—the comic and sublime faces, as it were, of a single "question mark" of meaning. But my point concerns the structural role of this questioning of identities within *The Birth of Tragedy* itself, as modeled at least in part after Plato's *Symposium*.[18] Clearly, the relation between Socrates and Dionysus is an intertextual one, which we may overlook only at our peril. We have already seen how Socrates represents the anti-Dionysianism that is internal to Dionysianism, how he represents, in effect, the frailty of all Greek idealism, including the Dionysian variety, whose truth (ideality) is concealed most of all from itself. We might note, however, that in his later reflection upon *The Birth of Tragedy*, in his "Attempt at a Self-Criticism," Nietzsche does not say that Dionysus is the solitary question mark of his first book. He is "*one more* question mark" ("Attempt," 3; emphasis added). By the same token, Socrates, instancing the collapse of structural opposites (of structure pure and simple), is nonetheless a structural effect, and not a self-sufficient cause. It is a challenge to account for his place in this framework, and his peculiar nonpertinence to it.

"Eternal" Phenomena: Culture's Illusions

Contrary to the impression that the last few pages may have given, Socrates does not "contain" *The Birth of Tragedy* within himself, like some fabulous Silenus; he is not its privileged center. In a way, Nietzsche's Socrates has the status ascribed to him by his fellow Athenians when they wished to deny his contemporary relevance and his exemplary Greek nature: that of a mere accident, a freak, a "superfoetation."[1] Incommensurable with what comes before him, he is also inexplicable in light of what follows: scarcely a cause or an effect, Socrates is rather the figure for the logic of causality, and for its self-exhaustion in the face of "causes apparently without effects, and effects apparently without causes"—such was Euripides' response, for example, before the spectacle of Greek tragedy, possibly his only accurate assessment of the genre (§14). We might see in the Socratism of Socrates the trivialization and banalization of a Platonic Idea gone rampant, flooding the disparate realm of phenomena, which it can no longer even contain. Indeed, with Socrates a crisis in the system of representation in *The Birth of Tragedy* is broached, literally an "internal bifurcation" (§22). All identities in *The Birth of Tragedy* are vulnerable to such complication, while their collective identity and their common source is not "the primordial unity" or "the primordial contradiction" (assuming these can be distinguished), but rather the "dissonance" that is man (§25). With the (re)appearance of Socrates, Nietzsche has difficulty keeping the strands of his narrative apart, not together. Apollo may be reborn as Dionysus, and indeed all the figures of his discourse begin to totter on the brink of individuation, over the abyss of a contradictory unity, in an unstable bond that is far more troubling than any promised metaphysical "reconciliation." "Dionysus," "Apollo," and "Socrates" are differences of reading only, slight accentuations and distortions of one another; all are separated by a scenario of birth that is either inverted (Dionysus as Platonic form) or miscarried in the course of its telling (Socrates as Dionysus, both equally "decadent"). The joins cannot hold. Like a "chain of paradoxes," the names of the gods and myths of *The Birth of Tragedy* dissolve into the rhythm of their configuration, pulsating in flashes of luminosity, but also decaying in faint after-images, the most blinding spots of all.[2]

Why, we might well ask, does Nietzsche insist so on misleading his readers with a narrative about the birth of tragedy? A quick answer may be found in the classical model that Nietzsche inherited from Aristotle in the latter's treatise on poetics, which likewise contains both a genetic narrative and its ahistorical, structural, and teleological undoing. It was Aristotle's authority, in chapter 4 of his *Poetics*, that sanctioned the theory that satyric compositions and dithyrambs were the historical source of the tragic form. The frailty of this reconstruction, or rather this story, is plain to see, and it has been attacked on several grounds.[3] But its schema is most easily questioned, one should think, by reading Aristotle's own distinction between literature and history back into his account of literary history. History unfolds as a sequence of events that are chronologically but not logically connected, "one thing after another" (*tade meta tade*); poetic events, by contrast, are causally connected, "one thing as a result of another" (*tade dia tade*; *Poetics*, chs. 10, 23). Now, Aristotle's account of the historical evolution of poetic forms is a causal account, an aetiology that unfolds according to its own necessary logic and comes to a final fruition in the telos that commands the sequence as a whole, the tragic form (ch. 4). So even by his own lights Aristotle cannot have given a history of the birth of tragedy; rather, he has invented a poetic story, a *mythos*, in the guise of a history about the invention of poetry. Nietzsche's treatise is, among other things, a commentary on Aristotle's critical fiction. Nietzsche nowhere says that he has replicated (and twisted) this paradoxical feature from his Aristotelian model. But in practice, this is exactly what he has done. Only now, Aristotle's finalism and essentialism are subjected to intense criticism, as was Kant's earlier (in the essay "Teleology since Kant" [1868]), while the organic consistency of the Aristotelian tragic form in Nietzsche breaks up into the fragments of its competing accounts, into the "ruin" of a poetics.

A more complex answer to the question why Nietzsche has constructed so misleading a narrative lies in his peculiar relationship to metaphysical speculation generally. For in portraying successive Greek cultural forms as an unfolding Platonic dialectic that ultimately comes to grief upon itself, dying a death "by suicide" like Socrates, Nietzsche ultimately puts a heavy burden on the governing logic of this sequence, not to say its plausibility. The coherence of Dionysianism is fatally compromised, but that should not disturb us. Pretending to have given an elaborate account of the Dionysian, Nietzsche gives us nothing of the kind. The problem with the Dionysian is not that it lies beyond what can be expressed in concepts but that it is the essence of conceptuality: it is too easily named and individuated as a phenomenon, too much a Platonic Idea. Dionysianism, and the metaphysics for which it stands, betrays its own internal antithesis, namely anti-Dionysianism (Socratism). Dionysianism thus proves to have been self-deforming, internally decadent, a crumbling edifice of logic and imagination that could never really stand from the very beginning. It is, quite simply, an incoherent theory, and self-consciously so. All of this makes it truly "impossible" to fit Nietzsche's arguments into the frameworks by which they are conventionally read. Nietzsche calls attention to this problem in his "Attempt," where he seems to be writing not out of resignationism but in despair at his readership's incomprehension. The 1886 preface to *The Birth of Tragedy* is, in fact, a directive for rereading: "How differently Dionysianism spoke to *me*! . . . I appended hopes where there was no ground for hope, where everything pointed all too plainly to an end!" and therefore, by the same token, not plainly enough ("Attempt," 6).[4]

In *The Birth of Tragedy* Nietzsche is not particularly out to refute Plato or even Schopenhauer for that matter. Philosophers, being victims of the phenomena they set out to describe and to transcend, merely systematize an urge to metaphysics that runs rampant through the whole of the cultural domain, with a necessity that is constant, if not "eternal" ("it is an eternal phenomenon"). The circularities within metaphysical logic thus point outward, toward a larger cultural circulation that is both debased and exalted, devoid of meaning and seduced into meaning, clear-eyed before itself and deluded by what it sees. And the pattern is repeated at another level, whenever a reader faces Nietzsche's text and endeavors to establish its sense from outside the metaphysics of its appearances.

Given the ambivalent role assigned to him by Nietzsche, we might say that Socrates is synonymous (but not identical) with the repetition—the return—that mars the perspicuous narration of a story about cultural and historical identities, pure and simple—or that impinges on unconditional, metaphysical identities once they have been set back into some matrix, some structure, or some history. Through Socrates, not exclusively but most difficultly through him, Nietzsche repeatedly tells a story not about self-identical historical moments, but about moments of self-complication. Hence, Nietzsche offers his readers at most a dissonant narration about the birth of tragedy that can only suggest another dissonance—not a deeper, concealed, more essential dissonance, like the self-divisions of primordial being, but just one more dissonance, comparable to any inscribed in *The Birth of Tragedy*. It is to the sources of dissonance in *The Birth of Tragedy* that we must next turn.

Primordial Fairy Tales

Fragments from an abandoned expansion of *The Birth of Tragedy* dating from early 1871 comment on the autopsical fairy-tale figure from the end of §5. The latter represents an impossible, totalized vision conferred by Nietzsche, as a privilege, on the primordial artist-genius of the world (as it were, "the primordial unity" in its creative aspect) and, derivatively, on the empirical artist in touch with this primal vision. No longer artist or genius but a "weird image of the fairy tale," the Will under this description "can turn its eyes at will and behold itself," simultaneously subject and object, at once artist, spectator, and spectacle (§5). Here the draft in fair-copy reads:

> Constrained as we are to understanding everything under the form of becoming, i.e. as *will*, we are now tracing the *birth* of the three different kinds of genius in the only world we know, that of appearances [these three kinds are presumably the world-genius or world-eye, *das eine Weltauge*, representing the primordial unity, then the Apollinian and Dionysian artistic types, all of which are mentioned in the preceding paragraph]: the thrust of our inquiry is the question, What are the most important *preparations* that the "will" needs in order to arrive at these [three states]? We have every reason to establish our point by way of the *Greek world*, which speaks to us about that process in a simple and suggestive way, as is its wont. (*KSA*, 7:10[1]; 335–36)

The continuation is preserved in a still earlier draft, and is valuable for being as frank as it is:

> [Let us] not [forget] that *this whole process is only our necessary form of appearance and to that extent utterly lacking in any metaphysical reality*; [and] that, however, with all our proofs we cannot get past these barriers, and at most we are able to recognize them as such. If above I dared to speak of Genius and appearance as if I had access to a knowledge surpassing those limits and as if I were able to look out from the *one*, great eye of the world [*Weltauge*], let me state after the fact that I don't believe I have stepped outside of the anthropomorphic circle with that figurative language. . . . *But who could endure existence without such mystical possibilities*? (*KSA*, 14, 541; *KGW*, 3.5.2, pp. 1060–61; emphases added)

Nietzsche's admissions here are remarkable, both for the light they shed on his own use of metaphysical language and for the way they qualify his view of the all-too-human desire for metaphysics generally. Mankind can be redeemed from the insupportable apprehension of existence stripped bare of all delusory features, a life "without any such mystical possibilities," but at great cost, at the price of renouncing an illusion that is necessary for life. This double compulsion, dooming mankind to metaphysical illusion and alienating subjects from this possibility through its (fleeting and then disavowed) invalidation, is the *actual*, or if you like, "primordial" ground of mankind's internal dissonance. What such a dissonance reveals is not the contradictoriness of the world or the world's being in contradiction with its appearances, but merely the noncoincidence of the self with itself.

One of Nietzsche's most haunting passages in *The Birth of Tragedy* brings us back to this very theme: "If we could imagine dissonance become man—and what else is man?—this dissonance, to be able to live, would need a splendid illusion that would cover dissonance with a veil of beauty" (§25). I believe that this anthropological dissonance lies at the heart of Nietzsche's first book, which in turn embodies and performs the dissonance named here. It is this condition that accounts for the metaphysical appearances of *The Birth of Tragedy* and for their simultaneous invalidation.

As noted above, the substitutability of "primordial contradiction" for "primordial unity" is one way Nietzsche alerts us to the suspect character of the metaphysical vision he seems to be espousing. His image of the Dionysian artist, likened to a fairy tale figure in §5, is another. Throughout, Nietzsche's language signifies in its very contradictoriness a rift that is primordial not in the sense of originating in a realm "beyond," but in the sense of typifying the irretrievable nature of human engagements with the world, and (for the same reason) that of their metaphysical characterization.[1] As Nietzsche later says, "The 'real world' has been constructed *out of the contradiction to the actual world*" (*TI*, "'Reason' in Philosophy," 6; emphasis added). But even this thought is incomplete, for it implies that the actual world might be in contradiction with itself. But the world in Nietzsche's view is not in contradiction with itself (which would be just a further metaphysical claim) but only with our construction of it. Contradiction has no objective reality for Nietzsche at any point in his career: it is rooted, rather, in the self-contradictions of all-too-human subjects. It is *we* who experience the world as a contradiction, Nietzsche is claiming, and we do this as a defense against the experience of our own inconsistency.[2]

The early notebooks from around 1870 and 1871 tell the same story: "We are the one Being itself."[3] "If contradiction is the true Being, . . . then we are Being [itself]—*and we must produce appearance out of ourselves*."[4] Nietzsche is exposing our anthropology and critiquing the character of representation. The world's contradictoriness is plainly our contradictoriness. In bringing out this point, Nietzsche invents, in a way that is characteristic of all his writings, a kind of conceptual primary scene. This is a thought-experiment whose object is the very nature of thought itself; it is a virtual allegory of conceptuality and its limits, only it is one that crucially depends for the completion of its meaning on us: we are both the frame and part of the picture. Accordingly, Nietzsche asks us to imagine the world as if it existed in a blank state, ready to accept our projections upon it. Aesthetic judgments are opposed to a basic state of indifference, of which they are the idealization. There is no beauty in nature, just as its opposite, ugliness, is not naturally given either: both are a projection of the mind onto nature. "Perception," after all, "is an aesthetic product."[5] What is intrinsic to nature, Nietzsche hypothesizes, is "an indifferent point" that subtends and even mocks every aesthetic judgment that is projected onto it: "There is no natural beauty, but there is indeed the distressing and ugly [*das Störende-Häßliche*], and an indifferent point."[6] This is what Nietzsche calls "the negative origin of the work of art."[7] The question is how to relate the painfulness of the distressingly ugly (identified as the "real" of perception, viz., "the reality of dissonance" in contrast to the ideality of consonance and harmony[8]) to the state of indifference.

If pain is a perception, a by-product of a representing apparatus that is shaped by the conventions of culture, then pain cannot be primary. Indifference, Nietzsche seems to reason, not the contrasting states of pleasure and pain, ought to have a claim to the title of the "real." But how is indifference to be imagined? One way to conceive of indifference is as a primary ground against which all further representations are based, as something like a zero-degree of representation, an affectless, blank indifference, a mere projective ground. Nietzsche, however, is not positing a metaphysical background, in part because indifference is the caricature of any such background, standing for its problematic vacancy. "Painlessness [viz., indifference] must, somewhere, be *produced*—but how?"[9] Indifference (like "chaos" or "the void") cannot be conceived independently of the conditions of representation, and for that reason it is not a reliable guide to the objective metaphysical character of the world (if the world indeed has any such character). On the other hand, indifference in Nietzsche's analysis can at times appear not as a source but as a goal: it is what nature "reaches"; it conjures up the painlessness not of a being that is free of pain but of a being freed *from* pain, as in a martyr's blissful rapture, a painlessness that "must, somewhere, be produced." There is a painlessness to be located within painfulness, but both cannot be equally primordial. What, then, is the status of indifference?

We might think of the theory of indifference as Nietzsche's way of bringing home, in the only effective way possible, an unsavory truth about representation—about its intrinsically falsifying nature, its ideality and irreality. If indifference cannot be imagined outside the context of sensation and representation, then (Nietzsche adds with a certain vengefulness) neither can representations be conceived of independently of the indifference—the nullity and negligibility—that likewise characterizes them. Indifference, in this sense, is the hypostasis of a condition of representation, namely its inconsequentiality. Indifference is not all there is, but that is not the point. Nietzsche is refusing to recognize an origin in a positive sense, but only a "negative origin." The thought he is pressing after is not whether there is indifference, but rather: Who could endure it if there were, in the absence of consoling illusions? This specter of absolute indifference is something of a recurrent obsession in the later writings, a principle that flaunts itself by assuming opportunistic guises, whether in the atomistic principle of "nothing is this more than that" (*ouden mallon*), or in its Cynic-based aretological counterpart (the *adiaphora* [indifference, apathy] of the sage),[10] or else in dark visions of meaningless chaos. It is an invitation to unwilling, unimaginable, and utter refutation:

> "According to nature" you want to *live*? O you noble Stoics, what deceptive words these are! Imagine a being like nature, wasteful beyond measure, indifferent beyond measure, without purposes and consideration, without mercy and justice, fertile and desolate and uncertain at the same time; imagine indifference itself as a power—how *could* you live according to this indifference? (*BGE*, 9)

Due to our incapacity to fathom absolute indifference, we convert the (hypothesized) unaesthetic and indifferent into aesthetic differences. "Here, comparison of the work of art to that indifferent point out of which it arises is important, as is the comparison of the world that arises out of a point empty of pain."[11] The world, thus drained of beauty, presents a horrifying prospect—it is "ugly" in the vocabulary of aesthetic perception (abject and dissonant), but ultimately it is indifferent to any aesthetic scale of values or measures. Ugliness and dissonance here seem to be not only a primary reaction to indifference but also a reaction to the difference of representation from itself, to its very own incoherence. Without straying too much farther afield into this (admittedly bizarre) set of reflections from 1870–71, let us consider the following further speculations:

> Is reality perhaps only pain, and that is how *representation* is born? Of what kind, then, is the *enjoyment* [that is taken in representation]? Is it of something that is not real but only ideal? . . . And what is that indifferent point that nature reaches? How is painless-

> ness possible? Perception is an aesthetic product. What, then, is real? What is it that has perception? . . . Is it possible [that the] plurality of pain and indifference to the same are conditions [i.e., states] of a being [*Wesen*]? What *is* the being [*Wesen*] in those points of indifference [*Indifferenzpunkten*]? (*KSA*, 7: 7[116]; 164–65)

> If, however, the flower, the person, the peacock's tail have a negative origin, then we are truly like the "harmonies" of a god, i.e., their reality is a dream reality. Then we need a being [*Wesen*] that produces the world as a work of art, as harmony; the Will then produces art as *Poros* ["Means"], as it were out of the void, *Penia* ["Lack"]. Everything existing is then its [sc., the Will's] image. . . . [12]

> If contradiction is the true Being, the pleasure of appearance, if becoming belongs to appearance—then to understand the world in its depths means understanding the contradiction. In that case, we are Being—and must produce appearance out of ourselves. (ibid., 7[169])

Nietzsche's claim, in the first of these two notebook entries, that the subjectivity he is describing is "not anthropomorphic but only a mundane one" ("we are the figures in the dream of God who divine the way he is dreaming") is belied by the subsequent entry, in which the same thought is couched in terms of a series of linked hypotheticals: if this is so, then we need the concept of a being, etc. The same concessive reasoning is operative in the third entry above. The logic is that of someone trying to manufacture a logical picture; but it also describes a different kind of logic, that of the psychological need to construct this kind of picture. The question of why we "need" a Being that produces the world as a work of art, as harmony, a dreaming god, and so on, is nowhere explicitly asked. But it is everywhere implied—for instance, in the uncertainties that are apparent throughout, and in the very urgency of the construction that is being performed, or rather that is being *acted out*, almost hysterically: "What, then, is real?" "What *is* the being?" and so forth. This desperation gives the "truth" to the series and is even truer than the claim, or rather the premise that Being in its true form is contradiction: that premise is a reflection of the subject of the scenario, its initial contriver, who with all consequentiality must assume the burden of contradiction in his own person. That subject, incidentally, is not Nietzsche, but "ourselves," as imagined and voiced (ventriloquized) by him.

Nietzsche's conceit—or rather his chain of speculations—is obscure and unruly, but it is ultimately aporetic and self-defeating. The "points" of indifference are modeled after atoms ("atoms of will") and they contain the flaws of the atomistic projection within themselves, in a way that is both theatrical and performative:[13] once again, there seems to be no way of going outside of or beyond representation and the conventions of culture. Nietzsche's speculations dramatize the attempt to do so and the circularities that are thereby entailed.

> We are the Will, we are figures of a vision; wherein lies the connecting thread? And what are living nerves, brain, thought, sensation?—We are at once the gazers—there is nothing besides the vision to gaze upon—we are the gazed upon, merely something gazed upon—we are the ones in whom the whole process begins afresh once more.[14]

We are will and representation, the gaze and its source, the gazed upon and the seat of the whole circular process.

This is the starting position of *The Birth of Tragedy*, and it helps explain the dissonant character of Nietzsche's two-sided critique in that work, which tries to take in at once both human pretensions or self-transfigurations (as in the self-glorifications of the Greek "'will,'" §3) and the felt poverty and pain underlying them. No narrative unfolding could capture these dissonances without doubling back on itself and ruining the foundations of the narrative line that describes them. Instead, Nietzsche resorts to a dissonant narration, one that is truer to the logic of false projections it exposes and that it matches with impossible and insupportable descriptions of the sort we have been noticing all along. As he says, echoing Heraclitus, "All things move in a double orbit" (§19). Nietzsche's narrative of a birth is complicated, even anticipated, by the prospects of a rebirth. The turns of his immense itinerary and his detours of meaning in *The Birth of Tragedy* are a return of sorts, just as *The Birth of Tragedy* is one more deflationary instance of the histories it narrates (of science, philosophy, and art), "*in order, having gone through the most enormous detours, to return to man.*"[15] That itinerary traces the "swelling up" of mankind to the level of macrocosmos ("the true Being"), in order to show that, when all is said and done, "'you are, in the end, what you are.'"[16] Such a knowledge is as comic as its tragic bearer and subject. Nor are we moderns exempt from this verdict in a way that our ancient forebears were not. It is, after all, *our* myth that *The Birth of Tragedy* tells.

Classical Mythologies in the Present Tense

The deflationary pattern witnessed just above is what most characterizes *The Birth of Tragedy*. We might say, then, that if the structure of Nietzsche's narrative there is Platonic, its thrust is in ways ultimately atomistic (in particular, Democritean and Lucretian): it is antimetaphysical, decidedly this-wordly, virtually an anthropology and a diagnosis of an all-too-human condition that is rooted in specific material and cultural configurations. In this light, *The Birth of Tragedy* can be seen to present not the truths of metaphysics, of a primordial will, or of transfigured perceptions, but mere simulacra of these same things, with immediate implications for the myths of culture that are their erased contexts. Nietzsche is in ways a sly mythographer. It is to this aspect of his writing in *The Birth of Tragedy* that I want to turn next. For it is here that Nietzsche's attitude toward the myth of classical antiquity comes to the fore.

We saw how, in notebooks exactly contemporary with the drafting of *The Birth of Tragedy*, Nietzsche explores some rather bizarre scenarios. Let us rephrase the results of those sketches. Emptying out the colorful contents of beauty, the sublime, and all intermediate shades, and putting on display their thinnest outlines, mere husks of aesthetic value, Nietzsche demonstrates in these notes how cultures manufacture out of indifference and via quantities of sensation entire scales and qualities of valuation. Abstract and esoteric speculative scenarios there thus throw into relief, with their dark (but purely hypothetical) illumination, the conditions of aesthetic and social meaning.[1] But cultures do not only manufacture values; they produce other cultures. To Nietzsche's mind, Hellenic culture is in many ways the manufacture of modern culture, a recent creation that is of the most insidious kind because it is the least conscious of all: it is the product of a misunderstanding. The modern image of ancient Greece, Nietzsche suggests in "The Dionysian Worldview," is too much in the debt of the Greeks' own models: it repeats, quite simply, an Epicurean view of ancient cultural life (which in Nietzsche's eyes represents a debased form of Democritus' more rigorously critical philosophy). Nietzsche's target, as always, is the naive but well-subscribed model of Greek *Heiterkeit*, blissful, carefree "cheerfulness," purveyed in contemporary culture at large and sanctioned by a neoclassical philology that dates from the age of Winckelmann and Goethe:

> Measured against the gravity, the sanctity, and the severity of other religions, Greek religion is in danger of being undervalued as a fantastical pastime—unless we call to mind an oft misrecognized trait of wisdom at its deepest, thanks to which that Epicurean vision of divinity suddenly appears to be the creation of an incomparable race of artists and almost the highest possible form of creation. ("DW," 560)

"Almost." Nietzsche's remark implies a subtle paradox that needs to be teased out. The modern image of Greek "cheerfulness," we might say, is too Epicurean, too eudaimonic and carefree, if only because it is not sufficiently Epicurean, or, as Nietzsche would say in his essay "Homer's Contest" (1872), not sufficiently "*Greek*": "I fear that we do not understand these people in a sufficiently 'Greek' way, indeed, that we would shudder were we to understand them for once in a genuinely Greek way" (p. 784).[2]

On the Epicurean view, as we have already seen, divinity is to be taken as an emphatically human invention: the gods are simulacral beings consisting of atomic films that strike chords of responsion within the mind, which is itself of eidolic status; they are mere reverberations of ourselves, like the supernatural beings conjured up by nature-dwellers who, as Lucretius relates with some humor, take every echo of their own *flatus vocis* to be of divinest origin:

> Some [utterances] beating upon solid spots are cast back, and give back the sound, and at times *mock us with the echo of a word.* And when you see this clearly, you could give account to yourself and others, in what manner among solitary places rocks give back the counterparts of words each in due order. . . . Such places the dwellers around fancy to be the haunt of *goat-footed satyrs* and nymphs, and they say that there are fauns, by whose clamor spreading through the night and sportive *revels* they declare that the dumb silence is often broken; and that *sounds of strings are awakened, and sweet sad melodies*, which the pipe pours forth, stopped by the fingers of players. . . . All other marvels and prodigies of this kind they tell, *lest by chance they be thought to live in lonely places, deserted even of the gods.* (*De rerum natura* 4.570–92; trans. Bailey; emphasis added)

The wisdom that reveals Greek divinity to be a mere aesthetic invention is embodied in the wisdom of Silenus ("DW," 560), himself one of the acoustic echoes that his wisdom in turn mocks. Such wisdom is the driving mechanism of all Greek tragic knowledge, and of all knowledge measured against its limitations, but it is the full, unregenerate burden of atomism in particular: "This was the *need* out of which the artistic genius of this people created these gods" (ibid.). The passage from "The Dionysian Worldview" quoted above continues, "It is the philosophy of *the people* [*des Volkes*] that the captive forest-god ["the *Dionysian* companion," sc., Silenus] reveals to mortals: '*The best is not to be; the second best is to perish quickly.*' *It is this same philosophy which forms the background of that world of gods*"—which is to say, of the Epicurean vision of divinity (*Götterwelt*) just described, and which modern readings of antiquity fail to grasp (ibid.).[3] This background (*Hintergrund*) is the "oft misrecognized trait of the Greeks" referred to by Nietzsche. The abysmal insight of Silenus opens onto the void of atomism. Knowledge like this, devastating in its indifference to appearances and to our habits of taking them in, has the bitter taste of wormwood; Lucretius knows how desperately his wisdom needs the sweeter charms of art if it is to be faced at all (bk. 4, init.).

Of course, the very blending of *horror* (repulsion) and *voluptas* (fascination, pleasure, desire) is one of atomism's cruelest traits: atomism is both minutely absorbing and vaguely remote, aloof, and disdainful. Hence Democritus' "sobriquet of the 'Laughing Philosopher,' moved to mirth by the follies of mankind, . . . first alluded to by Cicero and best known from Horace [*Epodes*, 2.1.194]."[4] Hence, the "shrill laugh" that accompanies the wisdom of Silenus trapped by King Midas (*BT*, §3) also brings to mind Democritus, who could resemble a Silenus in different ways. In one analogy from Nietzsche's *Democritea* from 1867/68, which recalls Alcibiades' image of Socrates from the *Symposium*, Democritus is likened to a Greek statue—"cold on the surface, yet full of concealed warmth."[5] In another note, Nietzsche retails an anecdote from Julian the Apostate. Democritus is said to have promised to the Persian King Darius that he would revive his departed wife if Darius could list on her tombstone the names of three mortal beings who had lived a life without pain. "Darius was unable to come up with these three names, and so finally Democritus *laughed* and *spoke thus* [*und also gesprochen*]: 'Aren't you ashamed of yourself, foolish man, for mourning to such excess, as if you were the only person to share in this misfortune, when in fact you cannot name anybody who is free from pain.'"[6] Thus spoke Democritus *ridens*.[7] Could Democritean laughter be the ridiculous, satirical, and even satyric side of the sublime (§5) that makes Nietzsche's first book so "impossible" to read? "This crown of the laugher, the rose-wreath crown; I crown myself with this crown; I myself pronounced holy my laughter. I did not find anyone else today strong enough for that. . . . To you, my brothers, I throw this crown. Laughter I have pronounced holy: you higher men, *learn*—to laugh!" ("Attempt," 7). Not optimism, but irony, is the most easily misread feature of *The Birth of Tragedy*.[8]

Together, Silenus and the atomists form a curious alliance. They form a darker "background" behind the world of the gods and its bright façades, representing its horrific frightfulness, even as from a modern perspective they are themselves images from that well-lit world—or else, in Nietzsche's language, its *veils*. Together they point not only to the durability of myths but also to their ideality, in the absence of which life would be depressingly barren (in Lucretius' words, "lonely" and "deserted").

There is a strange circularity here, but it is no stranger than the atomistic myth of a turbulent world that empties out the myths of culture. Atomism points to the banality of metaphysical assumptions, yet as Nietzsche elsewhere shows it is itself one.[9] Seemingly remote from the consolations of a realm beyond, atomism in Nietzsche's eyes is in fact an object lesson in the *irretrievability* of metaphysical characterizations. Because all hints of this background are missing in the modern image of Greek cheerfulness, that image is more than just deficient: it is all too "*unambivalent*" ("DW," 561; emphasis added). Hence, the misprision of the modern perspective, "the yearning of the modern man for that age in which he *believes* he can hear the complete unison between nature and man" (ibid.; emphasis added). The moderns reinvent the very gods that the ancients invented, out of the same *horror vacui*, and they "dare to excuse, and even to honor," that invention "with the word 'Greek'" (ibid.). The modern view of antiquity, in other words, is too *full*.

Nietzsche is unafraid of exhausting ambivalence, and this last kind of remark from "The Dionysian Worldview," set in the context of ruminations on the origins of tragedy, is a clarion call to reading guardedly. It echoes several disparagements of an idealized reunion of man and nature in *The Birth of Tragedy*, all of which go flatly against the belief "that there was a primitive age of man when he lay close to the heart of nature" (§19). Such myths, which Nietzsche condemns as "unaesthetic," are the result of a "yearning for the idyllic, the faith in the primordial existence of the artistic and good man" (ibid.). Yet the yearning denounced here in §19 of *The Birth of Tragedy* as weakly and modern ought to be the same impulse that precipitated Greek tragedy (that yearning is, after all, called a "sentimental trait" in an earlier section) and which (Nietzsche "hopes") will precipitate its regeneration in German music "now at last, upon returning to the primitive source of its being" (ibid.). Hence Nietzsche can hold, with some apparent inconsistency, that "the *satyr*, like the idyllic shepherd of more recent times, *is the monstrous product* [*Ausgeburt*] *of a yearning for the primitive and the natural*" (§8; trans. mod.; emphasis added), while "at the very climax of joy" in Dionysian ecstasy "there sounds a cry of horror or a yearning lamentation for an irretrievable loss. In these Greek festivals nature seems to reveal a sentimental trait" (§2). The anachronism is unmistakable. "Here we should note that this harmony which is contemplated with such longing by modern man, in fact, this oneness of man with nature (for which Schiller introduced the technical term 'naïve'), is by no means a simple condition that comes into being naturally and as if inevitably" (§3).[10]

The problem with statements like these is not their contradictoriness, as if this might easily be sorted out, but their ambivalence, which penetrates the whole of Nietzsche's exposition of the birth of tragedy, and indeed of the invention of antiquity in the modern mind. We are in the same orbit as reflections on the classical ideal, inherited from Wilhelm von Humboldt, and their associated disavowals, which are all but on the surface as well: the modern nostalgia for an original and now lost condition is "an idyllic reality which one can at least always imagine as real," even if "one perhaps at some point suspects [*ahnt*] that this supposed reality is nothing other than a fantastically silly dawdling" (§19; trans. mod.).[11] "Self-forgetfulness" (§1) is the perfectly adequate description of this condition. "That is why the modern subject hankers after that age in which it *believes* to hear the complete unison between nature and mankind; that is why 'Hellenic' is the redeeming word for all those who have to look around for shining paradigms for their conscious affirmations of the will; that, finally, is why the concept of 'Greek cheerfulness' was created . . . , so that a playful life of laziness could dare to excuse, and even to honor, itself with the word 'Greek' in so shameful a manner" ("DW," 561; emphasis added).

Nietzsche's vision of a return to the primitive and the natural disintegrates in his own hands. The Dionysian experience of the ancients may be painted in uncompromising colors: "Not only is the union between man and man reaffirmed, but nature which has become alienated, hostile, or subjugated, celebrates once more her reconciliation with her lost son, man" (§1). Yet this image of transfixion is one which Nietzsche explicitly rejects as an idyll. It is all too "modern," indeed too "comforting" (§19). Like other similar images, the idyll is disguised by the very naiveté with which it is presented:

> Under the charm of the Dionysian not only is the union between man and man reaffirmed, but nature . . . celebrates once more her reconciliation with her lost son, man. Freely, earth proffers her gifts, and peacefully the beasts of prey of the rocks and desert approach. The chariot of Dionysus is covered with flowers and garlands; panthers and tigers walk under its yoke. . . . Now the slave is a free man; now all the rigid, hostile barriers that necessity,

> caprice, or 'impudent convention' have fixed between man and man are broken. (§1)

The passage, celebrating this return to primordial oneness, reads like a parody of itself. Its likely background is the processions of Eastern Greek mysteries aped (and ridiculed) in nearly identical terms by Lucretius in *De rerum natura* 2.600–628:

> Of her days of old the learned poets of the Greeks sang that <born on from her sacred> shrine in her car [Cybele] drove a yoke of lions, teaching thereby that the great earth hangs in the space of air nor can earth rest on earth. To the car they yoked wild beasts, because, however wild the brood, it ought to be conquered and softened by the loving care of parents. . . . Now the image of the divine mother is carried in awesome state through lands far and wide. On her the diverse nations in the ancient rite of worship call as the Mother of Ida, and they give her Phrygian bands to bear her company. . . . Taught timbrels thunder in their hands, and hollow cymbals all around, and horns menace with harsh-sounding bray, and the hollow pipe goads their minds in the Phrygian [viz., ecstatic] mode, and they carry weapons before them, the symbols of their dangerous frenzy, that they may be able to fill with fear of the goddess's power the thankless minds and unhallowed hearts of the multitude. And so as soon as she rides on through great cities, and silently blesses mortals with unspoken salutation, with bronze and silver they strew all the path of her journey, enriching her with bounteous alms, and snow rose-blossoms over her. (Trans. Bailey)

Lucretius' description of this florid procession ends on an abrupt note:

> Yet all this, albeit well and nobly set forth and told, is nevertheless far from true reasoning. . . . If any one is resolved to call the sea Neptune and corn Ceres, and likes rather to misuse the title of Bacchus than to utter the true name of the vine-juice, let us grant that he may proclaim that the world is the Mother of the gods, if

> only in very truth he forbear to stain his own mind with shameful religious awe (644–45; 655–59).

It is hard to read the passage from *The Birth of Tragedy* §1 with a straight face, and not just the last quoted sentence, which won't square with the aristocratism of that work (according to which Greece degenerates into democracy when "the fifth estate, that of the slaves, now comes to power, at least in sentiment" [§11]), not to mention the Aryanist racial fantasy that by implication colors the whole of the text and all of its attendant discriminations (e.g., between man and woman, Aryans and Semites, sacrilege and sinfulness, "active sin" and reactive, "mendacious deception" [§9]).[12] Other accounts of orgiastic, violent oneness in *The Birth of Tragedy* give the lie to this idyll of unison, for instance the pandemonium of the Dionysian festivals described in §2, with their "horrible 'witches' brew' of sensuality and cruelty," transfigured to be sure under the Apollinian and distinctively Greek influence, but palpable in "the similar impulses" that the Greek festivals shared with their savage Eastern counterparts nonetheless. We will come back to these underlying elements of violence at the end of this study.

Still other accounts of the primordial celebration of Dionysus sound a more cautionary and less credulous note, and some of these have been hinted at above. They are often disguised by the very naiveté with which they are presented. In §8, again, Nietzsche contrasts "the true human being" (an ideal required by Dionysiac worship as its premise) and "the man of culture" (a counterideal that is *just as urgently required*), which is to say, the "real truth of nature and the lie of culture." The contrast, which on the surface is so naively laid out, contains its own artful irony. It enacts, before the reader's eyes, the very construction of these ideals, and thus masks and unmasks, at one and the same time, the lie of the "truth" and the truth of the "lie." Not only is "the satyr the monstrous product of a yearning for the primitive and natural." It was "thus [that] he *had* to appear to the painfully broken vision of Dionysian man" (emphasis added). Desire produces the only difference that matters: its own unattainability. Moments later Nietzsche takes up a defensive posture, as though injured by the imagined objection that what he has described is a mere phantasm ("a fantastically silly dawdling," as he will soon object to the modern ideal himself, §19)—only to give away in the next instant what he has set out to defend: "The sphere of poetry does not lie outside the world as a fantastic impossibility spawned by a poet's brain: *it desires to be just the opposite*, the unvarnished expression of the truth, and must precisely for that reason discard the mendacious finery of that alleged reality of the man of culture" (§8; emphasis added). The logic reeks of disavowal. Nietzsche's own mendacious logic and hyperboles ("here the true being was disclosed, the bearded satyr") are woven into the unconscious prevarications of his "poet." Only, somehow the enactment of this massive "lie" becomes invisible and forgotten in the course of its own production, and all that is retained is its direct parallel, the better known metaphysical contrast between "the eternal core of things" ("the thing in itself") on the one hand, and "the whole world of appearances" on the other (ibid.). It is important to see that what are born here at a single stroke are two ideals, that of the Dionysian and what it would negate, born in the simultaneity of their opposition, in a "superfoetation." The sequel—everything that follows in *The Birth of Tragedy*—is not so much a consequence as a reenactment, a *redramatization*, of this fatally flawed logic, spread out now over time (much like Nietzsche's parable-like scenarios of the logic of Schopenhauer from "On Schopenhauer"). And Nietzsche's fictive present, which is reenacted whenever he is read, is one more instance of the same instant. Indeed, it is unclear whether this instant even exists outside of Nietzsche's (and consequently our) reading of it.

It should not be forgotten that the Dionysiac celebrant, whether in fact or in our "picture" of him ("perhaps" it is our picture of him only: "so we may perhaps picture him"), is lost to his intoxication, to his "mystical self-abnegation" and his denial of the *principium individuatio-*

nis, to his communion with his fellows and newly found peers: "Now, with the gospel of universal harmony, each one feels himself not only united, reconciled, and fused with his neighbor, but as one with him" (§1). Yet he is all this only on condition of being individuated, "alone and apart [!] from the singing revelers" (§2); and whatever visions he attains in this Dionysian state, as he "puts his ear, as it were, to the heart chamber of the worldwill" (§21), are got through "a *symbolical dream image*" (§2). There is, in fact, not a single passage or line in *The Birth of Tragedy* that is not similarly affected, not dissociated, like a Dionysian reveler, from the "purport" of the text, just by virtue of the text's most uncertain logic, which makes it difficult even to *suppose* "that there was a primitive age (*Urzeit*) of man when he lay close to the heart of nature" (§19). One can make this supposition, but it will always be in the form of an idyll. The primordial condition (*Urzustand*) that is the object of the will or else is objectified in it, a notebook from 1871 reads, "stands to the world as the idyll stands to the present-day": "The *will* that moves beneath all feelings and cognitions and that music represents is a *primordial condition, paradisiacal and full of presentiments*."[13]

Elsewhere, Nietzsche would suggest that these idylls of Dionysiac intoxication are in fact a symptom of idealism, pure and simple:

> Worship of *wine*, that is, worship of narcotism. This is an idealistic principle, a way to the annihilation of the individual. Strange idealism of the Greeks in their worship of narcotism. (*KSA*, 7:3[43]; 72, 1869/70)

It is an idealism that persists into modernity.[14] And with this, Nietzsche's reflections take an emphatic turn from myth to culture, from art to politics, and from idylls to ideologies. In another note, Nietzsche explicitly links these ancient idylls to the ever-burning question of political ideology. The correspondences between antiquity and modernity are disturbingly close:

> The goal of science is the annihilation of the world. This entails, to be sure, that the next effect is that of *small doses of opium*: heightening of world-affirmation. This is where we stand politically at this stage. It can be shown that the process was already carried out in Greece on a small scale, although the significance of Greek science is [relatively] minor. (*KSA*, 7:3[11]; emphasis added)

As the very persistence, in ideological form, of this idealism into the present suggests, and as Nietzsche's later writing confirms (for instance, the passages in *The Gay Science* on "European narcotics"[15]), the "background" that ultimately matters to him is not metaphysical but anthropological and cultural; and the violence of politics is only one of the arenas in which the ramifications of cultural violence make themselves felt. "All that we call culture," after all, "is made up of these stimulants" to forgetfulness (§18). In a draft that never found its way into the second preface, Nietzsche puts forward what he deems to be "one of the most difficult *psychological* questions: out of what *needs* did the Greek *invent* for himself the satyr?" (*KSA*, 14: 45; emphasis added). The answer ought to be related to the insight that "it was in order to be able to live that the Greeks had to create these gods from a most profound need" (§3), which brings us back to the Lucretian psychology of dreams announced in §1. It was the same question into need-driven behavior that had directed Nietzsche's philological and philosophical speculations while he was a student at Bonn and Leipzig. What Nietzsche discovered there is equally true here too: the question can only be reflected back onto the historical present.

Power and Appearances

Nietzsche's strategies of narration and argument (the one can often carry the other) are as devious as the "strategy of the Hellenic will"

("DW," 560) they set out to describe. Nietzsche's writing everywhere operates on different levels simultaneously, and even to isolate the strands of his narrative logic on one level is to risk running them back together on another. In the first place, Nietzsche is patently making an affront to contemporary classical tastes. The very postulate of a Hellenic "strategizing" is one such affront. But his main objective is to expose not a unified strategy but a doubling of appearances—anything to thwart an "unambivalent" picture of Hellenic culture. Thus, we are asked to contemplate not only the myth that basks in Olympian serenity but also the myth of its putative other and of their implacable feuds. Nietzsche's own strategy is to substitute one myth of the past with another less stable but no less incredible myth.

On another level, the strategies of the Greek will exposed by Nietzsche are more deviant and more devious than they at first appear. Behind the mythical façade of aesthetically pleasing congruences, and beyond the churning counterforces of Dionysus, Nietzsche reveals the rapacious force that had to be applied just to maintain the regime of tranquil appearances—a force that, upon reflection, must have been equal in potency, if not identical in substance, to its suppressed content. We may recall the Titans in chains, the various compromises struck with Dionysian elements, all the myths of a terrifying pre-Olympian order (or disorder) thankfully hidden from view: these are but the ways in which "the Delphic god *interpret*[*ed*] the Greek past" from the bulwarks of "*a political structure* [*that was*] *so cruel and relentless*" (§4; emphasis added). With this kind of commentary, Nietzsche is not striving to secure sympathies or to promote the image of a positive Dionysianism. Here, a suspicion of a deeper, more complicitous and duplicitous strategy of self-presentation on the part of the Greek spirit is justified. If earlier we saw how Dionysianism may be construed as an invention of Apollo, here Nietzsche is suggesting how this invention is politically "strategic." Apollo, after all, "shows us how *necessary* is the entire world of suffering" (§4)—the suffering for which Apollinian culture is in no small way responsible as well. What must be denied for the lie of culture to assert itself? Is the Dionysian not simply one of these lies? In this light, Nietzsche's *Birth of Tragedy* begins to look like a critique of the culture of violence and of the violence of culture, and of the ruses of their dissimulation.

Nietzsche's remarks on Apollinian forcefulness can be most unsparing at times. It pays to isolate some of these. Recalling them will restore some of the "hard, historical actuality" of Greek tragedy that Walter Benjamin felt to be missing from Nietzsche's treatment of it.[1] For instance, we can read how "in the Greeks the 'will' wished to contemplate itself . . . ; *in order to glorify themselves*, its creatures had to feel themselves worthy of glory; they had to behold themselves again in a higher sphere, without this perfect world of contemplation acting as a command or a reproach" (§3; emphasis added). Of course, just to mention this wish is to stimulate a reproach: can it be that the Greeks ever or fundamentally were unworthy of glory? The tale of self-aggrandizement is an undeniable element of the complex Hellenic will, which knew how to "ma[k]e use of [the Olympian world] as a transfiguring mirror" (ibid.). Indeed, self-aggrandizement—out of a constitutive *lack*—is just what "the ingenuous strategy of the Hellenic 'will'" is all about. That this is so is clinched by "The Dionysian Worldview": the mention of the "strategy" there occurs as a gloss on precisely the statement from *The Birth of Tragedy* in which the Greeks are said to have contrived a way of enduring existence by "surrounding [themselves] with a higher glory" (§3).

A notebook entry from the time puts this into even clearer focus

> The glorification of the will through art [was the] goal of the Hellenic will. And so the Greeks had to see to it that artistic creations were possible. Art is the free, excessive force of a people, the force that is not squandered in the struggle for existence. Here we arrive at the *cruel* reality of a *culture*—insofar as it builds its triumphal arches on top of enslavement and annihilation. (*KSA*, 7:7[18]; cf. *BGE*, 229)

Where in all of this now, one might like to ask, is the Dionysian realm, with its truths, its ecstatic revelations, its promises of redemption? All that is described is a cool and calculating cultural policy. And yet Dionysus would always have enjoyed a central role in this scheme simply by furnishing a useful contrast and a deflection, by playing the part of an ideologically imagined other to a no less ideologically imagined self.[2] Such ruses are a part of the nature of a differently conceived Greek humanity, with all its intrinsic ambivalence (its *Doppelcharakter*) and its conflicted and competitive motives, as the opening paragraph of "Homer's Contest" (1872) amply restates. The essay famously makes competition (*agon*) into the defining trait of Hellenic culture:

> When one speaks of *humanity*, one imagines, deep down, that humanity is that which *separates* man from nature and is his mark of distinction. But in reality, there is no such separation: the "natural" properties and those properly called "human" are indissociably fused together. In his highest and noblest powers, man is all nature and bears its uncanny double character [*Doppelcharakter*] within himself. His frightful and inhuman capacities are perhaps even the fruitful foundation, and the only one, from which all humanity can body forth in its movements, its deeds, and its works.
>
> So it is that the Greeks, the most humane people in antiquity, have in them a trait of cruelty, a tiger-like lust for destruction. ("HC," 783; cf. *BGE*, 229)

Apollo's role in all of this is lightly disguised. Far from forever beaming with light and sunshine, Apollo has a fierceness that occasionally breaks through the surface of his appearances. Hence his *peculiar lack of focus* in *The Birth of Tragedy*, for all his apparent clarity: "This is the Apollinian state of dreams in which the world of the day becomes veiled, and a new world, *clearer, more understandable*, more moving than the everyday world *and yet more shadowy*, presents itself to our eyes in continual rebirths" (§8, ad fin.; emphases added). Hence, too, the Doric manifestations of Apollo, with its "art so defiantly prim and so encompassed with bulwarks, a training so warlike and rigorous, and a political structure so cruel and relentless": "For to me the *Doric* state and Doric art are explicable only as a permanent military encampment of the Apollinian" (§4). We might compare "The Greek State," an essay from 1872, in which Apollo is remembered as he appears for the first time in Greek literature, bringing plague and death to the Greek warriors at Troy in book 1 of the *Iliad* ("the righteous consecrating and cleansing god of the state").[3] Sparta is only the most famous example of Dorian culture, and hardly a shining instance at that. In "Homer's Contest" from the same year, Nietzsche accuses Sparta of having "betrayed the Hellenic" character and of hastening the decline of Greece.[4] The Spartan constitution is praised in "The Greek State"; its self-destructive logic is implied by the example of Apollo just mentioned and in the delusiveness of the contest culture that is celebrated and evacuated in this essay, too:

> So overcharged is this [destructive] impulse amongst the Greeks that it forever starts to rage against itself afresh again and clamps its teeth into its own flesh. This bloody jealousy of one state toward another, of one party toward another, the murderous avidity of those little wars, the tiger-like triumph over the corpse of one's slain foe . . . , to what does all this naïve barbarity of the Greek state point? (p. 771)

These flarings-up of the Greek competitive spirit, its acts of cruelty toward others and above all toward itself, are but "the incessant renewals of those Trojan scenes of war and atrocity"—of that epic war waged in the name of an "ideal" (*BT*, §3), if not a phantom, Helen (p. 772), who is merely a symbolic instance of "the noble delusions [*Wahnbilder*] of artistic culture" (p. 765). These delusive phantoms, like cruelty in general, are a generic trait of all culture, of which Greek culture is merely a convenient paradigm.[5] Theognis, the fallen Megarian noble and one of the sources, for Schopenhauer and for Nietzsche alike, of the terrible wisdom of Silenus ("better not to have been born"), is another (similarly dubious) example of Dorianism. Indeed, he is an example of the modern Dorian racial fantasy whose actuality and fragility (and anxiety-ridden quality) Nietzsche attests to explicitly in §9 of *The Birth of Tragedy* and implicitly in the earlier sections of that work.[6]

Plainly, Apollo has a "double character" of his own, one that (I want to argue) preempts our need to have recourse to Dionysus so as to account for the shadowy aspects of Greek culture—for what is shadowy about Greek culture is precisely what appears to be so brilliantly illuminated in it. This is the (dark) core of Apollo's illusory appearances, whose goal is to appear naively as "the 'shining one,' the deity of light" and "the ruler over the beautiful illusion of the inner world of fantasy" (§1). And if it is true that "his eye must be 'sunlike,' as befits his origin," there is in turn a sternness to this imperatival must, as well as, so to speak, an illusoriness to the illusions of Apollinianism: "Even when [Apollo's eye] is angry and distempered it is still hallowed by beautiful illusion" (ibid.). For "still hallowed" we might just as well read "denied" and "disavowed." Is this what "the appearance of appearance" finally means? Apollo represents the fantasy of power "without command or reproach" (ibid.), which is to say, *power transfigured.*[7] That this fantasy has modern sources in the contemporary classical imagination in Germany and is caught up in the perplexities of nineteenth-century political projects (of which nationalism and racism are only the darkest, most fateful, and often most disavowed examples), and that the fantasy incorporated into *The Birth of Tragedy* describes not a return to antiquity but, more to the point, "a return of the German spirit *to itself*," its "blessed *self*-rediscovery" (§19)[8]—all this ought to go without saying.

The Myth of Mythlessness

We have begun to see how in *The Birth of Tragedy* and in other writings at the time Nietzsche exposes, and so gives the lie to, the noble simplicity not only of inherited forms of classicism but also of his own accounts of a counterclassical antiquity. The divisions and disparities within the myth of ancient Greece are replicated in his accounts of Apollo, which render Dionysianism strangely redundant, another appearance of divinity, another dream or fantasy of antiquity. Behind Apollinianism and Dionysianism, as we just saw, there seems to lurk a vast ruse that the Greek spirit perpetrates upon itself in the name of its self-glorification. The aim here, which is perhaps largely unconscious, is that the Greek might "feel himself a god," as through a kind of psychical investment (a "transference") and imaginary "acting" (§8), and so might "walk about enchanted, in ecstasy, like the gods he saw walking in his dreams," "no longer an artist" but "a work of art" (§1). On a third level, what we find in Nietzsche's first book is an inexorable attack on the credibility of all myths. Here we detect a sense of strain, of extremity: plausibility is taxed, myths counteract myths and all but cancel each other out in an overwhelming dubiety—all but, because myth can never cancel out myth, but can only perpetuate itself in another form. Everything points to the fact that Nietzsche is seeking to erase the modern myth of the Greeks by exposing its mythical and (as we now see more clearly) political "underbelly." That he is doing this is not quite stated but it is at least suggested by the following, which turns on the question of the moderns' receptivity to myths in general:

> It is probable, however, that almost everyone, upon close examination, finds that the critical-historical spirit of our culture has so affected him that he can only make the former existence of myth credible to himself by means of scholarship, through intermediary abstractions. *But without myth every culture loses the healthy natural*

> *power of its creativity: only a horizon defined by myths completes and unifies a whole cultural movement.* (§23; emphasis added)

Here, as in so many other places, Nietzsche is advertising the fictionality of his undertaking. *The Birth of Tragedy* is not about the birth of Greek tragedy so much as it is about the "rebirth of German myth" (ibid.). Its idealities, passed off as Greek, are those of the modern world; described are modernity's utopic longings and anticipations of a metaphysical Beyond and the location of this Beyond in an ahistorical myth—the myth of Greece, in the form of a "comfort [that] appears in incarnate clarity in the chorus of satyrs, a chorus of natural beings, who live ineradicably, as it were, behind all civilization and remain eternally the same, despite the changes of generations of the history of nations" (§7). Part of the comfort surely resides in the *ahistorical* assurances of the vision, which thus guarantee its accessibility and relevance to the modern world. Hence Nietzsche's claim from a contemporary notebook that "what we [Germans today] *can* do is interpret the world for ourselves *in a purely Dionysian way*," which is no contradiction but a complete confirmation of his previous critique of "pure Dionysianism": "*Pure Dionysianism is impossible.*"[1] What force and what violence perpetuate the contemporary myths of antiquity?[2]

The surrounding materials from Nietzsche's philology invite the question by themselves. There, he toys with various inversions of his own mythology of the Dionysian by bringing it into proximity with characteristically modern, not ancient, developments. The alliance of the Dionysian phenomenon with music is a case in point. It has sometimes been objected that, whatever else he may have known in his capacity as a philologist, on the question of music and its modalities Nietzsche failed to grasp the fundamental differences that set apart the classical Greek and modern European systems.[3] Nothing could be further removed from the reality. Compare the following from a contemporary lecture course, held in the summer semester of 1871 (and announced for 1873/4) under the title *Encyclopedia of Classical Philology*, in a segment on "Rhythm and Meter": "The error [of modern philology] lies in having taken our music to be identical to ancient music."[4] Nietzsche recognized, well in advance of other philologists, that in music the differences between the two cultures are as unbridgeable as they are on the question of time and rhythm, and for the very same reasons. Music, for Nietzsche, is a litmus test of culture, and indeed lies at the root of cultural perception generally; and so the statement is a strong assertion of cultural difference.

In the *Encyclopedia* lectures he is resuming his thesis from his studies on ancient, especially Greek, rhythm and meter, which began their life as lectures in the previous semester and then evolved over the next year or two into an ambitious project on "the history of sensation" that never saw the light of day. In the notebooks on rhythm, which are principally devoted to reconstructing the ancient sense of time (a sensibility we no longer share), Nietzsche sketches out an attack on the essence of modern music, melody. The very idea of Greek melody, in our sense of the word, is unthinkable; it is a sheer contradiction in terms: "The concept of *melody* is nonexistent (*and if melody existed*, then there was no *appreciation* for it)."[5] All modern melodic conventions, resting as they do on a harmonic as opposed to monophonic conception of music (the latter being based on the melodic line), are unknown to the Greeks. Counterpoint and harmonic dissonance, not to mention the consonance of chords, must be forgotten if a clear view of the Greek practice is to be attained: "The nature of classical music must be reconstructed. . . . Originally (in citharodic music), the note functions as a measure of time."[6] It is the proportional, quantifying, and purely temporal characteristics of the Greek sensibility that are erased, Nietzsche claims, by the introduction of the criterion of the ictus (the dynamic accent), counterpoint, and harmonic consistencies, all of which run through the emotional intonings of the modern scholarly establishment. Philology, which traditionally sought to recapture the accentual rhythms of Greek music and verse and thus to draw these phenomena into closer proximity to the modern understanding, is here shown to rest on an unconscious, or else willfully ignored, anachronism.[7] Nietzsche's irony in his reconstruction of Greek sense of time, rhythm, and music is that the Greek art forms are not only irretrievable and permanently lost (*unwiderbringlich*), to quote from a somewhat later notebook (1875),[8] but also a priori unintelligible to us today. The later chapters of *The Birth of Tragedy* are devoted to the alleged "rebirth" of tragedy "out of the spirit of music." But surely this hope for a return *ad fontes* and to a musical spirit that could be reclaimed today as "ours" is overshadowed by the very sorts of impossibility Nietzsche is demonstrating in his lectures on rhythm at the very moment he is composing his first book.

What is perhaps worse, in his notebooks on rhythm, the distinctive features of Dionysian music are explicitly conjoined with more recent "innovations" in "tonality," which is to say the modern expressive medium. The same tendency is reconfirmed in the second section of *The Birth of Tragedy out of the Spirit of Music* (as the full title of the first edition reads), where we find Dionysus associated with "tone," "melody," and "harmony," the characteristic triad of the modern musical sensibility for Nietzsche, at least in his notebooks on rhythm:

> *The song and pantomime of such dually-minded revelers was something new and unheard-of in the Homeric-Greek world*; and the *Dionysian music* in particular excited awe and terror. *If music, as it would seem, had been known previously as an Apollinian art, it was so, strictly speaking, only as the wave beat of rhythm*, whose formative power was developed for the representation of Apollinian states. *The music of Apollo was Doric architectonic in tones, but in tones that were merely suggestive, such as those of the cithara.* The very element which forms *the essence of Dionysian music* (and hence of music in general) is carefully excluded as un-Apollinian—namely the emotional power of the *tone*, the uniform flow of the *melody*, and the utterly incomparable world of *harmony*. (*BT*, §2; emphasis added)

What is remarkable about this passage is not only that it pressupposes the breakthrough discovery of Nietzsche's notebooks on Greek rhythm and music; it plainly alludes to the particulars of this thesis. Apollo represents the formal architectonics ("proportionality") of classical Greek temporal restraints *prior to their degeneration* into modern accentual and polyphonic vocality and music. The cithara, with its monophonic tones, designates the original, classical form of rhythm. As we saw, "originally (in citharodic music), the note functions as a measure of time"; and "music, as it would seem, had been known previously [prior to its radical transformation] as an Apollinian art," which is to say "only as the wave beat of rhythm." This is plainly a restatement of the hypothesis of classical quantitative rhythm and its eventual (and violent) erosion. No less remarkable is the fact that Dionysianism, by virtue of being opposed to Apollinian music and by being placed chronologically after the latter's demise, represents characteristically *modern* musical traits: the emotional tone, melodic flow, and "the utterly incomparable world of harmony." And later on, Nietzsche repeats this judgment about "the infinitely richer music known and familiar to us," against which Greek music in all its forms falls irremediably short (§17). The conclusion seems inevitable: Dionysus is, musically speaking, a historical anachronism, a projection of the modern sensibility (indeed, an instance of "sentimentality" in the Schillerian sense [§2]) onto a mythical background. Later, in §17, Nietzsche goes on to underscore the failings of Greek art: "What the [Greek] word-poet did not succeed in doing, namely attain the highest spiritualization and ideality of the myth, he might very well succeed in doing every moment as creative musician." The concealed irony here is that *it is our ideals the Greek poets fail to measure up to*; they are failed instantiations of our own projections. As if to supplement what they lack, "we are almost forced to construct for ourselves by scholarly research the superior power of the musical effect" which they "might very well" have succeeded in attaining. (In his notes on rhythm, Nietzsche acidly criticizes modern scholars for trying to do just this: there, Greek music is no longer even sensuously imaginable, so removed is the modern sensibility from its ancient counterpart.) But "even this musical superiority, however, would only have been felt by us had we been

Greeks," and so we are forced to "*imagine* we hear only the youthful song of the musical genius modestly intoned" (§17)—a statement that is full of untold ironies and complication.[9]

One of these ironies is the not very widely known fact that Nietzsche is both rehearsing a prejudice of Wagner's and turning Wagner's analysis on its head. In his essay "Zukunftsmusik" from 1860 (published in 1861), Wagner had already anticipated many of the same general claims that Nietzsche is making both here and in his notebooks on rhythm—the claims about the distinguishing differences between ancient and modern music; about what Wagner calls the "incomparable" superiority of the modern innovations in "harmony" (which he says was "entirely unknown in antiquity") and "melody" (viz., "polyphony"); and about the "essential" feature of ancient melody, namely its "uncommonly lively and changeful rhythm," owing to its nearness to dance: for the Greeks, "music is only an accompaniment to dance"; worse still, "Greek music can be regarded as only dance expressing itself in tones and words."[10] So far, Nietzsche seems to be faithful to the maestro's musical analysis. But the complication lies in the fact that where Wagner had referred to a "rebirth" of the fine arts in the Christian era (meaning painting and music), and where he viewed the developments of Italian opera, with its reintroduction of the more primitive but by then "incongruous" role of rhythm and "dance melody," as a "*relapse into paganism*,"[11] Nietzsche wants to view Wagner's perfecting of the opera form as *deriving* from "the spirit of *ancient* music," which needless to say has something to do with the orgiastic dithyrambic dances of Dionysus (§§5, 8, 9, 21, etc.). The compliment cannot have been entirely well received, even if the ecstatic transports of Dionysianism had their appeal. And anyone who cared to inspect Nietzsche's categories and wished to sort them out would have been facing a similar puzzle: the pieces are all familiar; they simply don't fit where they ought to belong. Dionysianism is being asked to stand for too many incongruous things. It is primitive; it is post-Apollinian; it is quintessentially Greek; and it is barbaric even to the Greeks. In a word, it is—*modern*.

In the *Encyclopedia of Philology*, Dionysus is more than a simple anachronism. The sign of a dark metaphysical tendency (and "need") that ripens over time and finally flowers in the Alexandrian age, Dionysianism runs the risk of being a retroactive construction of the Christian modern world itself and its *Jenseits*-yearnings: "With Alexander, this impulse [to the Beyond] sets in once again: it is characterized by the expansion of Dionysus-worship." As the ages go by, down to late antiquity, the tendency ripens, only to blossom in the late antique "mysteries of Dionysus, Hecate, Venus, Sabazius, Isis, Mithras—everyone [living at the time] is unanimous about that. As a result, the character of the here and now [*Diesseits*] changes." Christianity is but a short step away. In fact, these Greek worshippers are essentially Christians, and Dionysus has metamorphosed into Christ, "for the goal of existence is [now] referred to a Beyond." In this way, a trait that had been developing ever since tragedy began to slip into decline at the end of the fifth century is finally realized.[12] Doesn't *The Birth of Tragedy* fulfill these yearnings for a *Jenseits* the way no Greek myth possibly could? Once again, the story of the birth of tragedy as told in the lectures stands the surface narrative of *The Birth of Tragedy* on its head. And yet, a close look at Nietzsche's book will confirm the tendency of the lectures even there. Compare the closing lines of section 12 of *The Birth of Tragedy*. After Socrates "put to flight the powerful god," Dionysus "sought refuge in the depths of the sea, namely the mystical flood of a secret cult which gradually covered the earth." There is little point in belaboring the obvious: the "secret cult" named here is nothing other than Christianity itself.[13]

But that is not all. Earlier, I made a supposition about the priority and exclusivity of the Apollinian realm of representation vis-à-vis the Dionysian realm of reality. The nineteenth lecture from the *Encyclopedia* lends further support to this idea. While tracing the historical evolution of Greek divinities in the Greek mind, Nietzsche at one point writes:

> The divine world of beauty *produces* [literally, "gives birth to," *erzeugt*] the chthonic divinities [viz., the "horrible" world of "Hades, Persephone, Demeter, Hermes, Hecate, and the Erinyes" and "then Dionysus"] *as its own supplement.* These latter, more formless in themselves [*an sich*] and more related to the Concept [*Begriff*], increasingly gain the upper hand and [then] cause the whole Olympian world to vanish together with the heroes, as symbols of *their* [sc., the chthonic gods' own] secrets.[14]

What is fascinating about this remark is the reversed genealogy it introduces into Nietzsche's proposed evolutionary scheme, rupturing it from within: the striking claim about the invention—the aesthetic creation—of the dark chthonic divinities out of the brighter Olympian world, the origination of the mysteries and of a realm beyond (*Jenseits*), not to mention ecstatic orgies, initially absent from the scene.[15] In short, this is the invention of the Dionysian godhead out of an Apollinian framework. The aesthetic supplement of the pre-Olympians, Nietzsche maintains, is at bottom philosophically motivated: it constitutes a response to a deep "metaphysical need," and it represents a movement toward intellectualization, toward Platonism (the invented gods are "closer to the Concept," to the peculiar formlessness of the Platonic Idea), and thus toward the (Romantic) idealism of modernity. The pattern described here is strictly correlative to Nietzsche's claim in *The Birth of Tragedy* about Prometheus' secrets, which intimate "a twilight of the gods" and betoken a "skepticism" on the part of the Greeks toward "the Olympians" (the reference is to Aeschylus). The "Dionysian truth" that Prometheus represents "takes over the entire domain of myth as the symbolism of *its* knowledge" in the form of tragedy and "dramatic mysteries"—but all this leads, at the same time, toward the decline of these fifth-century forms. "The feeling for myth perishes" (§10).[16]

A further correlation is the claim in *The Birth of Tragedy* that the appearances of art are "not merely an imitation of the reality of nature but rather *a metaphysical supplement* of the reality of nature, placed beside it for its overcoming" (§24).[17] Art exists both to seduce us into discovering the deeper mysteries of reality and to protect us from ever attaining them: "The brightest clarity of the image did not suffice us for this seemed to wish just as much to reveal something as to conceal something" (§24). Both images are an illusion—both the clarity of the Apollinian veil (which in itself is a mere aesthetic illusion) and the illusion the veil creates of a depth lying beyond itself. As with Parrhasius' *trompe l'oeil*, the veil is nothing more than the idea—the suggestion—of a hidden depth: "Its revelation, being like a parable, seemed to summon us to tear the veil and to uncover the mysterious background; but at the same time this all-illuminated total visibility cast a spell over the eyes and prevented them from penetrating deeper." The veil conceals nothing, or rather (to recycle a cliché that nonetheless is uniquely applicable here), it conceals the fact that there is nothing to conceal. The reality of nature for Nietzsche, at least on the position he challenges us to imagine for ourselves, consists not in a metaphysical primordial condition (for this is but a "supplement") but rather in a world conceived in the absence of metaphysics (to the extent that this can be so conceived). What does the world look like in the absence of Apollo, which is to say, without its Apollinian transfiguration? The thought is literally unthinkable, and the ecstasies of Dionysianism are a protection against this knowledge.

If the situation today is in no way different from the Greece depicted by Nietzsche, there are good reasons for this parallelism. Whence, after all, does the image of Greece stem?

> We were *comforted* by indications that nevertheless in some inaccessible abyss the German spirit still rests and dreams, undestroyed, in glorious health, profundity, and Dionysian strength, like a knight sunk in its slumber; and from this abyss the Dionysian song rises to our ears to let us know that *this German knight is still dreaming his primordial Dionysian myth in blissfully seri-*

> *ous visions*. Let no one believe that the German spirit has forever lost its mythical home when it can still understand so plainly the voices of the birds that tell of that home" (§24; emphasis added)[18]

To gaze into the veil of appearances is to see nothing, or rather, it is to see nothing but one's self. The veil returns the self-reflection of any subject who looks into it. It sends back what in places Nietzsche calls the Apollinian *Wiederschein*[19] and what in *The Birth of Tragedy*, at its close, he calls a *Widerspiegelung*. The effect is palpable to anyone, "provided he has ever felt, if only in a dream, that he was carried back into an ancient Greek existence. Walking under lofty Ionic colonnades, looking up toward a horizon that was cut off by pure and noble lines, finding *reflections of his transfigured shape* in the shining marble at his side . . . " (§25; emphasis added). And what modern subject could resist this invitation to escape from the duller hues of a more familiar, more banal reality?

The entirety of *The Birth of Tragedy* could and perhaps should be accounted for as a myth projected back by a culture eager with anticipation for a "rebirth" of certain expressive possibilities (a rebirth of tragic art), whatever kernels of historical truth the myth may contain. In other words, Nietzsche's book seems to project a myth drawn with a deliberate perspectival distortion and in line with "the typically Germanic bias in favor of anything called 'ideal'" (§7), and not least of all in favor of the Platonic ideal, of which Greece—the idea of Greece—is the paradigm.[20]

Paradigm, but also delusive mirror. "When we speak of the Greeks we involuntarily speak of today and yesterday: their familiar history is a polished mirror that always radiates something that is not in the mirror itself" (*HA*, II, 281). This thought is perfectly available to Nietzsche during the time of his studies at Bonn and Leipzig, and it is unlikely that he suddenly forgot about it or its significance when he was writing up *The Birth of Tragedy*. Dionysianism is plainly a mirror of modernity's yearnings for a Beyond. However, the image in which modernity sees itself is crucially inverted, and hence misrecognized as other than it is. The disguising of modernity's longings as pagan and pre-Christian masks, but also at the same time names, what they really are: merely inauthentic. Another name for this inversion is Apollinian appearances, the luminous, if darkly shaded, cloud in which classical antiquity appears "today"—as "our" historical Beyond. It is in this sense that the supposition I put forward earlier concerning the priority (and exclusivity) of the Apollinian realm of representation is to be understood. If Dionysianism represents a longing for reality, Apollinianism represents what this longing cannot represent to itself. Appearances are indeed deceiving. Nietzsche's text is the incorporation of this truth once more. And so, to read *The Birth of Tragedy* in all of its unreadability, one must read self-consciously and skeptically. One must be aware of the work's transparent doublings and duplicities, of the history that distances Greeks from "us" (thus ruling out any "certain immediate vision"), and of the piling-up of lenses upon lenses and of "borrowings" through which we read—or invent—a vanished cultural phenomenon.

There are good reasons why we resist reading *The Birth of Tragedy* in this way, and these reasons, too, are anticipated by the work. If calling for a "rebirth" flatters the instincts of his readers with their own possibilities, the desirability and the need for any such reawakening brings them unflatteringly back to the decadence of a culture that is theirs ("the restless, barbarous, chaotic whirl that now calls itself the 'present'" [§15]).[21] The vantage opened by cultural possibilities can be a delusive one. Moreover, Nietzsche takes this plight of mankind, which spirals vertiginously in representations and "objectivations," and is punctuated or stalled by fleeting communions with nature ("an overwhelming feeling of unity"), to be a universal condition for all historical variation: this pattern persists "ineradicably, behind all civilization . . . eternally the same, despite the changes of generations and of the history of nations" (§7). *Plus ça change . . .* [22] Because its preconditions are persistently the same, all historical narration can be seen to be underlain by a universal irony, a repetition of appearances ("it is an eternal phenomenon"). This irony compounds the difficulties of unraveling the myth of history in Nietzsche's narrative—the more so since even this assurance of universality has already been exposed as a myth of "romantic" ideology: "This harmony . . . , this oneness of man with nature . . . is not a condition that, like a terrestrial paradise, *must* necessarily be found at the gate of every culture. Only a romantic age could believe this" (§3).

Not even Schopenhauer would have been taken in by Nietzsche's Dionysian myth. Schopenhauer, in fact, expressly takes issue with what it purports in his bemused reflections on Greek and Roman sarcophagi depicting "festivals, dances, marriages, hunts, animal fights, *Bacchanalia*." All these images are impressed with the stamp of "the most powerful impulse to life," the extremest form of which is the "copulation between satyrs and goats": these are so many vain attempts to divert the mind from mourning, to ward off the specter of death, and to betoken "the immortal life of nature and thereby to indicate . . . that the whole of nature is an appearance and at the same time the fulfillment of the will to life."[23] Such rituals are, to be sure, not Schopenhauer's recommended way to redemption from suffering. Precious time and energies, he feels, are wasted in such activities, but some benefits are to be gained as well, given "the double neediness of mankind"—its need for solace and for distracting pastimes. And so, he concedes, "this fantastical intercourse with a dreamt-up world of spirits" is "the bonus of all superstitions and not at all to be despised."[24] The concession is perhaps telling. Schopenhauer is susceptible to other superstitions and to other myths, as we have already seen, and now we may add one more: namely, his assumption that he is beyond such susceptibility altogether. Schopenhauer, the deluded metaphysician, is a good example of the "faith" that one "is altogether incapable of intoxication" (*GS*, 57).[25] Schopenhauer emphatically claims that his exposition is not historical, and "not mythical, but rather philosophical" (*W*, 1.1, §64). The mythological garb in which Schopenhauerianism is cloaked (and exposed) in *The Birth of Tragedy* therefore has added point: it names Schopenhauer's philosophy as the mythology it is.

"It is the fate of every myth to creep by degrees into the narrow limits of some alleged historical reality, and to be treated by some later generation as a unique fact with historical claims. . . . For this is the way in which religions are wont to die out: . . . one begins apprehensively to defend the credibility of the myths" (§10). One of the paradoxes operated by Nietzsche here is that myth becomes credible only when it is no longer believed in. Perhaps the "skeptically minded" Greeks never really believed in their myths. If so, then Nietzsche adds a further twist: this distrust was only theoretical; they only *believed* that they did not believe in their myths; in practice, they did. Thus, tragic metaphysics is a compensation for disbelief in Olympian divinity, the way Presocratic metaphysics is a compensation for rational demystification, and the way Platonic metaphysics is a compensation for the censure of art. In this, their capacity for self-deception, which is one of the most potent mythopoeic forces there is, the Greeks are again exemplary for modernity.

Here, at last, we can get a glimpse of what Nietzsche's "inversion" of Platonism amounts to. It is a recoiling from the remote and permanent reality of the Ideas and Forms and a validation of what invalidates them: "life in appearance [is] the goal." But it is more than this as well, because it suggests that the remoter reaches of Platonic reality just are an appearance posing as a nonappearance. When Nietzsche writes that "Plato, the thinker, arrived by a detour where he had always been at home as a poet," he does not simply have in mind the poetic accoutrements that Plato used "to represent the idea which underlies this pseudo-reality" (§14). He means *this very idea of a transcendent reality itself*. That is the ultimate poetry Plato created: his own thought. Nietzsche literally stands Plato on his head. And for the same reason, Platonism turned around on its own axis is the inversion of Schopenhauer's metaphysics: everything that Nietzsche holds against Plato holds for Schopenhauer as well. Platonism is metaphysical just because it is so deeply (and blindly) aesthetic in its posture toward reality; and Nietzsche's getting hold of reality from the opposite end, that of pure appearance, is no less metaphysical, and no less suspect. It may be that "it is only as an aesthetic phenomenon that existence and the world are eternally justified" (§5). But as we saw, Nietzsche does not actually get hold of reality in appearances, nor does he even make that his goal. On the contrary, he continually reminds us how desperate, and desperately thin, this justification is—and how difficult it nonetheless is to escape the psychological and finally the cultural truth of his own dictum. Philosophy is a mythology. But who can live in the absence of metaphysical or mythological "comforts"?

Nietzsche's attitude toward myth can be briefly described. Myths are the inevitable by-product of existence. To exist means, for Nietzsche, to be able to "stamp" life with the impress of one's character. To exist in an active way means to stamp life (the "immediate present") with all the force of conviction, to press upon the flux of the world "the stamp of the eternal" (§23). This, too, remains a tenet for Nietzsche from first to last, as he himself recognized and could even rightfully boast: "That every strengthening and increase of power opens up new perspectives and means *believing in new horizons—this idea permeates my writings*" (*WP*, 616; emphasis added). The word "horizons" tells ever so slightly against the upbeat tone of the statement. It brings to mind not simply the conquest of new territories, but the limits of conquest itself. And from *The Birth of Tragedy* we now can add a further meaning to "horizons": it designates the presence of myth. For "without myth every culture loses the healthy natural power of its creativity: only a horizon defined by myths completes and unifies a whole cultural movement" (*BT*, §23). And so too, within a year of the quotation from *WP* above, Nietzsche could write, expressing an apparent heresy with regard to his own "later," presumably anti-metaphysical dogma: "*To impose upon Becoming the character of Being*—that is the supreme *will to power*" (*WP*, 617; first emphasis added; 1886/87).[26]

Nietzsche's concessions to idealism are unsettling, nor can they be explained away. The corollary of this idealism, however, is its momentary and repeated nullification. For it is not enough to lend the world the stamp of the eternal and the impress of conviction: one must, *and perhaps can only*, continuously (and disruptively) perform this act, again and again ("eternally"), with equal conviction, and not just from one *saeculum* to the next but with each new moment and each new perception. Only so can the genuine threat of an indifferent world be in some sense stilled, and the "metaphysical drive," which is an innate part of our constitution or at the very least an ineluctable part of our "representational apparatus"—"our 'unconscious metaphysics'" (§23)—be safeguarded against its own metaphysical pretensions and delusions. This is the abstract lesson to be learned from the early critical essay on Schopenhauer and from the subsequent notebooks down to the publication of *The Birth of Tragedy*. Nietzsche's "first book" does no more than dress up, in another set of mythological trappings, the same insight into the ambivalences of human nature. And both kinds of reflection, philosophical and mythological, point back to the contemporary present.

Now if it is true that the moderns live trapped in their own historical consciousness, this is not because they have forsaken all myths. It is because they have adopted a new myth, one that is on the surface incompatible with all prior myths, and is in fact the most transparent and therefore most invisible myth of all: the (characteristically modern) *myth of mythlessness*. It is this myth of historical consciousness which is saturated with fictions (whether "Alexandrian," "Socratic," or "scientific"), that Nietzsche is out to puncture, in part by provoking the self-appointed "mythless man" of the present into open self-contradiction: "And now the mythless man stands eternally hungry surrounded by all past ages, and digs and grubs for roots, even if he has to dig for them among the remotest antiquities" (§23). What Nietzsche is describing is "our mythless existence" today (§24). Nietzsche's final position is not an invitation to metaphysical thinking, but an invitation to mythical, indeed to "mythopoeic" thinking (§17), in the face of its plain falsity and deceptiveness.[27] It is an invitation to acknowledge (not embrace) the disguised metaphysics of thought that is being practiced in the contemporary present. The prospects for success in this venture are undoubtedly bleak, and are best encapsulated in the trio of names that Nietzsche gives to the "mothers of being" who act as the titular guiding spirits (and virtual epigraph) of the project of his book: *Wahn*, *Wille*, *Wehe*, "Delusion, Will, Woe" (§20, ad fin.). To put it bluntly, Nietzsche's invitation is a test that nobody can possibly pass.

To be able to recast the present, the mundane, and the indifferent as a willful myth—this is the sign of great myth-making and great cultural capacity. It is also the sign of a great need, and of cultural degeneracy.[28] To be able to recast the past (our vision of it) once more, and then again and again, is the sign of this capacity and this decadence exponentially raised. Nietzsche shows why the Greeks are a necessary myth in our culture. He shows why it is equally necessary for us to reconsecrate their image through a smashing of the idols, and through an even more iconoclastic regeneration of their fragments. But above all, he shows why we can never do so completely or to our complete satisfaction. What compels us to myth also forces us to shrink back in horror from it. The pattern will continue so long as the most unendurable of glimpses is not into the mysteries of some essence, but into the unvarnished, unreflective, and distortion-free surface of the present. And that spectacle, Nietzsche suggests, can be glimpsed only through another, through the myth of its possibility.

Reference Matter

Notes

INTRODUCTION

1. Ritschl to Kiessling, cited in Stroux 1925, 32–33; Kaufmann, Translator's Introduction to *BT*, p. 13.

2. Haunting—and vexing—is the question of just when his insanity sets in. One of Nietzsche's early physicians later opined that his patient's insanity commenced at the time of *Human, All Too Human* (see Hayman 1980, 203); at the other extreme, after visits to the insanatorium in Jena, Nietzsche's friends frequently denied that he was insane at the time (see the testimonials reproduced in Hayman 1980, 340–41). Others would place the onset of Nietzsche's insanity already in 1872, for instance his teacher Ritschl, who privately found Nietzsche to be touched with "ingenious vertigo" and "megalomania" (Ritschl's diary entries, cited in Hayman 1980, 146). Clearly, a medical approach to the problem is of limited value, for what would it prove? Nietzsche's self-identity in his writings throughout his career is constitutively unstable; see Porter 1998, 183–84 with n. 62.

3. Lange 1866, v. All future references to Lange will be to this edition unless otherwise noted.

4. *W*, 1.1, §25.

THE PROBLEM OF PERIODIZATION: NIETZSCHE'S APPEARANCES

1. *GM*, Pref., 3.

2. Letter to von Gersdorff, end of August 1866. Compare a later notebook entry: "Kant has in a certain sense had a destructive contributing impact, for the belief in metaphysics is a thing of the past. Nobody will be able to count

on his 'thing in itself' as though it were a binding principle," and knowledge i now dangerously without reins (*KSA*, 7:19[28]; 1872/73). Compare the fol lowing early statement by Nietzsche, in which the contrast between appear ances and things in themselves is indirectly put into question: "What right d we have to take the mode of appearance [*Erscheinungsweise*] of a thing, e.g., c a dog, to be pre-existent? The form is something [that exists, has meaning] fo us. Once we conceive [the form] as a cause, *we lend to an appearance the value a thing in itself*," that is, of a transcendental ground ("TSK," 389; emphasi added). The contrast between appearances and things in themselves is radi cally put into question in the essay "On Schopenhauer" (on which, see below

3. Letter to Deussen of April/May 1868.

4. "TSK," 372. Cf. *HA*, I, 19: "We continue to feel ourselves compelled t assume the existence of a 'thing' or material 'substratum'. . . . Here too ou sensations divide that which moves from that which is moved [cf. *GM*, I, 1 on the "doer" and the "deed"], and we cannot get out of this circle because ou belief in the existence of things has been tied up with our being from tim immemorial."

ABYSSAL METAPHYSICAL SURFACES: F. A. LANGE

1. Thus, if it is the case that "the contrasting inclinations and opinions tha are deeply grounded in human nature" can never be resolved, they can at leas be "incredibly softened and to a certain extent reduced to a harmonious antag onism" (!)—so Lange hopes in his foreword (1866, p. iv). On the general his torical trajectory traced in Lange's study, see Porter 2000, ch. 1.

2. "Epicurus showed . . . a more genuine philosophical spirit than an other of the philosophers of antiquity" (so Kant, detailing some of the point of overlap between his system and the atomist's).

3. "That in which the sensations can be posited and ordered in a certai form, cannot itself be sensation" (A20/B34).

4. In fact, Jacobi, in 1787 (Jacobi 1812–25, 2:291–310), was the first t raise this worry, which subsequently became a standing issue in Kant criticism See Vaihinger 1881–92, 2:35–55; esp. 36–38, 53.

5. The metaphor of limit for Kant's "rule" is in some respects un-Kantian as is the exploitation of the ambiguity in the meaning of *Grund*: "(empirical cause" / "(transcendental) ground." In the later edition (1873–75), the argu ments borrowed from Ueberweg are silently dropped, and the shrill urgenc of the passage is toned down, doubtless because of the influence, which Lang

openly acknowledged (1974, 2:498; cf. ibid., 576 n. 35), of Hermann Cohen's more refined analysis of the first *Critique* (1871). But these conceded weaknesses of the first edition (they are in fact its source of polemical and rhetorical power) do not touch the larger doubt as to the objective a priori validity of the Kantian categories. This is a critical position that Lange never recanted (cf. Lange 1974, 2:577 n. 37), and it has had more recent exponents (e.g., Guyer 1987, 98, 369; Waxman 1991, 290).

6. A statement from Nietzsche's notes, dating from late 1867 to early 1868, reads: "Philological 'objectivity' . . . is nothing but 'subjectivity' on another level [*auf einer weiteren Stufe*]" (*BAW*, 3, 324). This is a direct translation of Lange into philology. The same process of endless projection has implications for the very style of Nietzsche's writings and the ways in which they are voiced; see Porter 1994, 220.

7. Lange 1866, 493 (where the word "indifferent" appears at all only because of this fundamental indifference to the question of essences).

8. See Lange 1866, v: because, as Kant shows, there is no way to grasp the unknown factor that is in part constitutive of our knowledge and experience, "it is quite certain . . . that metaphysics as a science is a self-deception for this very reason, even as the value of metaphysics resides in providing the architecture of our concepts, indeed in constituting one of the most essential needs of mankind." Cf. ibid., vii, literally italicizing the unhinderable "*impulse* [Trieb] *to produce divinity*," which is "*deeply rooted*" in human nature; "*related to the jenseitiges nature of things*," this impulse is the source of all our fantasies, without which life is literally unthinkable. And yet Lange will have nothing of such mysticism (and "personifications" [ibid., 374–75]). He is a profoundly enlightenment-style thinker (as is Nietzsche's Democritus). Schopenhauer, too, knows about "metaphysical needs" and even about the inescapability of representation; but Lange is highly critical of Schopenhauer, and Nietzsche will follow suit (see below).

9. Whence Nietzsche is said to be able eventually to "surpass" Lange, by abolishing finally (or else, explicitly) the contrast between appearances and things in themselves; so Salaquarda 1978, 245 (Lange's *Zwischenposition*); and Stack 1983, 60, 218 ("implicit in Lange, . . . explicit in Nietzsche") and p. 219 n. 36 (dating Nietzsche's critical stance toward things in themselves to "as early as" *Human, All Too Human* [1878], when it in fact goes back as far as the materials covered in the present book). In all these studies there is, moreover, a failure to distinguish between Lange's first and second editions (see n. 5, above). A laudable exception to this orthodoxy is Meijers 1988, 388.

10. Once again, Lange is giving Kant a materialist twist, but he is also sub-

tly reweaving a thread in Kant's thought. The concepts of subject and object which for Kant are convergent upon a mutually inaccessible thinghood (the subject qua Thing being formally correlative to the object qua Thing), for Lange in fact share a mutual (and we might say, material) identity: "The concept of the self is, initially and in its spontaneous nature, completely indissociable from the concept of the body; and this body is the diorama-body, the retinal body, fused with the body of tactile sensations, the feelings of pain and pleasure" (p. 490). Kant's "commerce [of the subject] with bodies" (*CR*, A346), which he places after the moment of spontaneous transcendental apperception (but before its representation as an idea), is in Lange now inverted: it comes before this apperception and is its spontaneous condition of possibility, but only in the wake of its being represented to the subject as an idea (as a possibility, and as inaccessible to the subject).

THE APPEARANCE OF METAPHYSICS IN 'THE BIRTH OF TRAGEDY' AND BEYOND

1. Nehamas 1985, 96–97.

2. See *GS*, 354 ad fin.; and cf. *WP*, 565: "Qualities are insurmountable barriers for us"; *KSA*, 12:6[13]: "We will get rid, last of all, of the oldest stockpile of metaphysics, assuming we *can* get rid of it—that stockpile that is incarnate in language and in the categories of grammar and that has made itself so indispensable that it may seem that we would cease to be able to think at all were we to renounce this metaphysics"; and "TSK," 372 (cited 168 n. 4); *KSA* 7:19[159] (1872/73): "We can free ourselves from *qualities* only with difficulty." These concessions and others like them have all-important implications for the theory of the will to power, a point that cannot be argued here.

3. "PTG," 846.

4. "PTG," 846; cf. p. 845, characterizing the Presocratics as steeped in "mythical thinking" (viz., that of their own philosophies) and as showing "highly volatile" imaginations.

5. "PTG," 813: "metaphysical article of faith [*Glaubensartikel*]"; and *KSA* 14, 109 (now, *KGW* 3.5.1, p. 859) from a draft of "PTG": Thales' "idea [*Einfall*]" is a "metaphysical assumption [*Annahme*]" expressed as a scientific hypothesis.

6. See Porter 1998 and 1999 for some arguments concerning the will to power.

7. This culturalist reading of metaphysics is prevalent from early on in Nietzsche, as was glimpsed above in the discussion of Nietzsche's Langean

cultural anthropology. Compare the following notes from 1872/73: "A cultural necessity is what drives Kant"; "in *philosophers*, knowledge comes into contact with culture again"; "truth appears as a social requirement"; "the realm of the virtues and of the arts—our metaphysical world"; Greek philosophy is a continuation of Greek culture (*KSA*, 7:19[34], [172], [175], [64], and [168]); etc. On the relentlessly "acquired" nature of unconscious impulses, present in dreams and waking reality alike, see *D*, 119.

8. Art steps in to fill the gap. Cf. *KSA*, 7:19[35] (1872/73): "*The philosopher of tragic knowledge* . . . erects no new belief. He *tragically feels the ground of metaphysics that has been pulled out from under him*, and even so he can never be satisfied with the colorful, dizzying play [*Wirbelspiel*] of the sciences. He works at building a new *life*: he gives back to art its rightful due." Further *KSA*, 7:19[39]: "The creation of a religion would reside in this, namely that someone *awakens faith* in the mythical construction that he has erected in the void (*Vacuum*)"; the note goes on to paint a picture more optimistic than is strictly warranted by Nietzsche's account and its premises of the indispensable role of "illusion" as a requirement of "life" and of "culture" (cf. ibid., 19[34]; [43]; [64]): "It is *unlikely* that this [resurrection of religious and metaphysical belief] will ever happen again" after Kant's critique of metaphysics. Nietzsche knows better. For art, which is a "metaphysical supplement" (*BT*, §24), fulfils exactly the same need, the same requirement of life; and indeed religion, metaphysics, and culture already in themselves constitute artistic solutions to this need (cf. *BT*, §15). That is, *metaphysics was already constituted by art to begin with*. Thus, "giving back to art its rightful due" is merely a matter of acknowledging art's constitutive role in the construction of metaphysics from the very beginning—and its continuing role in the same construction even after this admission is made.

9. *W*, 2.1, §17.

10. *KSA*, 7:19[72] (1872/3). The quoted words are preceded by: "Significance for culture." Cf. *BAW*, 3, 277, where we find Nietzsche's gloss for the Democritean ideal of "well-being" (*euestō*, of which Democritus was the living embodiment, according to some of his portrayals in antiquity): "he did not let himself be frightened by *eidōla*," viz., by atomic films or images, which is to say, by the theoretical reduction of appearances to such films. There is thus an irony built into the hypothesis of atomism itself, which functions as a test of our moral and intellectual character: the threat, and the daring, of atomism lies in the mere assumption of its truth; simply to *contemplate* the hypothesis is to confront its horrors and to test (or confirm) one's achievement of philosophical tranquility and happiness (the highest form of pleasure). See Lucretius, *On the Nature of Things*, Book 3, 25–30: "But on the other hand, the quarters of

Acheron are nowhere to be seen, nor yet is earth a barrier to prevent *all things being descried, which are carried on underneath through the void* [*per inane*] *below our feet*. At these things, as it were, some godlike pleasure [*voluptas*] and a thrill of awe [*horror*] seizes on me, to think that thus by thy power nature is made so clear and manifest, laid bare to sight on every side" (trans. Bailey). Nietzsche would reconfigure this "testing" of metaphysical commitments after his own fashion.

11. Cf. *BGE*, 11, on how Kantian synthetic judgments can be a priori possible: "Such judgments must be *believed* to be true, for the sake of the preservation of creatures like ourselves; though they might, of course, be *false* judgments for all that!"; and *WP*, 517: "The fictitious world of subject, substance, 'reason,' etc., is needed" to think and act. These positions are standard for Nietzsche in his later writings. Contrast the difference in tone in Schopenhauer: metaphysics is truth and it is ethically necessary; "therefore, one can set up as the necessary *credo* of all the righteous and the good, 'I believe in a metaphysics.'" It is this credo, inter alia, that allows Schopenhauer to reject the "destructive" implications of physical reductionism, e.g., of atomism (*W*, 2.1, §17).

12. Cf., however, Blondel 1986, esp. 40–43, for one exception.

13. Henceforth, references to *The Birth of Tragedy* will be given by section number only, with "Attempt" standing for the second preface. Kaufmann's frequent overtranslation of *Schein* as "mere appearance" is regularly (and silently) given here as "appearance." I will abide, moreover, by Kaufmann's rendering of *Apollinisch* with "Apollinian" rather than "Apollonian," which (like "Apolline") is as valid as the Latinizing German original.

14. Cf. *TI*, IX, 10–11; *EH*, V:1; *KSA*, 12:2[110–13]; *WP*, 798, 799, 1049, 1050. Some of these passages are discussed below.

15. Kaufmann 1974, 129, 235; Lloyd-Jones 1976, 8; Silk and Stern 1981, 118; Deleuze 1983, 14, 18.

16. See n. 18, below. Kaufmann's claim (1974, 281) that "the 'Dionysian' of *Götzen-Dämmerung* [*Twilight of the Idols*] is no longer that of *The Birth of Tragedy*" is hard to construe given Kaufmann's own admission (ibid., 177) that the precise nature (and even number) of these principles and their relations is hardly self-evident within *The Birth of Tragedy* itself. That Dionysianism involves "passion *controlled*" (p. 129) and not limitless frenzied passion (p. 282) is nothing new in Nietzsche. See Porter 2000 for arguments why Dionysianism represents a classicizing, not an anticlassicist, principle.

17. *UM*, II, 3, ad fin. Cf. *HA*, II, Pref., 1: "All my works are to be backdated" (trans. mod.), and see n. 22 below.

18. In the final sections (§§16–25) we can read, for instance, about "the playful construction and destruction of the individual world as the overflow of a primordial delight" or "the primordial [Dionysian] joy experienced even in pain" (§24); and we find a critique of Aristotle's theory of tragic effect, catharsis (e.g., §17 init. and §22), which the later theory of "overflow" and "excess" is presumed to replace, but which is already effectively in place in the earlier work. For an overview of the stages of revision and a careful critique of the view that the later additions to *BT* come unforeseen and unprepared for, see Silk and Stern 1981, 31–61, esp. 58–59. Still, like Kaufmann (cf. his n. 11 to *BT*, §15), they find the later portions of the work comparatively "less tidy" than the rest. See further von Reibnitz 1992, 36–53.

19. *KSA*, 7:19[115] and [117].

20. Some continuities cannot be denied. It is simply false, for instance, to assert that "Apollo" disappears from view, as if eclipsed by a new Dionysian intensity. The two deities, for instance, are named together twice in the passage from *Ecce Homo* above. Apollo, "the god of rhythm," is discussed in *The Gay Science* (p. 84; cf. *BT*, §2), and his tranquilizing, orderly attributes are praised. He is implicit, however, in the invocation of "the whole Olympus of appearance" that Nietzsche finds in the Greek adoration for the surface of "forms, tones, words," the outer "fold" of skin (*GS*, Pref. 4). In the same work, at §370, Nietzsche's personal copy contains two marginalia that fill out the opposition that is in any case implied. Between the "Dionysian," "the desire for *destruction*, change, and becoming, . . . an expression of overfull, future-pregnant strength (my term for this is, as one knows, the word 'Dionysian')," and "the will to *eternize*," Nietzsche wrote into the margin of his copy, "—the Apollinian, as per my old formula—" (*KSA*, 14:275). Nietzsche likewise annotated the phrase that follows about the "spreading [of] a Homeric light and glory over all things" with the parenthesis that balances the parenthesis on Dionysus above: "(in this case I speak of *Apollinian* art)." Kaufmann asserts that such marginalia, being mere "afterthoughts," needn't reflect Nietzsche's "final views," but it would take a special brand of *Afterphilologie* to divine just where to draw such fine, problematic lines as would establish Nietzsche's "final views."

There are extensive restatements of the Dionysian/Apollinian thesis in the later notebooks, as for instance in an entry from 1888 (*WP*, 798: "*Apollinian-Dionysian.*—There are two conditions in which art appears in man like a force of nature," etc.); Apollo is credited with standing for "*the highest feeling of power*," the will to power in its "classical" form (*WP*, 799); and even the earlier set of notes to the "Attempt," dating from 1885/86 and titled "On *The Birth of*

Tragedy" (*KSA*, 12:115–18), offer a more positive extension and assimilation of the earlier work than does the final preface itself. See also Nietzsche's "review" from 1888 of *The Birth of Tragedy* in *KSA*, 13:224–30 (14[14–26]; incompletely reproduced as *WP*, 1050), which is reworked in a fair copy, ibid., 520–22 (17[3]; imperfectly rendered in *WP*, 853); *KSA*, 10:8[15]; 336 (1883); letter to Overbeck, 13 July 1885 (see pp. 201–2 n. 14). Another way of putting the problem is that if Apollo all but "disappears" in the later writings, Dionysus only reappears at the time when Nietzsche begins contemplating the reissue of *The Birth of Tragedy*, as Wolfram Groddeck has shown (see Reibnitz 1992, 341). The sudden effloresence of Dionysiaca in the later Nietzsche (beginning with *BGE*, 195) is indisputably tied to this philological fact. But has Dionysus in fact disappeared between 1872 and 1885–86? It would be equally wrong to tie down Nietzsche's texts (before or after 1886) to strict denominations of the contrast between the two gods, as the example of "the entire Olympus of appearances" shows, and as does, e.g., the description of "the modern spirit, with its restlessness, its hatred for bounds and moderation," which brings to mind nothing so much as the Dionysianism of *The Birth of Tragedy* (and with good reason, as will be argued for below), and to which are now opposed, as representative Greek traits, "artistic conscientiousness," "charm," "simplicity," and self-imposed "constraint" (*HA*, I, 221); or else the continuities between passages such as *D* 72 and *A* 58 (which presuppose an identification of Dionysianism with Christian mysteries, on which see the final section of the present study); not to mention the presence of the contrast in all but name in the lectures, *Encyclopedia of Classical Philology*, to be discussed at the end of this study. Clearly, what we look for, whether consciously or not, will precondition what we find.

21. Nietzsche glosses what is meant by "a pessimism of strength" in the immediate sequel thus: "An intellectual predilection for the hard, gruesome, evil, problematic aspect of existence, prompted by well-being, by overflowing health, by the *fullness* of existence," etc. "Pessimism" is plainly an ambiguous term; indeed, it is doubtful whether it has any literal meaning, not least of all because Nietzsche (I believe) feels that pessimism is an incoherent position for anyone to hold. See nn. 22, 26, 27 below.

22. Nietzsche says as much himself, in notes that eventually find their way into his second preface to *HA* from 1886, alluding to further, secret tensions (notably with Wagner), but also echoing notes contemporary with *The Birth of Tragedy* (*KSA*, 12:6[4]). The notes are conceived as projecting—remarkably—a book of prefaces. In the final version (*HA*, II, Pref., 1), all that remains of the statement about *BT* is the following: "All my writings are to be backdated" (in

the notes he more strangely says, "*are* backdated"), inasmuch as they contain ideas already palpable in earlier writings, the way the first three *Untimely Meditations* "go behind even" *The Birth of Tragedy*, "as it will not be concealed from the view of anyone who subtly observes and compares" both works: Schopenhauerian pessimism had in *The Birth of Tragedy* already been "vanquished" (*überwunden*) by the doctrine of the Dionysian (*KSA*, 12, 233). *The Birth of Tragedy* bears this out, as do surrounding notes. Apart from *KSA*, 7:19[52] (1872/73): "Absolute knowledge leads to *pessimism*: art is the antidote," which recapitulates the view of *The Birth of Tragedy* completely, cf. the earlier notes: *KSA*, 7:3[95] (1869/70), "Pessimism is impractical and can have no coherent consequences! Not being cannot be a goal"; ibid., 3[32], "Tragedy is the natural curative against the Dionysian. *Life* should be possible: thus, pure Dionysianism is impossible. For pessimism is practically and theoretically illogical. Because logic is only the *mechanē* [instrument] of the will"; and ibid., 3[55], "Pessimism as an absolute yearning for non-being is impossible: [it is possible to yearn] only to be better!" This pessimistic view of pessimism might imply optimism, but Nietzsche's position is more complex; and the alternatives, so put, are too simple. For a defense of Nietzsche's newly won optimism in *The Birth of Tragedy*, see Goedert 1978 (with Müller-Lauter's comments in the appended "Discussion"); Kaufmann 1974, 131 and n. 3 to §7 of his translation; Lea 1957, 42–43; Lloyd-Jones 1976, 9; Love 1963; Nussbaum 1991. Young's dissenting view (1992) is that *The Birth of Tragedy* is ultimately "life-denying," on the grounds that its optimism is aesthetically and not morally grounded. The labels "pessimism" and "optimism" are susceptible to endless stipulation, which is one of their weaknesses.

23. "I don't want exactly to say that I fully belong to these philologists of resignation [*Resignationsphilologen*], but as I look back on the way I traveled from art to philosophy and from philosophy to scholarship, and how in philology I find myself in an ever narrower field, it nearly looks like a conscious act of renunciation on my part" (*BAW*, 5, 251 [1868/69]); cf. ibid., 3, 297–98.

24. *KSA*, 12:9[42] (*WP*, 1005).

25. Schopenhauer, *W*, 2.2, §46. See ibid., §37, where he complains that Greek tragic figures fail to take the last, proper step toward resignation: they refuse to give up on their will to life. The relevance of these passages from Schopenhauer to *The Birth of Tragedy* is likewise pointed to by Cartwright 1991.

26. Briefly, subjects as a rule are for Nietzsche constituted by their divided allegiances to affirmation: there are no intrinsically life-affirming acts and no values that are intrinsically worth affirming; on the other hand, subjects can-

not help but affirm life, not even in the attempt to unwill life (cf. *GM*, III, 28). I cannot make this point here; I discuss it in a study in preparation (*The Seductions of Metaphysics*).

27. *KSA*, 7:3[42], [62]. Likewise, Heraclitus is the "opposite" of a pessimist; but neither is he an optimist ("PP," 281).

28. "Tragedy, with its metaphysical comfort, points to the eternal life of this core of existence, which abides through the perpetual destruction of appearances" (§8).

29. Nehamas 1985, 43; similarly, Fleischer 1988. This characterization of Nietzsche's shift in his thinking about metaphysics from early to later periods is clearly stated in Heidegger 1961, 1:180; cf. pp. 622–25. Heidegger's temporary solution (perspectivism) resembles more recent treatments, until the suspicion of something deeper (*Verborgenes*), a concealed essentialism, gains the upper hand (as on p. 626). Thus, while Heidegger is right to point out the lingering residues of metaphysical thinking in Nietzsche, he is wrong to assume that Nietzsche believed that these residues could be dispelled. The relevant issue is not whether the contrast between appearances and reality is present but what causal relations the contrast implies.

30. Benjamin 1979, 102–3.

31. Lacoue-Labarthe 1971, 66; Kofman 1977, 202; 1979, 63–76; Shapiro (1989) labels Nietzsche's advance after *BT* an "epistemological break" (p. 14), but then goes on to use the evidence of *BT* ("It is a dream. I will dream on"), as the paradigm for Nietzsche's position "after" the break (pp. 27, 34); Blondel (1986, 52–54) vacillates unclearly (but see pp. 40–43); Clark (1990) constructs careful arguments in favor of the developmental view, but skims lightly over the writings prior to *The Birth of Tragedy* that exhibit, for example, Lange's preemptive influence, only (unwittingly) to saddle Nietzsche in the end with a Langean doctrine of the *Standpunkt des Ideals* (p. 203): this would mark not an evolution in Nietzsche's thought but a reversion. Pautrat's is a subtle version of these approaches, all of which require a kind of literalism that the text will not support; his position is that Nietzsche's corpus slowly "realizes" the *impensé* that remains concealed and nonfunctional in its early "unconscious" (Pautrat 1971, 108, 115). De Man (1979, 79–102) strives to get beyond these habits of exegesis, mainly by circumventing, rather than confronting, the narrative surface of *BT*: in an odd departure from deconstructive method, the registers of the extratextual and the explicit statement are summoned so as to bring about the resounding deconstruction of the metaphysics of meaning within *BT* (87–88, 100–103, 117, a "detour" into the surrounding *Nachlass*). De Man is surely right to question the narrative authority of *BT*, but his reading

disappoints, chiefly because it assumes that Nietzsche's reasons for deconstructing his own text are improbably, like de Man's, to establish the purely semiological and rhetorical, viz., structural and nonreferential, nature of language, and therefore Nietzsche's texts can have nothing to do with "problems of psychology or of historiography," let alone culture and ideology. The result is a reading that, for all its momentary brilliance, remains reductively thin and hermetic. A more careful balancing of evidence prior to and outside of *The Birth of Tragedy* may be found in Böning 1988. See also the brief discussion in Hamacher 1986, 314.

32. At the extreme, Nietzsche's metaphysical gestures can take the form of self-quotation. One graphic example will suffice. Echoing notes from 1870/71 ("The world is an enormous, self-engendering [*sich selbst gebärender*] and self-sustaining organism" (*KSA*, 7:5[79]) that is endowed with aesthetic instincts (7[167–68] and *passim*), Nietzsche can in 1885/86 contemplate "the world as a self-engendering [*sich selbst gebärendes*] work of art" (*WP*, 796).

33. Nehamas 1985, 42–43. Apart from the fact that this sounds like a paraphrase of some of the positions held by the later Nietzsche (including the *GS* passage just quoted), I take Nehamas's stronger claim to be that Nietzsche meant this contrast in a metaphysical way earlier but not later (cf. ibid., 80). But this, too, is open to objections, some of which are supplied by Adorno 1966, 171–72 (English version, pp. 169–70). Adorno defends the distinction between essence and appearance not because of its objective validity (it is, on the contrary, "fallible"), but because it corresponds to experience ("the measure of which is what subjects objectively experience as their suffering," as the felt pain of experience) and to a distinction between the "essential" and the "inessential," in the absence of which cognition remains "stagnant and unproductive." This is Nietzsche's position, exactly. See further n. 36 below.

34. "One must even *want illusion*: the tragic lies in this" (*KSA*, 7:19[35]). This "must" is a requirement that is partly volitional and partly given by the condition (and fate) of human nature.

35. Of course, if Nietzsche's view of the thing in itself is that it does not name a "transcendent" entity that points to a metaphysical beyond, but is a "transcendental" critical concept that accounts for the mind's "immanent" operations (cf. *CR*, A296–97/B352–53; and Lange 1866, *passim*), the question of the relationship of things in themselves and appearances takes on an entirely different look. On the fallacy of assuming for Kant a realm "behind" and "beyond" appearances, see Prauss's emphatic treatment (Prauss 1974) and Allison 1983. A corollary of the transcendental view, which this view in fact presumes to expose, is the "natural" and "inevitable" nature of certain metaphys-

ical "illusions" conditioned by the nature of human reason (A298/B354f.); see also Guyer 1987, 397; Allison 1983, 250, 252. In this respect, too, Nietzsche stays within the bounds of Kantian critical philosophy.

36. Cf. also *HA* I, 20 ("A few steps back"): upon liberating himself from metaphysics, a person "needs to take a *retrograde step*: he has to grasp the historical justification that resides in such ideas, likewise the psychological; . . . without such a retrograde step he will deprive himself of the best that mankind has hitherto produced." Best . . . and worst (ibid., 18)—that is Nietzsche's (divided) position throughout his career. Cf. further p. 170, n. 2.

37. Blanchot 1969, 231. Contrast *EH*, III, "Why I Am So Clever," 9, where Nietzsche speaks of the "antithetical capacities" within himself and his cultivation of these: "Order of rank among capacities; distance; the art of dividing without making inimical; *mixing up nothing*, '*reconciling*' *nothing*," etc. (emphasis added). This only begins to describe the tense oppositionalities lived out by Nietzsche and exhibited in his thinking. Cf. *KSA*, 10:7[21] (1883): "The *other* movement, my movement, is *au contraire* the sharpening of all oppositions and gaps, the casting aside of equality, the creation of individuals of superior power," etc.

38. See "HC," 789 for a general benediction of the Greek sense of inclusive conflict as opposed to the "exclusivity" of the modern form of conflict; the contrast is between contest culture, which breeds socially productive conflict, and individual contest, which eliminates conflict. Blanchot 1969, 209, writes: "Jaspers was the first to alert us to the principles any interpretation of Nietzsche must respect so as not to render him complicitous with the forces that he never ceased to oppose." Complicitousness cannot, however, be effaced like this, as Nietzsche knew (and constantly demonstrated). See *EH*, I, "Why I Am So Wise," 1: "I know both, I am both"—both decadence and its wished-for opposite; further, Porter 1998 and 1999.

THE COMPLICATION OF APPEARANCES

1. Cf. *BGE*, 289: "Does one not write books precisely to conceal what one harbours? . . . Every philosophy is a foreground philosophy. . . . Every philosophy also *conceals* a philosophy; every opinion is also a hideout, every word also a mask."

2. "With the Apollinian art sphere [the aesthetic spectator] shares the complete pleasure in mere appearance and in seeing, yet at the same time he

negates this pleasure and finds a still higher satisfaction in the destruction of the visible world of appearance" (§24). Nietzsche is here describing not mere art, but rather "a metaphysics of art" (ibid.).

3. The logic of appearances in *The Birth of Tragedy* will prove closest to the following Hegelian insight: "The supersensible therefore is *appearance qua appearance*" (Hegel 1970, 118; emphasis added).

ANTICIPATIONS: THE PHYSIOLOGY OF DREAMS

1. Cf. *KSA*, 7:7[106] (1870/71): "On the theory of dreams: Lucretius 5 and Phidias, Heracles, then Sophocles." Beyond book 5, there is book 4.722–822 and 907–1036 on dreams and fantasies. And, of course, the theory of simulacra is found in the whole of Lucretius. See Long and Sedley 1987, 1:139–49, for sources on the later atomistic tradition.

2. 68A77–80 and fr. 166 DK.

3. See Nietzsche's observation that the "full potency of thought and inquiry is exhibited by Democritus. But in all of this he never loses his *poetic sense* of things. This is proved by the character of his own expositions [and] by the judgment he passed on poets, whom he looked upon as prophets of truth (by which he understands prophets of *natural facts*)" (*BAW*, 3, 336; emphasis added; cf. ibid., 364). To this, Nietzsche then adds: "We do not believe in fairy tales, but we are sensible nonetheless to their poetic power." That this posture will have an obvious bearing on *The Birth of Tragedy* almost goes without saying (see below).

Even so, only occasionally is it acknowledged by scholars that Democritus' theory of poetic *afflatus*, enthusiasm, and insanity, as recorded by Cicero and Horace among others, neither accounts for nor exhausts Democritus' view of poetry. That view is better seen as a comment on the *physiological* sources of poetic inspiration, which ultimately is expressed in a poem's technique and structure (fr. 21 DK). See Zeller 1856–68, 1:645; Russell 1981, 72–74; and cf. Lange 1866, 67–68, with whom Nietzsche is in complete agreement: "The enlightening effects [of Democritus' philosophy] did the entire [Greek] nation good; it was carried out in the simplest and most sober [*nüchternsten*] view of things initially available to our thought, a view that has not lost its value today even after having gone through the most various transformations: in *atomism*." Lange is obviously Nietzsche's source for the epithet "lucid" ("sober").

4. For discussion of Lucretius and Epicurus on this question, see Long and Sedley 1987, 1:144–49, commentary to §23 ("God"); for Democritus, see Guthrie 1965, 478–83; and Henrichs 1975.

5. See also fr. 166 DK, where the dream images (*eidōla*, *phantasiai*) of gods are described by Democritus in identical language: they are literally "of marvelous appearance and prodigious size" (*megala kai huperphua*). The language in both authors, incidentally, is that of the sublime, as a glance at "Longinus," *On the Sublime* will confirm. See also n. 10 below.

6. *BAW*, 4, 54; cf. 4, 78: "Democritus gives the doctrine [of atomism' founder, Leucippus] an *aesthetic* [*schöne*] exposition. His is a poetic mind. Lik Lucretius'." On Democritus and Empedocles, see *BAW*, 3, 349; on Lucretiu and Empedocles, see "ECP," 409. Further, Porter 2000, ch. 2.

7. See Henrichs 1975, 103, 104 n. 50. Long and Sedley (1987, 1:148) suggest that the evidence for Epicurus' statements about the perishability of th gods is ambiguous and possibly calculatedly irresolvable; they take the position that gods for Epicurus are ultimately a human conception ("thought constructs," 1:145) and an ethical symbol, not real. This was Lange's view too a view that Long and Sedley avowedly reproduce; see ibid., 2:490; and Lang 1866, 25 (on Epicurus), 374–75 (speaking more generally about the construction of the supersensual domain, whether of gods or fantasies).

8. See Cicero, *On the Nature of the Gods*, 1.43–49 (= Long and Sedley 1987 1:141–42); and Long and Sedley 1987, 1:145: "We do not need to make an conscious effort to form this idea [of gods]. The idea of such beings is 'innate, in the sense that it is part of our very nature to conceive it" (emphasis added)

9. Sextus Empiricus, *Against the Professors* 9.45; trans. Long and Sedle (Long and Sedley 1987, 1:143).

10. It is worth noting that the phrase about "the glorious divine figures that "first appeared to the souls of men . . . in dreams" (§1) gives the first mention in Nietzsche's published writings of an Overman creature ("*übermenschlicher Wesen*"). *Zarathustra* is universally taken to be the work in which th Overman-"doctrine" is first officially announced. Perhaps the better way t put this is to say that the Zarathustran teaching plainly echoes this earlier passage from *The Birth of Tragedy*. Cf. *Z*, II, 13 ("On Those Who Are Sublime") "Then your soul will shudder with godlike desires, and there will be adoration even in your *vanity*. For this is the soul's secret: only when the hero has abandoned her, she is approached in a dream by the overhero (*Über-Held*)" (emphasis added).

11. Letter to Rohde, 4 August 1871, replying to Rohde's letters from 1 July and 1 August 1871 (here, *KGB*, 2.2, 406). The scholar in question wa Otto Ribbeck, Rohde's colleague at Kiel at the time and the future editor o Ritschl's writings. The opposing view still has its proponents. Cf. Calder 1983 250: "Wilamowitz proved that the book had nothing to do with scholarship.

12. Cf. §23: "To purify our aesthetic insight we have previously borrowed from them the two divine figures who rule over separate realms of art."

13. *KSA*, 7:19[97].

14. A healthy exception to this rule is Jacobs 1978, esp. 12, 121 n. 2 (referring to the passage just cited), 123 n. 17, and 124 n. 25; as is, at a more general level, de Man's critique of "genetic" narratives in *The Birth of Tragedy* (de Man 1979, 79–102).

15. See Lange 1866, 4: "Mythology, which appears to us in the cheerful and light garb of the Greek and Roman poets, was neither the religion of the people nor that of the formally educated. . . . The people believed far less in the whole realm of Olympus, which was populated by the poets, than in the popular local divinities of the towns and countrysides, whose images in the shrines were revered as especially holy. It was not the resplendent statues of famous artists that captivated the praying masses, but the old, venerable, and misshapenly carved statues hallowed by tradition." What is more, Lange continues (p. 20), with the rise of philosophy, religious beliefs were reduced to rational abstractions, which were then echoed (given popular, religious form) in new mystery cults. See Porter 2000, ch. 4.

16. Lange in a sense repaid the compliment and validated this idea in the second edition of his book, in which he actually cites Nietzsche's *Birth of Tragedy* (Lange 1974, 1:49 with n. 44) in connection with the rationalization of religious beliefs in fifth-century Athens—a view that Nietzsche would have found confirmed in Lange anyway (Lange 1866, 20); see previous note.

17. Cf. "ECP," 437 (1871/74): the Greeks are, "to our astonishment, as *deep* as they are simple. . . . That is, they are *naive*." See Porter 2000, ch. 5, on Nietzsche's semiconcealed classicism and the inheritances at play here, beyond those that plainly come from Schiller (whose aesthetic practice is said to be "deep" and "idealistic" in "ITS," 25).

"DELICATE BOUNDARIES"

1. Cf. §2: "We can hardly refrain from assuming even for their dreams . . . a certain logic of line and contour, colors and groups, a certain pictorial sequence reminding us of their finest bas-reliefs. . . . "

2. For the inverse argument, which claims to show that Apollo is himself an internal effect (and "externalized projection") of Dionysus, thus preserving (wrongly, in my view) the "originary" character of Dionysus ("*origines dionysiaques*"), see Kofman 1979, 72. But our positions are similar

insofar as we agree that the (il)logic of representation produces metaphysical beliefs.

3. *KSA*, 13:14[18].

4. Ibid., 14[24].

5. See "The Problem of Periodization," n. 2, above.

6. "*. . . wenn er plötzlich an den Erkenntnisformen der Erscheinung irre wird.*"

7. See below on the Lucretian parody of Eastern cultic worship in *BT*, §2 and on the critique made in *The Birth of Tragedy* of its own idyllic Romanticism.

8. Cf. §8: "In its vision this chorus beholds its lord and master Dionysus."

9. There are near-parallels with Schopenhauer's narrative of the will, but Nietzsche diverges from Schopenhauer when he introduces the idea of *Urlust* into that of the *Ur-Eine* (§§5, 24), itself a complication of Schopenhauer (see p. 58 below).

10. The failure to make this second inference is a common mistake (which is one of oversimplification). It is made, for example, by Deleuze (1983, 11), who writes: "The contradiction in *The Birth of Tragedy* is between primitive unity and individuation, willing and appearance, life and suffering. This 'original' contradiction bears witness against life, it accuses life."

11. All three suggestions are of course compatible with the notion that "'being in itself' is a contradiction," as Nietzsche would later put it, with reference to the conceptually flawed procedures by which the notion of being is derived (*WP*, 580). But that is his earlier position, too.

12. "DW," 571; see ibid. on the "indifference toward appearances" that is the strict equivalent of the demotion of appearance.

13. *KSA*, 13:14[46] and [47] = *WP*, 799 and 821 (trans. mod.). This is to be compared (but not clearly contrasted) with what is described in another note as "the transfiguring power of intoxication," an intoxication that, moreover, "does well to lie about itself" (*WP*, 808).

14. On the sensation of incongruence, see *KSA*, 7, 366 (labeled there as being the result of a "depotentialization"). As an entry from late 1870 reads, "*Insofar as we view the contradiction, i.e., that which is unconciliatory* in this image, we experience, as it were, how the scene depicting the possessed youths *provokes* the transfiguration" (*KSA*, 7:6[3]; emphasis added). See *BT* §11 on Euripides: "With this gift, with all the brightness and dexterity of his critical thinking, Euripides had sat in the theater and striven to recognize [anything at all] in the masterpieces of his great predecessors, as in paintings that have become dark, feature after feature, line after line. . . . He observed *something incommensurable* [*Incommensurables*] *in every feature and in every line*, a certain deceptive distinctness and at the same time an enigmatic depth, indeed an

infinitude, in the background. Even the clearest figure always had a comet's tail attached to it which seemed to suggest the uncertain, that which could never be illuminated" (§11; trans. mod.). Euripides merely failed to respond to this feature of appearances with a metaphysical attitude: he clung to the surface. This same incommensurability "in every feature and in every line" is the "fine line" dividing appearance from itself. It is its "illogical element," which "as the father of every knowledge also determines the limits of that knowledge" and thereby, in the play of limit and transgression, "supports life" and "seduces to life" (*KSA*, 7[125]; 183).

15. See "The Complication of Appearances," n. 3, above, and compare Žižek's gloss on Hegel: "The suprasensible essence is the 'appearance *qua* appearance'—that is, it is not enough to say that the appearance is never adequate to its essence, we must also add that *this 'essence' itself is nothing but the inadequacy of the appearance to itself*, to its notion (inadequacy which makes it '[just] an appearance')" (Žižek 1989, 206). This recognition is precisely what the "depotentialization" of appearances is all about. As this book was going to press, I came across the following: "The standard Idealist reduction of reality as such, in its entirety, to the mere appearance of some hidden Essence falls short here: within the domain of 'reality' itself, a line must be drawn which separates 'raw' reality from the screen through which the hidden Essence of reality appears, so that if we take away this medium of appearance, we lose the very 'essence' which appears in it" (Žižek 1999, 59). Isn't this line drawn within the field of appearances the very Apolline line that produces in Nietzsche the appearance of appearance and, at the same stroke, the metaphysical (Dionysian) realm beyond?

16. Cf. *BT*, §22: "For [the attentive subject] will recollect how with regard to the myth which passed in front of him, he felt himself exalted to a kind of omniscience, as if his visual faculty were no longer merely a surface faculty . . . and as if he now saw before him, with the aid of music, the waves of the will," where the hypothetical character of this process suggests its delusory character as well.

17. Pliny, *Natural History* 35.65.

"ON SCHOPENHAUER"

1. Schopenhauer at times seems uncertain as to whether the will really does designate the thing in itself he claims it both names and identically is. See "OS," 357, quoting after Schopenhauer (*W*, 1.1., §22): the will "is the clearest, most . . . immediately illuminated appearance of the thing in itself." Young

(1987) argues that the gap between the will and the mysterium "beyond the will" (*W*, 2.2, §50) is an essential component of Schopenhauer's project. Perhaps it is. But in *W* 1.1., §22, at least, Schopenhauer defends his choice of terms: if "'will' stood as a mere sign for an unknown quantity," for some "thing in itself," then the term we used would be a matter of indifference; but it is *not* a matter of indifference: such a "thing" or "essence" is just what "the word 'will' designates," and we have direct and "immediate" knowledge of this essence. Similarly, e.g., *W*, 2.1, §25: "*Die . . . jenseit der Erscheinung liegende* Einheit jenes Willens, *in welchen wir das Wesen an sich der Erscheinungswelt erkannt haben*," etc. Thus it is equally likely that Schopenhauer is simply inconsistent in his theory, and in fundamental ways.

2. See discussion in Porter 2000, ch. 2.

3. Nietzsche makes no positive claims about things in themselves, because he has none to make. He is simply examining the way in which the concept has been positioned in the past (by Kant, by Schopenhauer, "their" thing in itself), and taking a hard look at the consequences of these views. The thing in itself whenever it appears in early Nietzsche (e.g., in *The Birth of Tragedy*) should accordingly always be read as though it were bracketed by quotation marks, but never as evidence for Nietzsche's metaphysics. Thus, Clark's reading of the thing in itself as ontologically grounded beyond space and time (1990, 57) perhaps holds true for Schopenhauer (some qualifications would need to be made), but not for Nietzsche, who is intensely critical of these commitments. Nietzsche nowhere holds to a "representationalist" model of cognition (ibid., 82–83); he attacks philosophical presuppositions, without making any truth claims of his own. It is not just in his later phase that Nietzsche comes to regard the thing in itself as "contradictory" or a contradiction in terms (ibid., 131), as the early essay on Schopenhauer shows.

4. Cf. *TI*, III, 6, where the second proposition of a thesis against contradiction reads: "The characteristics which have been assigned to the 'real being' of things are the characteristics of non-being, of *nothingness—the 'real world' has been constructed out of the contradiction to the actual world*," etc. Cf. *HA*, I:1, where oppositions are said to have meaning only in metaphysics; and ibid., I:16, where the concept of a thing in itself is ridiculed for being "empty of meaning." All this is evidence, moreover, that Nietzsche recycled the contents his own earlier (and sometimes earliest) notebooks.

5. "*Dieser Trieb ist nicht unter das* princip. indiv. *eingegangen*," sc., in the way that it should have been subsumed (p. 352).

6. As he also later holds; *KSA*, 7:5[123], 128(1870/71).

7. Similarly, *WP*, 552: "Man projects his drive to truth, his 'goal' in a certain sense, outside himself as a world that has being, as a metaphysical world, as a 'thing in itself,' as a world already in existence [*als bereits vorhandene Welt*]." This obviously has a different ring to it than Schopenhauer's monistic identification of "will" with the "world, life, just the way it is [*gerade so wie es dasteht*]" (*W*, 1.2, §54 init.), viz., "all that exists" (*das Vorhandene*) (ibid., §53).

8. See *W*, 2.1, §17 ("On the Metaphysical Need of Man"), where man is said to be an "*animal metaphysicum.*"

9. This "tangle of possibilities" and the causal nexus it delimits (*Grundgewebe*) constitutes the "fourth" in a series of fatal objections to Schopenhauer's philosophy. It is introduced, with some deviousness, as mitigating the previous three points, and as turning the tables back in favor of Schopenhauer; but it nonetheless remains the fourth of the four fatal objections (cf. "OS," 352: "*Der Versuch ist mißlungen*"). My view departs from the more conciliatory pictures drawn in previous readings of this document, e.g., by Böning 1988, 5; Crawford 1988, 95–104; and even Love 1963, 41–47, 51–52, 56–57, who gives a clear account of Nietzsche's growing disenchantment with Schopenhauerian metaphysics in this period, but without reading Nietzsche's revision of that metaphysics as itself a further critique of Schopenhauer's system, and not its positive and mystical replacement. Similarly, Barbera 1995, 133 n. 37, in an article that documents the imprint left on Nietzsche by Rudolf Haym's 1864 critique of Schopenhauer ("Arthur Schopenhauer"; rpt. in Haym's *Gesammelte Aufsätze* [Berlin 1903] 239–355). Lea 1957, 47, puts the accent where it belongs: Schopenhauer's system "could be justified, if at all, only as a work of art"; but it remains, like all philosophical ideas, what Nietzsche designates as a "'metaphysical comfort,'" a mere "'illusion'" and "mirage."

10. This possibility is overlooked by Gerratana 1988, in a richly documented and often perceptive essay on Nietzsche's early apostasy from Hartmann and Schopenhauer.

11. *KSA*, 7:7[175].

12. Lange 1866, 274–75; emphasis added.

13. For the reference and the date, see the commentary in *KSA*, 14, ad loc., and Kaufmann's discussion in a note to his translation of the *WP* fragment. As argued above, the earliest writings, dating even before the essay on Schopenhauer, point to Nietzsche's demystification of metaphysics by the time of *The Birth of Tragedy*. "It is impossible to assert that, in *The Birth of Tragedy*, Nietzsche is plying a naive metaphysics after a Schopenhauerian model" (Crawford 1988, 179). This is true; defining its sophistication is harder. Nietzsche's ter-

minological vacillation, e.g., between primordial unity and contradiction (ibid., 161 n. 9) is noteworthy, not as a sign of Nietzsche's confusion or indecision, but as indices to a tactical deployment of concepts.

14. *KSA*, 7:7[148] (1870/71): "*der Wille ist etwas metaphysisches.*"

15. If my rendering of Nietzsche's *Urvisionen* by a "primordial gaze" ("the autonomous activity [*das Sichbewegen*] of the ur-visions imagined by us") calls to mind Lacan's "gaze of the Other," the association is perhaps not entirely misplaced. It is Nietzsche, in fact, who has surprisingly anticipated Lacan on the question of "the dialect of appearance and its beyond," as for instance when Lacan suggests that "if beyond appearance there is nothing in itself, there is the gaze" (Lacan 1981, 103). That Lacan has Nietzsche firmly in mind is clear from the reference to "the pacifying, Apollonian effect of painting" (p. 101), which describes a saturation of appearances with no recourse to a beyond, and the simultaneous birth of the visual object; from the allusion to "the mask" as constitutive of the beyond ("man, in effect, knows how to play with the mask as that beyond which there is the gaze," p. 107); and possibly from the reprise (on p. 115) of the analogy from *BT* §5, ad fin., between the limits of consciousness and a battle scene depicted on canvas (viz., an aggression acted out in the imaginary for an unconscious instance or Other).

16. *KSA*, 7:8[2].

17. See Nietzsche's essays on Kantian teleology, "OT" and "TSK."

18. *P&P* 5:167, and n. (II:§85).

19. This is a conceptual pun. Schopenhauer describes Kant's thing in itself as that which is "left over" when the form of appearance is subtracted from what is given in experience (*W*, 2.1, §17).

20. See *W*, 1.1, §22, where Schopenhauer denies the very charge that Nietzsche makes against him. Nietzsche has this passage in mind ("OS," 357).

21. "Apollo, however, again appears to us as the apotheosis of the *principium individuationis*, in which alone is consummated the perpetually attained goal of the primal unity, its redemption through appearance."

22. *KSA*, 7:5[80]; 114; emphasis added.

23. Ibid. I am construing "it" (*es*) as a reference to "representation." The next sentence reads, "Not to be confused with the representational mechanism in sensible existence," confirming this reference and indicating that Nietzsche has some deeper level of representation in mind.

24. *KSA*, 7:26[11]; 575 (1873); *KGW*, 2.4, 339–40 (1869–76).

25. The phrase is likewise borrowed from Schopenhauer and used against

him. It also appears in Nietzsche's critical appreciation of atomism. See Porter 2000, ch. 2.

26. Letter to Deussen, February 1870.

TRANSFIGURATION

1. Cf. *KSA*, 12:6[23] (1886/87), which explores the aporetic logic of "appearance as appearance" in terms of the "perspective of perspective": "Belief [viewed] as belief" is no longer belief, for belief is incompatible with a view of appearance as appearance or a view of perspective as perspective. This is part of a discussion of the distinction between appearances and essences, a distinction that could only be traced to "the contradictory character" of our intellect: those who put forward claims about appearances in relation to things in themselves "pretend to know much too much, they imagine that they know [something], as if the distinction that they presume between an 'essence of things' and a phenomenal world were valid. To be able to make such a distinction our intellect has to be saddled with a contradictory character: it has to be conceived on the one hand as endowed with a perspectival vision" in order for it to be able to live, and "on the other, as simultaneously endowed with a capacity to grasp this perspectival vision as a perspectival vision and appearance as appearance. . . . In short, we shouldn't conceive our intellect as so contradictory that it simultaneously is [viz., implies or enacts] a belief and a knowledge about this belief as belief." He is recapitulating ideas first aired in "On Schopenhauer" and in notebooks from around the time of *The Birth of Tragedy*. We might add that although knowledge cancels out belief, Nietzsche also knows that belief persists in a disavowed form, which in turn compromises knowledge and converts it into a self-imposed ignorance: I know that the distinction I claim to know (between appearance and reality) is illegitimate, but I act as if I believe in it just the same (and thus effectively don't know what I know). Thus, we always "know too much" and simultaneously "believe too much." Such is the self-conflicted and self-compromised (and ultimately "contradictory") nature of subjectivity that Nietzsche critiques in all his writings. More on this below.

2. "R," 427, 446. See Porter 1994, 226–27, 238. The philosophical equivalent of this figure is given by the Presocratics, and especially the atomists, who waged a virtual campaign against the false reasoning of mankind which

"sets effect for cause" (Lucretius, *On the Nature of Things*, 4.832–33). Schopenhauer's *prōton pseudos* names the same paralogism.

3. I have borrowed the phrase "world within a world" from a notebook entry dating from 1870/71 (*KSA*, 7:7[116]), which describes the rapturous ecstasies of a holy martyr freed from pain and the idealities of representation. Winckelmann has a strikingly close conception (Löhneysen 1987, 103–4), but the immediate reference is undoubtedly to Lange and to Nietzsche's Langean critique of Schopenhauer (as discussed above). Cf. *KSA*, 7:7[175], for the same thought transposed into atomistic reflections (a part of Nietzsche's Schopenhauerian experiments at the time), quoted on p. 63 above.

4. The theme of appearance as excess can be traced throughout Nietzsche, starting with the following: "*Beauty* or the overflowing of an outline attracts us" (*BAW*, 2, 255 [1863]). "Art is never form, shape, or image without at the same time, in its morphological surplus, leaving form behind, disfiguring shape, and surrendering the claim of the image to reproduce or produce a reality. . . . The phenomenalism of the sign opens itself in art onto the unseemly [*dem Scheinlosen*, "the nonphenomenal"]. If anything there still gets shown, presented, lit up, then it is the extinction of phenomenality, of the *eidos* ["form"], and of meaning itself" (Hamacher 1986, 331; trans. 134). The category of "excess" is integral to Nietzsche's analysis of the aesthetic, and even more explicitly in his notes from 1870/71. Cf. *KSA*, 7, 145; 7[27]: "Every Greek statue can teach us that *beauty is only negation*" (emphasis added). The contours of the statue's shape do not merely define an "excess" (beauty is always in excess: ibid., 7[46]; 7[201]; cf. the "*excess* of Apollinian force," *BT*, §22); they also create this excess and exceed it at the same time. My point is not only that form is a leftover of this excess, but that its metaphysical implication is as well. The climax of dithyrambic ecstasy is, for example, the loss of individuation, a rhythming of sensations to the point of indifferentiation—a moment that is never attainable, for "there always remains, even in this area of the feelings, an indissoluble remainder" ("DW," 572), one that therefore appears to be primordial (so Schopenhauer) but in fact is an effect of the process itself.

5. Trans. mod. Kaufmann dodges the circularity by rendering *zur Erzeugung gedrängt* with "impelled to *realize*."

6. "Attempt," 3; emphasis added. This reading stands in contrast with one typified by that given by Sallis, which, bypassing Nietzsche's references to "ground of being," treats the Dionysian as an unequivocal figure for ecstatic, abyssal groundlessness, "in excess of (the) metaphysics (of presence), echoing, resounding, from beyond being" (1991, 75). This view is doubly perplexing,

because it lands Nietzsche's "own" theory with features that are central to the very Schopenhauerian metaphysics that Nietzsche is also assumed to have vehemently critiqued (ibid., 63; cf. 67). (Regarding Schopenhauer, cf. the will's "groundlessness" and excessiveness with respect to representation, *W*, 1.1 §20; this is acknowledged, ibid., 135.) Either Nietzsche is hopelessly self-contradictory here or else he is critiquing the self-contradictions of Schopenhauer. But in either case, the image of an exotic "beyond" is for him a phantasm, and a metaphysically determined one at that.

BEYOND METAPHYSICS—TO ITS BANALITY

1. A similar reading results from the fragments contemporary with *The Birth of Tragedy*; see esp. Jacobs 1978, 7. Look as we might for a ground of appearances, Nietzsche leaves us only with two gradations of appearance and illusion, whose distinction is problematical in any case: "*Dionysian appearance* [*dionysischer Schein*]" and the Apollinian reflection of the same (*apollinischer Wiederschein*) (*KSA*, 7:10[1]; 335). But this kind of speculation about the primordial ground goes nowhere, as does the worry whether the valorization of pain and pleasure is reversed from early to late Nietzsche (these are misdescriptions in any case: at neither period is either state privileged, let alone clearly distinct from the other; cf. "the primordial joy" and "delight" of §24), or whether the one is metaphysical and the other is not (Fleischer 1988). It is contradiction that is primordial, and the source of contradiction lies in us: cf. "the primordial Being . . . that we are" (*KSA*, 7:7[174]; 207).

2. Commenting on this passage, Silk and Stern (1981, 290) rightly note that all three "solutions," including "even the Dionysiac," are "illusory," but then on the next page we read: "Apprehension of the truth is necessary, but only the Dionysiac instinct can achieve it" (p. 291).

3. De Man 1979, 99; see already Lea 1957, 47, for the same point (albeit differently phrased) about the significance of this passage. Pace de Man, the "dissonances" here and elsewhere in *The Birth of Tragedy* are not linguistic or rhetorical: they are anthropological. Cf. *BT* §25: "If we could imagine dissonance become man—and what else is man?—this dissonance, to be able to live, would need a splendid illusion that would cover dissonance [lit., "its own essence"] with a veil of beauty." More on this below.

4. The statement that "we have need of lies in order to conquer this realty" (*WP*, 853), an insight likewise available to the early Nietzsche (e.g., *KSA*, 7, 19[48] (1872–73): "We live only through illusions"), is equivocal: it hovers

between joyous celebration and damaging critique. Cf. the sequel, with its hymn to the "artists' triumph" and the will to power of the deceiving (and self-deceiving) subject; or *EH*, V "The Birth of Tragedy," 2: in contrast to "the strong man," who can face up to truth, "*décadents need* the lie—it is one of the conditions of their existence." See further Porter 1999.

5. "Grades of illusion [*Stufen der Illusion*]" all too vividly recalls Schopenhauer's "grades of objectification [*Stufen der Objektivation*]" (*W*, 1.1, §25); Nietzsche has made Schopenhauer's metaphysics into the illusion that it is. Cf. ibid., §24, where Schopenhauer protests—too much—against the possible empty content of his philosophical principles—thereby revealing *his horror vacui* (see n. 7, below). Lea (1957, 47) is to my knowledge the only commentator to note the dissonance that the passage from §18 quoted here injects into the supposed Schopenhauerianism of *The Birth of Tragedy*; but this observation is not explored, and Nietzsche's dissent from orthodoxy is relegated to a dim awareness "at the back of his mind."

6. See *KSA*, 14, 55 ad loc., for the textual variants. Kaufmann's worries, in a note to his translation (ad loc.), about "Buddhistic" and its penciled-in variant "Brahmanic" ("both . . . depend on some misconception; neither seems to make much sense") are unfounded. Buddhism (Nirvana, etc.) opens the way to an orientalism beneath tragedy—that is, to new layers of illusory depths. Buddhism is a frequent component of Nietzsche's notebook speculations, cf. *KSA*, 7:5[102]: "The background illusion of tragedy is that of Buddhistic religion," which defines just one more set of "delusions." Nietzsche is exposing the Schopenhauerianism of his conception as an exotic delusion; that is the irony of his conceit.

7. Schopenhauer certainly could not. See *W*, 1.1, §24, referring to the Kantian forms of experience that mediate between the subject and its objects and give content to everyday encounters with the world: "Now, if the objects that appear in these forms are not to be mere empty phantoms [*leere Phantome*], but rather to be possessed of significance, they will have to point to something, be the expression of something, that is not in turn like themselves an object, a representation, a mere relative subjective thing, . . . but instead is a *thing in itself*." Lange and Nietzsche's principle of the metaphysics of the surface is here being objected to in advance of its formulation.

8. Cf. *Z*, III, 13, 2, on the "disgust with all existence [*Überdruss an allem Dasein*]" and the resulting "nausea." A note from 1883 confirms that this is what Nietzsche had in mind eleven years earlier (Nietzsche quotes this very passage from *BT*). Indeed, it has been, he says, his *Grundgedanke* all along: "*the redemption of man from himself*"; "limiting the focus to the human, in contrast

with 'the world process' and 'a world behind [*Hinterwelt*],'" which are just so many metaphysical escapisms; disbelief in an "impulse for knowledge in itself"—*War alles schon vorhanden* ("Everything was already there") (*KSA*, 10:16[11]). This does not strike me as a creative reinterpretation of his own past. It does, however, invite us to speculate further about the role of the Dionysian in *The Birth of Tragedy*.

9. Cf. *BGE*, 230; and Porter 1999.

10. Cf. §24: the Dionysian wisdom of the tragic myth "says to us: 'Look there! Look closely! This is your life, this is the hand on the clock of your existence.'"

NARRATIVE APPEARANCES

1. *KSA*, 14, 541.

"RAVING SOCRATES"

1. *KSA*, 7:9[10], [88], and [92] (1871). On Hölderlin, see Warminski 1987; for a discussion of these notes from *KSA*, see Jacobs 1978, ch. 1; also de Man 1979, 118: "The Dionysian vocabulary is used only to make the Apollonian mode that deconstructs it more intelligible to a mystified audience." Some of the historical evidence for this fact is collected in Baeumer 1976.

2. This is how Plato characterized the Cynic and "minor Socratic," Diogenes of Sinope, according to an anecdote told by Aelian, *Varia Historia* 14.33; cf. Diogenes Laertius 6.54. See further at n. 9, below.

3. The metaphor appears in Schopenhauer in connection with natural science (*W*, 2.1, §17), and in *BAW*, 3, 349 (1867/68) in connection with Democritus. In each case, a contrast between the covering and the uncovered is straightforwardly drawn, unlike here.

4. This is, needless to say, Nietzsche's Socrates, his construction of the problem of Socrates. But the image he arrives at is formed in a gap in the evidence that continues to trouble scholars today, while Nietzsche's Socrates is ultimately a name for this very gap. For a recent attempt to reconstruct the historical Socrates in Plato, see Vlastos 1991. On Nietzsche and Socrates, see further Nehamas 1985, ch. 1.

5. At a purely formal and syntactic level, the *Symposium* is structured by embedded levels of reported, indirect discourse (represented by nested infinitive-clauses).

6. The centaur remained an image of literary hybridity into later antiquity; Lucian (*Twice Accused*, 33) describes his own dialogues as "centauric." For Nietzsche, the centauric form inevitably smacks of *modernity*. See *BT* §21 (on "the Lucians of antiquity") and n. 8, below.

7. "HCP," 249, 251, 253.

8. Ibid., 251–52; emphasis added. The last thought is carried over to a notebook from 1869/70 that anticipates *BT* (*KSA*, 7:3[3]). In "GrS" (p. 765), the centaur-image is a sign of modernity's deficient cultural and intellectual fusion with antiquity.

9. A strand of cynicism seems to run through the Platonic ancestry of this Socrates as well, on Nietzsche's portrayal: "An instance of this is Plato, who in condemning tragedy and art in general certainly did not lag behind the naïve cynicism of his master" (§14).

10. Nietzsche cites only A. W. Schlegel in *BT*, §7. But see §14: "Indeed, Plato has given to all posterity the model of a new artform, the model of the *novel*"; and compare Friedrich Schlegel's theory of the novel (*Roman*), conceived as the core of all (which is to say, in absolute terms, Romantic ["*romantische*"]) poetics, in his *Gespräch über die Poesie* (Dialogue on Poetry), a theory later adopted by Bakhtin (1981, 22). Bakhtin cites Schlegel as holding that the Socratic dialogues were "'the novels of their time'"; and in the *Gespräch* Schlegel writes, "Indeed, I can scarcely conceive the novel as anything other than a mixture of narration, song, and other forms" (Schlegel 1958–: 1.2:336). Is Plato possibly a *proto-Romantic, or even a Romantic*, for Nietzsche? That this is nearly the case will be argued for further below.

11. *KSA*, 7:8[13] (1870/71–1872). Later, Nietzsche would show the reversibility of this relationship, holding that the figure of Socrates was a "semiotic for Plato" (*EH*, VI ["The Untimely Essays"], 3).

THE PLATONISM OF 'THE BIRTH OF TRAGEDY'

1. *W*, 1.1, §51, ad fin. But of course, as we saw above, Schopenhauer disapproves of the Greeks' life-affirming stance toward tragedy. Needless to say, Greek drama provided the model and precursor to the *Gesamtkunstwerk* (Richard Wagner, letter to Berlioz, February 1860).

2. Cf. *EH*, V ("The Birth of Tragedy"), 1. See also Hegel's *Lectures on Aesthetics*, esp. pt. II, §2, ch. 2 (on the individuation of the gods, which is fateful and tragic). The affinities between *The Birth of Tragedy* and Hegel's treatment of the birth of the classical ideal and its simultaneous fruition and exhaustion

(and self-mourning) in Greek tragedy, in a complex interplay of the beautiful and the sublime, are too close and too absorbing to be considered here. The nineteenth lecture of Nietzsche's *Encyclopedia of Philology* is governed by an overtly Hegelian schema, at least in its narrative pattern (see Porter 2000, ch. 4 and p. 103 below). In general, readers of Nietzsche have been too quick to dismiss the "offensive Hegelian smell" of his writings, and his—admittedly secondhand but nonetheless working—knowledge of Hegel. One key instance was given earlier (see "The Complication of Appearances," n. 3, above). A final example is a passage from the preface to the *Phenomenology* that I have never seen cited in connection with *The Birth of Tragedy*. It is remarkable not only for its fusion of Apollinian and Dionysian features but also for its indecision between the ideals of classicism and romanticism, an indecision that Nietzsche is keen to expose: "Appearance is the coming into and going out of being, which itself does not come into or go out of being, but rather is in itself and constitutes the reality and movement of the life of truth. The truth is thus the giddy Bacchic transport [*der bacchantische Taumel*] in which no member is not drunk; and because every member immediately dissolves the moment it is isolated, this transport is at the same time a transparent and simple tranquillity" (Hegel 1970, 46).

3. The relation between Kant's and Plato's conceptions is one of proximity: "to be sure, though not identical, nevertheless [they are] very closely affined [*verwandt*]" (*W*, 1.1, §31). One might speculate a philological connection here. Creuzer 1836–43, vol. 4 (1st ed. 1810–12), contains numerous anticipations of Schopenhauer and of Nietzsche, from the veil of māyā (p. 157) to discussions of various forms, in Greek mythology, of the emanation of, and desperate attempted returns to, an idea incorporating divinity in its highest form (pp. 21, 168, 408–9). Creuzer's theories and interests vaguely reflect both the diffuse Neoplatonism of his later Greek sources and the Hegelianism of the contemporary German academy. I am not aware if Schopenhauer read Creuzer, but it seems likely that he did. The impulse may be traced back at least to Moritz's *Götterlehre* (1795). See Moritz 1981, 2:639: "Because . . . the imagination is predicated on no particular sequence of its appearances, often one and the same divinity will manifest itself repeatedly in different guises." See further, n. 9 below.

4. Nietzsche's hostility to Platonism is evident throughout, from his earliest philological championing of Democritus (against Plato and Plato's heirs) to his later writings. Cf. "*Beiträge zur Quellenkunde und Kritik des Laertius Diogenes*" (1870), §8 (*KGW*, 2.1, p. 223), where Nietzsche sides with a later doxographer, Diocles of Magnesia, against Plato's "antipathy to Democritus"; *BAW*, 3, 347 (1867/68): "Theologians and metaphysicians have heaped on

[Democritus'] name the inveterate grudges that they hold against material ism," where "the divine Plato" is adduced as a paradigmatic instance (h sought to destroy by fire the writings of Democritus—so a piece of anecdota testimony from later antiquity); and *EH*, V ("The Birth of Tragedy"), 2: "I wa the first to see the real antithesis—the *degenerated* instinct which turns agains life with subterranean vengefulness (—Christianity, the philosophy c Schopenhauer, in a certain sense already the philosophy of Plato, the whol idealism as typical forms)."

To be sure, Nietzsche's undermining of the Platonic Ideas in *The Birth c Tragedy* is subtly complicated by a number of factors, not the least of which i the ever-uncertain relationship between "the divine Plato" (§12) and "the Pla tonic Socrates" (§15) the latter being in any case more prominent than the for mer. It won't pay to belabor the question here, for instance the way both Plat and Socrates fundamentally share the same mistrust of appearances ("th pseudo-reality," §14; "the essential perversity and reprehensibility of wha exists," §13) and seek cognitive refuge in a realm beyond (a "sublime meta physical illusion," §15) that, against their better instincts, is equivalent to a aesthetic justification of reality; or the fact that this intimate proximity of the metaphysical thinking is confirmed in Nietzsche's lectures on the Platonic dia logues (see "ISPD," §5, p. 152 on Socrates' "*despising of reality*"), where th derivation of Plato's "Socratic *eidē* [Ideas]" (p. 55) is elaborately argued ou (cf. §5, "Influence of Socrates"; §7, "The Socratic Concepts"; §17, p. 163; an *passim*).

What is also of interest in these lectures and more relevant to my argumer here is something else, namely the contrast that Nietzsche draws between th Platonism of Plato and that of Schopenhauer. Schopenhauer's Ideas are a "aesthetic" version of Plato's (p. 158); they rest on an "intuitive comprehen sion of the universal," which is to say on an inner perception (the Ideas ar concepts that are "*anschaulich*"; cf. *BT*, §1, init.), whereas for Plato Ideas ar precisely nonintuitive and nonaesthetic concepts; he did not deduce the from the visible world, but only from its rejection and by recourse to a pure cognitive, and dialectical (and to this extent Socratic) grasp of higher realit (§§10–16, pp. 154–63); and Plato's attitude toward art is corresponding symptomatic (§13, p. 160). As we shall see, Nietzsche's inversion of Plato à Schopenhauer's "aesthetic Ideas" will entail a corresponding inversion (ae theticizing) of Schopenhauer. Equally of interest here is the way in whic Nietzsche traces Plato's philosophical development between, as it were, tw forms of skepticism: first, there is his skepticism toward the apparent world, i his early, Heraclitean phase (p. 43), and in the end there is his skepticis toward his own theory of Forms (pp. 125, 127) and his flirtation with its abandonment (p. 84). Racked by doubts, Plato makes for an instructive case-study of *homo metaphysicus*. His response to his dilemma is a form of the dilemma itself—namely, *metaphysical recidivism*, in the face of an even greater horror: "The assumption of the Ideas creates many difficulties ["knowledge of them is doubtful"]. But the alternative is even worse for philosophy," for "the non-assumption of the Ideas is equally unreassuring" (p. 125). Plato cannot step free of metaphysics in part because he never really could do so to begin with (the first of his skeptical moves represented a plunge into metaphysics) and in part because Plato's first plunge was motivated by the very *horror vacui* that plagues him to the bitter end (where it is framed as the unacceptable alternative of a life without metaphysics).

5. *KSA*, 7, 7[156]. Cf. ibid., 6[14] (late 1870): "Belief that the concept reaches the essence of things: Platonic Idea, whence the metaphysics of logic: identity of thinking and being. . . . *Delusion* [*Der Wahn*]." Cf. ibid., 7[28]: "The Platonic Idea is the thing with the negation of impulse (or with the *appearance* of the negation of *impulse*)," viz., it is an image of things generally, conceived as drained of all instinctual impulses, hence an etiolation of reality and a negation of life. Similarly, "ISPD," 163: "Even the Idea of the Beautiful in Plato is completely bodiless and colorless; it is not to be compared with any particulars, be they corporeal or spiritual."

6. *W*, bk. 3, is subtitled *Representation, Independent of the Principle of Sufficient Reason: The Platonic Idea: The Object of Art*. It covers §§30–52 of *W*, 1.1. Indeed, for Schopenhauer, art (the "work of genius") is a privileged contemplation of Platonic Ideas, the pure paradigm, as it were, of the scientific syntagm (§35). Schopenhauer can be critical of Plato, and especially of the way in which Plato phrases some of his conclusions (as in §41); but he never challenges the centerpiece of Platonism, the eternal Ideas, which he simply makes over in his own image.

7. *KSA*, 7:8[19]; and *WP*, 419.

8. The Greek term *typos* brings to mind *eidos* and *idea* in Plato, the official designations for Platonic Ideas or Forms, at least to the German ear. Cf. *EH*, V ("The Birth of Tragedy"), 2: "the philosophy of Plato, the whole of idealism as typical forms"; cf. Weininger 1919, 9: "auch das Objekt der Wissenschaft ist der Typus, die platonische Idee."

9. *KSA*, 14, 50 (see now *KGW*, 3.5.1, pp. 142–203, for the previously unpublished portion of this ms; here, pp. 172–73). This underlying schema, though it is obvious upon reflection, is attested elsewhere in Nietzsche's notes. Cf. *KSA*, 7:3[73]; 80: "Dionysus and Apollo. . . . The mythological exemplars

[*Vorbilder*] of the Platonic Idea," where *Vorbild* is meaningfully ambiguous, suggesting "prototype," "example," and "ideal." The possibility that Platonism underlies *The Birth of Tragedy* is rarely considered long enough to be even denied (as in Lea 1957, 41: Nietzsche "will have nothing of the doctrine of Ideas"), the universal assumption being that Nietzsche's work is a refutation of Platonism (an "inverted Platonism," *KSA*, 7:7[156]). Cf. Riedel 1995, 53–54. Young 1992, 32 (cf. 43), rightly picks up on the Schopenhauerian/Platonic association with respect to Apollinian appearances, but then drops it again when he considers the Dionysian (pp. 32–33). Finally, for a somewhat parallel logic, cf. the notebook entries from *BAW*, 5, 221–22, 231 (1868/69) on the "ideal" personalities with which the ancient Greeks endowed their most revered poetic figures, Homer and Hesiod, and which became the "masks" of the latters' identities: "Homer [was made into] an ideal entity [*Idealwesen*], just like Hesiod. . . . What might explain this idealization? . . . From this [came] the name of the 'Homeric' Hymns, which were performed by way of the mask of Homer," etc. Similarly, *KGW*, 2.2, 351.

Creuzer 1836–43, 4:116, in a discussion of Dionysus Zagreus, treats Apollo as a "unity," but only insofar as he is the unity of the collected fragments of the—in Schopenhauer's terms, individuated—god Dionysus (cf. ibid., 196). Here, the notion of a "Dionysian Apollo," attested in antiquity (ibid., 36), takes on the typical philosophical traits of German idealism, while Dionysus is treated as the final "emanation" of divinity *simpliciter* (ibid., 21), which ultimately points the way to Christianity and its peculiar, unpagan problematics: "the sanctification of the will" (ibid., 409–10). On Schopenhauer's probable use of Creuzer, see n. 3, above.

10. See Behler 1989, 155, who writes that "Socratism" is synonymous with the artform in which it "inheres" and "out of which it stems." Behler goes on to locate the source of tragedy's demise in its "dialectical" component of dialogue, originally missing from tragedy (*KSA*, 1, 545), a contestable premise (see next note). Even by his own logic, however, dialogue is not "an element introduced from without" that kills tragedy off. The admission of this element into tragedy stems from tragedy's deepest mainsprings and fatalities (such as will be described below). Tragedy dies, after all, by "*suicide*"—"tragically" (§11, init.).

11. "Socratism is older than Socrates; his influence, which dissolves art, makes itself felt already much earlier. The element of dialectic, which is characteristic of him, had crept into musical drama long before Socrates and it wreaked havoc on that beautiful body" ("Socrates and Tragedy," *KSA*, 1, 545). Drawing attention to this point, Behler (1989, 149) also cites a letter from

Romundt, Nietzsche's alter ego, from 25 March 1870 (*KGB*, 2.2, 176), in which the "Socratism" of Nietzsche's lecture is called "an *eternal* disease," "pre- and post-Socratic" (emphasis added). Romundt was a better reader of Nietzsche's thought than most subsequent readers would prove to be. As was Richard Wagner, who upon reading the same lecture sought to encourage Nietzsche in his project: "Now go and show what the purpose of philology is, and help me bring about the great 'Renaissance' in which Plato will embrace Homer and Homer, filled with Plato's Ideas, will at last truly become the greatest Homer of all" (letter of 12 February 1870). Riedel 1995, 53 cites this remark and then comments, "Indeed, Wagner, one has to say, did not at all understand the consequences, for Nietzsche's revaluation of classical Greece, of the distinction" that he had made in his lecture between Plato's "'philosophical drama'" (oddly, the phrase is found in *BT*, §14 and in a note from 1869, but not in "Socrates and Tragedy") and Greek tragedy. See further *KGW*, 3.5.1, pp. 112–13, outlining an envisaged project entitled "Socrates and Instinct":

Introduction. The "cheerful" neo-Hellenism

1. Morality in the service of the will: pessimism impossible.
2. Greek idealism, e.g., idealized sexual drive (concept of friendship)
3. Fatalism perishing in beauty.
   Idealistic views of the past, e.g.,

   Pythagoras Orpheus Lycurgus.

   Homeric stories with an idealistic stamp.
   The Platonic Idea before Plato. (In the instinctual life of the ancient Greeks, the biological curse, etc.)
   Denial of the individual in the Bacchic cult.
   History and philosophy of the *bios theōrētikos* [life of the mind].

This paradox was deeply rooted in Nietzsche's mind, and indeed foundational to his conception of Greek tragedy and culture. Cf. *KSA*, 7:1[15], an entry from 1869: "Socrates was the element in tragedy, and of musical drama generally, that dissolved tragedy—*before Socrates was alive*" (emphasis added).

Behler is right to connect "dialectic" with "dialogue," but wrong to equate them. Their proximity is, as it were, a near miss of meaning and part of the contortions of Nietzsche's text. Cf. *BT*, §9 on the tragedy of Oedipus and "the genuinely Hellenic delight at this dialectical solution," viz., Oedipus' self-undoing by logic and the "marvelously tied knot of a trial," and on *Oedipus at Colonnus*, this "divine counterpart of the dialectic," which is productive of "the most profound human joy." Dialectic, or if you like, *pre*-Socratic Socratism, is plainly tragedy's characteristic (its *eigenthümliche Element* [*KSA*, 1, 545])—and its eventual downfall. See "'Eternal' Phenomena: Culture's Illusions," n. 2, below.

12. "IST," 9–10.

13. Ibid., 12. Further, the tragic chorus is for the Greeks (or in fact) not an individual, but a "concept" (ibid., 26), pace what Nietzsche had claimed earlier in the same lectures. The generic identity (viz., *eidos*) of tragic forms and their representational coherence, from before Aeschylus onward, are viewed as a Platonic Idea: in tragedy proper, "the unity of the whole lies no longer in the unity of an event [as in pre-Aeschylean "lyric tragedy"] but in that of a *being* or of a *thought* (genre as Platonic Idea)" (p. 37). It is in this same context that Nietzsche appears moreover to have given his first analysis of the Dionysian and Apollinian in tragedy (pp. 11, 16), and not in "The Dionysian Worldview" (Behler 1989, 150), which was composed in June/July of 1870 and must have been a crystallization of these lectures, which were given in the summer semester (May to July) of the same year. In the lectures, the Dionysian element is seen as deriving from popular poetry (the *Volkspoesie der Masse*), as "tamed" by "moderate Apollo," and then as undergoing a "rebirth" and intensification in tragedy (p. 16). Such a derivation is literally deconstructed in the earlier essay, "Homer and Classical Philology," in terms that strikingly anticipate the later, Dionysian vocabulary. Take, for example, the presentation of *Volksdichtung* and of *eine dichterische Volksmasse* as a presumably "deeper and more original force than that of the singular, creative individual": the "hypothesis" of a "mysterious discharging, [of] a deep and artistic national impulse," is a fantastic notion about Greek *Phantasie*, an "intoxicant" for its modern exponents but not for Nietzsche ("HCP," 258–61, and *passim*). Nietzsche finds this mass psychology "unpretty and unphilosophical" (p. 261) and plumps instead for a cagier aesthetics of deception, of which he is himself a practitioner (see Porter 2000, ch. 1). Nietzsche's vacillation is to be taken as a further instance of his general ad hoc style of argument and as a salutary warning against trusting in the appearances of his meanings.

14. See further "IST," §9, which adds complications of its own (Sophocles "alone" is "genuinely tragic," while Aeschylus is "still epic," viz., displaying a "naive optimism" that "will be reintroduced later by Euripides as Socratism"; but "Sophocles follows in Aeschylus' wake" and confesses to have "imitated" him). Or see "Socrates and Tragedy," *KSA*, 1, 549 (where Sophocles exerts a reverse, deleterious influence on Aeschylus). In general, however, here and elsewhere Nietzsche is inclined to view Sophocles as a conscious exfoliation of

Aeschylus' unconscious instincts and tendencies and not as their contradiction; see *BAW*, 5, 219 (1868/69); *BT* §12.

15. See *BT*, §11, on Aristophanes' play *Frogs*. Nietzsche alludes broadly to this tradition; cf. §12: "even if Euripides has been punished by being changed into a dragon by the art critics of all ages"; ibid., "the poetic deficiency and degeneration, which are so often imputed to Euripides in comparison with Sophocles." The modern tradition is surveyed in Behler 1986; see also Henrichs 1986. Nietzsche's portrait of Euripides is a brilliant exaggeration of this tradition, and no more or less informative, philologically or critically, than his portraits of the remaining tragedians. It also constitutes a subtle critique of the modern tradition, as *BT*, §13 begins to suggest: Aristophanes' poetic lynching of Socrates is "to the consternation of modern men, who are quite willing to give up Euripides, but who cannot give sufficient expression to their astonishment that in Aristophanes Socrates should appear as the first and supreme *Sophist*, as the mirror and epitome of all sophistical tendencies." See further n. 17 below.

16. "IST," 39.

17. The claim about the oracle is presented in §13 with reference to Socrates and Euripides only. Then comes a new and unexpected paragraph, adding Sophocles to the list and emphasizing the forced nature of Nietzsche's embroidered account. The paragraph reads: "Sophocles was named third in order of rank—he who could boast that he *knew* what was right. Evidently it is precisely the degree of the brightness of this *knowledge* which distinguishes these three men in common as the three 'knowing ones' of their time." Interestingly, Nietzsche seems to be reversing Friedrich Schlegel's judgment that Socrates was "a philosophical Sophocles" (see Behler 1986, 339, citing Schlegel 1958–, 1:634). But Schlegel's view of Greek tragedy is complex (see Behler 1986), as is Nietzsche's view of the Schlegel brothers. Where Nietzsche most diverges from the Schlegels is in his elevation, partly à la Schopenhauer, of dissonance and not harmony as a positive feature of the Greek tragic form (contra Schlegel, ibid., 246–48, 301; cited in Behler 1986, 341–42). Nietzsche's aesthetics has little to do with the organic formalism of the Romantics (which has no place for *illusion*), and his metaphysics lies elsewhere too. These points are not sufficiently brought out by Behler.

18. "Such magic transformation is the presupposition of all dramatic art. In this magic transformation, the Dionysian reveler sees himself as a satyr, *and as a satyr, in turn, he sees the god* . . . ; he beholds another vision outside himself, as

the Apollinian complement to his own state. With this new vision, the drama is complete" (§8).

19. Needless to say, Apollo provides the framing "architecture" for the Dionysian image: the circular "form of the theater" generates the illusion of "a luminous cloud formation" present to the (imagined) Bacchants. Such is "the splendid frame in which the image of Dionysus is revealed to them" (§8).

20. *KSA*, 7:3[53].

21. *KSA*, 7:8[19].

"THE GOAL OF THE ANTIPODES"

1. See "The Platonism of *The Birth of Tragedy*," nn. 10 and 11, above.

2. Cf. *KSA*, 7:3[3]: "Art as the jubilee of the will is the most powerful seducer to life. Science likewise stands under the rule of the impulse to life: the world is worth knowing: the triumph of cognition holds [mankind] fast to life" (1869/70); identically, "HCP," 251–52.

3. *KSA*, 7:5[32].

4. Cf. *KSA*, 7:5[38].

5. "Profound *illusion*": §15. The Greeks' "worship" of wine (their "narcotism") is labeled a symptom of their idealism in *KSA*, 7:3[43] (1869/70) (quoted on p. 141, above).

THE SOCRATIC FALLACY

1. Lange (1866, 489) speaks of the fantasy of subjective identity (consciousness and the self) as a *fingiertes Wesen* and compares it to a perspectival illusion of the kind that is produced in a diorama or in a camera obscura.

2. KSA 7:6[11], 7[131], 9[132]; emphases added. Cf. further 5[108] ("the tragic man"); 7[41] ("the tragic man—Empedocles") and [101] ("*tragic* knowledge," like Empedocles' suicidal desire to know; "knowledge *without measure* and limits"); 8[14] and [15] ("a music-making, *i.e.*, *an artistically productive* Socrates"). Cf. 8[19] (1870/71): " . . . the deepest affinity of this Socrates with the Platonic Idea of the Hellenic. If we merely take a closer look at the mythical representatives of the Hellenic, the greatest of these figures recall nobody else but Socrates. He is at once Prometheus and Oedipus, but Prometheus before his theft of fire and Oedipus before he solved the riddle of the Sphinx. Through him is inaugurated a new reflection of those two representatives . . .

All are "masks of the original hero, Dionysus" (*BT*, §10). Oddly, the identification is already anticipated in Schlegel, 1958–, 1: 244, n., following up on a prior suggestion: "Hemsterhuys speaks about a philosophy that is similar to the *dithyramb*. . . . I would call the [Platonic dialogue] *Simon* of this philosopher *Socratic poetry*; its 'arrangement' is '*dithyrambic*.'" Only, as Schlegel understands this philosophy to involve "the freest outpouring of moral feeling, a communication of great and good intentions," the thought is quite removed from anything found in *The Birth of Tragedy*.

3. Cf. §13: "*The dying Socrates* became the new ideal, never seen before, of noble Greek youths: above all, the typical Hellenic youth, Plato, prostrated himself before this image with all the ardent devotion of his enthusiastic soul." In this sense, too, "Plato is a Socratic work of art" (*KSA*, 7:8[13]), fashioned after his own ideal. (The notebook entry is a study for this passage from *BT* §13.)

4. *BAW*, 3, 68. Cf. "HC," 790, where the dialogue is showered with praise again—this time by Plato himself.

5. See "IST," 37; *KSA*, 7:9[17].

6. Cf. "HCP," 257, where this assumption is ridiculed, though Nietzsche's ridicule doesn't affect or even adequately reflect his argumentative strategies here in *BT* or in the earlier essay.

7. See Silk and Stern 1981, 148, on the problem of the "discrepancy between the seriousness of the dithyramb as we know it and the apparent frivolity of the satyr," which is not limited to the uncertainties of Nietzsche's historical construction—it invades his theory at its core.

8. *KSA*, 1, 549; emphasis added.

9. Both the sublime and the comic are "a step beyond the world of beautiful appearances," though they do not coincide with truth, but only with its illusion and concealment ("DW," 567). See further notes from 1869/70–72, where the proximities of tragedy and laughter, two kinds of excess, are well attested: *KSA*, 7:3[31] ("The curse and laughter"; "The horrible and the ridiculous"; "Terror, nausea, laughter"); 5[119] ("why Attic comedy [arises] out of tragedy") 7[27] ("The *beautiful* is a smiling of nature, an excess of power and the pleasurable feeling of existence," but it is also "only negation"); 8[9] "*point of union*: Archilochus: the Dionysian-Apollinian artist. Sublime and ridiculous").

10. Xen. *Symp*. 4.19.

11. "Well, something much more painful than a snake has bitten me in my most sensitive part—I mean my heart, or my soul, or whatever you want to call

it, which has been struck and bitten by philosophy," etc. I owe this last obse vation to Sunil Agnani. The intimation of sex is, moreover, germane to th Silenic analogy.

12. "DW," 544; emphasis added.

13. *KSA*, 14, 54. Cf. *GS*, 153.

14. Cf. the letter to Overbeck of 13 July 1885, where Nietzsche remar how he continually finds himself reverting to earlier "decisions" regardin "the *fundamental* problems" in his thinking. The same decisions "are already place in my *Birth of Tragedy*, where they are *concealed and obscured as much possible*, and everything that I have learned in addition since then has grow into [that frame] and become a part of it" (last emphasis added). This appea to have been Nietzsche's prime compositional method even before *The Bir of Tragedy*. See his letter to Deussen of April/May 1868: "here [in an essay c the synchronicity of Homer and Hesiod], my Homeric *paradoxa* come to lig for the first time," viz., in concealed form. See Porter 2000, *passim*.

15. "Attempt," 1. At *KSA*, 7:6[11], under the rubric and question, "Ho can Socrates make music?" (§2), Nietzsche refers to the "cheerfulness Socrates in the Platonic *Symposium*, his irony."

16. *BAW*, 2, 420–24; here, 423–24.

17. See "DW," 444.

18. See the brief notice by Silk and Stern 1981, 208. Kofman (1989) di cusses some of the implications of Alcibiades' speech in her chapter on Plat without exploring the strategic uses of this allusion in *The Birth of Tragedy*. F her, there is a *dionysisme caché* (recalling Pautrat's *la dionysie cachée* [Pautr 1971, 224]) in the Apollinianism of Socrates, who "*ne peut être, pour Nietzsch 'apollinien' sans être en son tréfonds* un tant soit peu *dionysiaque*" (ibid., 304–5 Socrates is, however, crucially Dionysian, and more than a little. It may be th Apollinianism is *un fantasme idéologique*, but so is Dionysianism. And anywa "pure Dionysianism is impossible" (*KSA*, 7:3[32]). Cf. Saß's fleeting questio responding to Kaufmann's mention of an "artistic Socrates," in the "Discu sion" to Goedert 1978, 25: "Isn't there even Dionysianism already wi Socrates? Put differently, is the Dionysian in fact as immoral as Nietzsche lat understands it? . . . More pointedly still: are the maieutic and the creative pri ciples mutually exclusive?" Less tentative, as I discovered only after this boo went to press, is Pierre Hadot in an article on "the figure of Socrates" in Plat Kierkegaard, and Nietzsche. Noting the abundance of Dionysian imagery su rounding Socrates in the *Symposium*, Hadot writes, "Thus we find in Plato *Symposium* what seems to be a conscious and deliberate ensemble of allusio

to the Dionysiac nature of the figure of Socrates. . . . We should not be surprised if, paradoxically, secretly, and perhaps unconsciously, the figure of Socrates comes, for Nietzsche, to coincide with the figure of Dionysos" (Hadot 1995, 170 [1981, 88–89]; the article first appeared in 1974). See also the brief but suggestive remark by Jacobs 1978, 124 n. 25: "The original Dionysian womb, the Originary One, was a necessary invention of the Socratic image of history." Finally, see the anticipation by Schlegel (in n. 2, above), which merely begins to point to the historicity of Nietzsche's conceit.

"ETERNAL" PHENOMENA: CULTURE'S ILLUSIONS

1. Socrates is "a monstrosity *per defectum* . . . in whom, through a hypertrophy [*Superfötation*], the logical nature is developed as excessively as instinctive wisdom is in the mystic" (§13).

2. In "Socrates and Tragedy," Nietzsche claims in fact that all of Sophocles' tragic figures are destroyed "not by the tragic," but thanks to "a superfoetation [*Superfötation*] of the logical [faculty]," preeminently among them, Oedipus (*KSA*, 1, 546). Socrates is not such an aberration after all.

3. See Winkler 1990 for an effective, because purely internal, counterargument: "Aristotle's 'literary history' is actually a complex argument about the possibility of giving a wholly naturalistic account of the generation of the genres of poetry" (p. 309). Silk and Stern's objections to viewing Nietzsche's account as a "literary history" (1981, 150) are applicable to Aristotle as well; see ibid., 227, 237.

4. On some of the ways in which Nietzsche may have been redirecting his readers' gazes through this added preface, see Nussbaum 1991, 97, 98–99; and Conway 1992.

PRIMORDIAL FAIRY TALES

1. It would be a mistake to trivialize such characterizations by taking them as proof of the ultimate "figurativeness" of language: Nietzsche is describing an experience of the world. Cf., for starters, *BT* §8: "For a genuine poet, metaphor is *not a rhetorical figure* but a vicarious image that he actually beholds in the place of a concept"; emphasis added. Further, §6 ad fin., discounting the symbolic medium of language altogether.

2. Pace, e.g., Müller-Lauter 1972, 7–9. That is one reason why Nietzsche

so often rejects "contradictions" in favor of "grades" of difference—but both are in fact subjectively constituted; see *BGE*, 24; *WP*, 560, 552c.

3. *KSA*, 7:7[201]; 214.

4. *KSA*, 7:7[169]; 204.

5. *KSA*, 7:7[116]; 165. Compare the parallel insight by Lange 1866, 544: "It is up to me whether I see chiefly imperfection or perfection in nature, whether I carry my idea of the beautiful into it and then receive it back again a thousandfold, or whether the traces of decay, diminishment, and battles of destruction confront me."

6. *KSA*, 7:7 [116]; 164. This is parallel to Nietzsche's later claim, which was quoted earlier, that "man has *humanized* the world." Cf. *TI*, "Expeditions of an Untimely Man," 19: "Man believes that the world itself is filled with beauty—he *forgets* that it is he who has created it. He alone has bestowed beauty upon the world—alas! Only a very human, all too human beauty."

7. *KSA*, 7:7[117]; 165.

8. *KSA*, 7:7[116]; 164.

9. *KSA*, 7:7[117]; 166.

10. The Cynic formula of virtue (living indifferently, *adiaphorōs*) is expressed most powerfully by the third-century B.C. philosopher Aristo of Chios, a figure well known to Nietzsche and a harsh (and Cynicizing) critic of the Stoa (cf. *KSA*, 7:35[4]; *GS*, 120; *BGE*, 190, with von Arnim, *Stoicorum Veterum Fragmenta*, vol. 1, fr. 343). *BGE*, 19, quoted below, reads like a paraphrase of Aristo's Cynicizing critique of Stoicism.

11. *KSA*, 7:7[116]; 165.

12. Ibid., 7[117]; 165. The allusions (*Poros* and *Penia*) are to Plato's *Symposium*, 203bc.

13. The notebook entry quoted from earlier, which begins, "we are on the one hand *pure perception* (i.e., projected images of a purely enraptured Being that enjoys unrivaled tranquility in this perception); on the other, we are the one Being itself," goes on for a bit and then reads, "as represented beings we do not feel the pain (?) [*sic*]. The person, e.g., as a sum of countless small atoms of pain and atoms of will [*Schmerz- und Willensatomen*], whose pain only the *one* Will suffers, and whose plurality is in turn the consequence of the rapture of the *one* Will" (*KSA*, 7:7[201]; 214–15). See p. 63 above and ibid., 7[204] ("The atom as [a] point, contentless, in every smallest moment becoming, never *being*. In this way the whole Will has become appearance and looks at itself") for a similar incorporation of the atomistic hypothesis within a Schopenhauerian scenario. This passage, incidentally, marks Nietzsche's first

innovative deployment of *Willensatomen*, "atoms of will," already in 1870–71. The next major occurrence will be in the notes to the will to power from the mid-1880s onward, which are no less strange (and estranging) than these early notebooks, and in many respects—too many to go into here—are strictly continuous with them as well.

14. *KSA*, 7:7[201]; 216.

15. *KSA*, 7:19[91] (1872–73); emphasis added. Cf. "TL," 251: "Just as the astrologer observes the stars in the service of men and in connection with their joys and sorrows, so such an investigator observes the whole world as linked with man; as the infinitely refracted echo of a primeval sound, man; as the reproduction and copy of an archetype, man."

16. *KSA*, 7:19[91] (1872/73). Cf. ibid., [71], for identical language, and where the analogy is partly to theater (the way an actor or dramatic poet "projects himself outwards" and calmly contemplates the world), partly to natural philosophy and perhaps to atomism. Cf. ibid., 19[91]: "All natural science is only an attempt to understand man, the anthropological element." Democritus, mentioned in an adjacent note (19[89]), is given two titles by the Suda, *The Great Diacosmos* (i.e., *The Great World Order*) and *On the Nature of the Cosmos* (68A31 DK), and is also reported to have written that "man is a microcosm" (fr. 34 DK). Nietzsche once briefly contemplated reducing the lineaments of the Democritean corpus, elsewhere reported as vast, to these two titles (*BAW* 3, 254–59); see discussion in Porter 2000, ch. 1.

CLASSICAL MYTHOLOGIES IN THE PRESENT TENSE

1. A fuller exposition of this material, which is closely tied to Nietzsche's ongoing interests in atomism, his scenarios of the will, and his speculations about aesthetics, will have to wait for another occasion.

2. Adorno, however, did, in Nietzsche's wake. See Adorno 1970, 81: "Cruelty [in Greek works of art] is part and parcel of their critical self-awareness."

3. Last two emphases added.

4. Guthrie 1965, 387.

5. *BAW*, 3, 349. Silk and Stern (1981, 194–95; cf. 285–86) make the intriguing suggestion that Socrates is consciously fashioned by Nietzsche against the background of Socrates' earlier alter ego in Nietzsche's writings, the embodiment of pre-Socratic rationality, namely Democritus, whose "lust for knowledge [*Wissenstrieb*]—lucidity—poetic abandon" (*BAW*, 4, 59) is cited

as evidence of his seemingly unlimited "versatility": this list "not only reads a shorthand for Socratism plus art, but is not so far from the triad Socratic–Apolline—Dionysiac itself." (To this list, one might add that Democritu "prose" was itself a kind of "poetry," while his desire for knowledge was once "inebriated" and lucid; *KSA*, 7:1[7]; 13 (1869); *BAW*, 3, 349.) The co presence, the argument runs, of contrasting impulses (scientific and artisti would have marred the "monolithic" image of Socrates that Nietzsche wante to preserve without any "unwelcome ambivalence": "but if art and thought ca so readily coexist as the case of Democritus might suggest, there is n dilemma, no paradox, no occasion for a paradox, and the painfully achieve mixed mode of *BT* itself is mocked." And so Democritus as a prototype had t be junked—until, that is, *The Birth of Tragedy* comes to take in its sights "a cu tural dilemma" (the recognition that "art and thought are, but should not b disjunct"), at which point another figure is needed, a centauric Socrates, musically minded Socrates—or should we say, a *Democritean* (not to sa Dionysian and tragic) Socrates? (See "The Socratic Fallacy," n. 2, above.)

This fleeting, if withdrawn, approximation of Nietzsche's project in his fir book with his earlier philology is undeniably suggestive, and more satisfacto than Kofman 1989, where Democritus is portrayed as one more instance the "Socratic repression of the Dionysian" (p. 304). But without going int detailed comment here, one would surely want to wonder whether the logi structure, and genesis of *The Birth of Tragedy* have been well diagnose whether the Platonic Socrates (or any rationalist) is in fact a "monolithic ratio nalizer" in Nietzsche's eyes, and whether this Socrates can be neatly sundere from a Socrates who practices music and poetry. There is indeed a dilemma the heart of *The Birth of Tragedy*. But Socrates is not to be located on one si of the dilemma. Rather, *the dilemma inhabits him*. Contrast the argument Behler (1989, 151), who connects up an ambivalent, self-divided Socratis ("in both a scientific-theoretical and in an aesthetic sense") with Nietzsche "early philosophy in the widest sense," although Behler too greatly (and incon sistently) relies upon "the foundational opposition of the Dionysian an Socratic" as the final arbiter of any understanding of *The Birth of Tragedy*.

6. *BAW*, 3, 265; emphasis added.

7. Cf. *BAW*, 4, 59: "[Democritus'] nicknames: *Gelasinos* ('Laugher') an *sophia* [wisdom]." Cf. *BAW*, 3:333, 4:59; "PP," 331.

8. In a "plan" to *Zarathustra*, IV from 1883, Nietzsche tentatively scrip his *dramatis personae* and writes: "also a jester (Epicurus?)," followed by "Th hallowing of laughter. Future of dance. Victory over the spirit of heavines (*KSA*, 10:21[3]; 599); and compare the "scientific satyr" of *BGE*, 26.

9. See Porter 2000, ch. 2.

10. "In this connection we need only avail ourselves of the expressions and explanation of Schiller. Nature and the ideal, he says, are either objects of grief, when the former is represented as lost, the latter unattained; or both are objects of joy, in that they are represented as real. The first case furnishes the elegy in its narrower signification, the second the idyll in its widest sense" (§19).

11. The constitutive role of disavowal in classicism is discussed in Porter 2000.

12. Compare the seamless transition from Schopenhauer to the apparent recommendations of slavery in a draft preparatory to *The Birth of Tragedy* from 1871 (*KSA*, 7:10[1]; 341), which eventually was reworked as the essay "The Greek State." On the apparent Aryanism of *The Birth of Tragedy*, see "Power and Appearances," n. 6, below.

13. *KSA*, 7:9[106].

14. The same language appears in the *Encyclopedia of Philology* passage to be discussed below: "With Alexander, this impulse [to the Beyond] sets in once again: it is characterized by the expansion of Dionysus-worship [*Dionysusverehrung*]" ("ECP," 417–18). Alexander inaugurates his eponymous epoch, which is ours, too: Alexandrianism ("our whole modern world is entangled in the net of Alexandrian culture," *BT* §18).

15. *GS*, 147. Cf. ibid., 86: "Theater and music as the hashish-smoking and betel-chewing of the European! Who will ever relate the whole history of narcotica?—It is almost the history of 'culture,' of our so-called higher culture."

POWER AND APPEARANCES

1. Benjamin 1979, 103.

2. The analysis of the political in Nietzsche by Warren (1988) seems to miss Nietzsche's habitual irony in this regard: culture and violence are inseparable, never opposed. There is a cultivation of violence in politics and a violence to culture that make it false to claim for Nietzsche, at any phase in his career, that "what *instigates* suffering is meaningless social violence" (ibid., 77). It is right to underscore the role, real or imaginary, of "prediscursive" factors (force, sensuous relations, etc.). But in order to avoid an overly polarized view of these, we might say that Apollo's regime masks its own nondiscursive ("Dionysian") aspects in the guise of self-standing cognitive ones (cf. ibid., 76). My own view comes closer to that of Sloterdijk (1989), whereby Dionysus is eternally set off in quotation marks (cf. pp. 24–25), and ultimately represents a

stage in the transfiguration of the commonplace and banal (pp. 55, 57, 60 Gratuitous parodic cynicism and free-play (privileged and applauded by Slo terdijk) are, however, not the only threat to human self-exaltation recognize by Nietzsche (cf. p. 70). Nietzsche is critical of cultural violence and not ju cynical toward it.

3. "GrS," 774.

4. "HC," 792.

5. "One thing is not to be forgotten: the same cruelty that we found at th core of every culture resides in the core of every powerful religion and, gener ally speaking, in the nature of *power*, which is always evil" (p. 768). The mod ern version of these delusions are those that concern the "value of the indivi ual" (p. 765)—or the illusion that the modern world can model the (presume humanity of its culture on that of the Greeks. Nietzsche's essay is often read a plea for retrograde aristocratism and an attack on contemporary liberal an socialist political programs. But the essay is in fact an exposure of the sel deceptions of his culture's cruelty. He knows very well that labor, tied in th present to the ideology of human worth, "has as its goal the destruction 'valuable' people" (p. 775) and that pretending this isn't so is the founding l of his own culture. What Nietzsche is in fact describing is the "warlike task the state" in its current form (ibid.). That is the lesson of *The Birth of Traged* too: "Let us mark this well: the Alexandrian culture," of which Nietzsche own is the most recent avatar, "to be able to exist permanently, requires a slav class, but with its optimistic view of life it denies the necessity of such a clas (§18; this remark is followed by further direct echoes of "GrS," p, 775). A Reibnitz (1987, 83) writes, "Sparta, not Athens, as the modernists wish to hav it, is Nietzsche's model for Bismarck's Germany." But Nietzsche was hardly proponent of Bismarck's Germany, even at this time. Nor is it the case th Sparta was an unpopular countermodel among classical philologists, and lea of all for K. O. Müller's devoted pupil Ernst Curtius, who is cited as a instance of the "modernists" here (ibid.). See next note, and see further "Th Myth of Mythlessness," n. 2, below.

6. Theognis, vv. 425–29; cf. *BT* §3; and Schopenhauer, *W*, 2.2, §46. C Theognis and Sparta as paradoxical figures for fallen potency; on the con flicted Dorian fantasy that was inherited and "historicized" by the classic philologist K. O. Müller, a central source in these passages in *The Birth Tragedy*; and for a reading of Nietzsche's use of this Aryanist racial fantasy *The Birth of Tragedy*, see Porter 2000, ch. 5.

7. Similarly, *GM*, I:10, two desperate moments that ward off the inn duplicity of Nietzsche's phantasmatic nobles: "Even supposing that the affe

of contempt, of looking down from a superior height, *falsifies* the image of that which it despises, it will at any rate still be a much less serious falsification than that perpetrated on its opponent—*in effigie*, of course—by the submerged hatred, the vengefulness of the impotent"; "*ressentiment* itself, if it should appear in the noble man, consummates and exhausts itself in an immediate reaction, and therefore does not *poison*." For analysis, see Porter 1998, 161–72.

8. Trans. mod.; emphases added.

THE MYTH OF MYTHLESSNESS

1. *KSA*, 7:9[10] (1871); and 3[32] (1869/70); emphases added.

2. Compare the following note from 1870/71: "I could imagine that the [Franco-Prussian] war, on the German side, was waged in order to free Venus from the Louvre, as a second Helen. That would be the pneumatic [viz., spiritual] interpretation of this war. The beautiful ancient immobility of existence was inaugurated by this war—now the age of seriousness begins—we believe it will also be one of *art*" (*KSA*, 7:7[88]). "Pneumatic" undoubtedly alludes, in addition to allegory of a Christian kind, to the mythological variants according to which the Helen fought over and defended in the Trojan War was an *eidōlon*, a phantom, formed of mere clouds and air. Given Nietzsche's general hostility to Bismarckian politics and to German classical aesthetics, it is hard to believe he meant this statement to endorse the German appropriation of antiquity.

3. Zuckerman 1974, 22. Zuckerman dates Nietzsche's eventual enlightenment to the time he wrote the self-critical preface to *The Birth of Tragedy*.

4. "ECP," 399.

5. *KGW*, 2.3, 321–22; cf. *KSA*, 7:1[54] (1869): "What characterizes the Hellenic is harmony, what characterizes the moderns is melody (as absolute character)."

6. *KGW*, 2.3, 322.

7. Nietzsche's arguments against this anachronism are unwittingly restated and confirmed by Zuckerman (1974, 20–21, 25). One irony here is that Zuckerman's account of the gap between ancient and modern music is in all likelihood derived from *Nietzsche himself*. Nietzsche's notes on Greek music, although never published, were nonetheless eagerly read *samizdat*, and his findings were posthumously assimilated by classical philologists, gradually accepted, and finally became canonical (see Porter 2000, ch. 3). The further

irony is that, apparently unbeknownst to Zuckerman, Nietzsche was antic pated in part by Richard Wagner.

8. "WPh," 5[156].

9. Emphasis added. There are further complications in Nietzsche exposition of the problem of music and rhythm, and these are discussed i Porter 2000, ch. 3.

10. Wagner 1871–83, 10:144–46. Wagner is resuming and clarifying h earlier *pronunciamento*, "*Das Kunstwerk der Zukunft*" (1849).

11. Ibid., 144, 145.

12. "ECP," 416–18. "Thus, not only is the general dissolution of paganis favorable to Christianity; one can also see countless approximations an pavings of the way [leading up to Christianity]. Especially important is the fa that the gods are now de-nationalized: next comes the general prejudice i favor of the Orient. Then, the goal of existence is referred to a Beyond [*Jen seits*]: its primary means are secret rites and a conscious morality that culm nates in ascetism," etc. (pp. 417–18); cf. ibid., p. 370, and (in detail) Port 2000, ch. 4, on the unexpected parallels and continuities between Dionysia ism and Christianity.

13. And not the hoped-for cult of Wagner (Reibnitz 1992, 341–42), whic at most represents an extension of the postclassical Christian mysteries name here in *BT* §12 ("Will it not some day rise once again out of its mystic dept as art?" *BT* §17).

14. "ECP," 415 n. 37; cf. 413, 414 n. 37.

15. "*Orgia* (originally not the ecstatic [kind])" ("ECP," 413).

16. The sequel runs, "and its place is taken by the claim of religion to hi torical foundations. This dying myth was now seized by the new-born geni of Dionysian music; and in these hands it flourished once more with colo such as it had never yet displayed, with a fragrance that awakened a longir anticipation of a metaphysical world." The pattern is familiar and laden wi ambiguous overtones: the metaphysical longing eventually culminates in t mysteries, then in Christianity, and finally in modern classicism (of which *T. Birth of Tragedy* is an instance).

17. Trans. mod.; emphasis added. "*Supplement*" here is paralleled in t *Encyclopedia* by "*Ergänzung*."

18. A later incarnation of this imagery is the subject who fails to rema deaf, like Odysseus, "to the siren songs of old metaphysical bird catchers wh have been piping at him all too long, 'you are more, you are higher, you are a different origin!'" (*BGE*, 230). See Porter 1999, pp. 166–67.

19. *KSA*, 7:10[1]; 335 (1871).

20. Moved by the "romantic" temperament, "one wants to go *back*, through the Church Fathers to the Greeks, from the north to the south, from the formulas to the Forms." "What happiness there is already in this will to spirituality, to ghostliness almost!" (*WP*, 419 [1885]).

21. None of this was lost on Nietzsche's contemporaries, for instance his teacher and mentor in classics, Friedrich Ritschl: "I belong, every inch of me, so decisively to the *historical* tendency and to the historical view of human affairs, that the redemption of the world never seemed to me to be found in one or another of the philosophical systems; [and] that at the same time I can never call the natural fading away of an epoch or a phenomenon 'suicide.'" (Ritschl to Nietzsche, 14 February 1872). Wilamowitz likewise found the implications of *The Birth of Tragedy* too "vaguely pessimistic" for his tastes (in Gründer 1969, 134; cf. p. 32). He would attempt to vitiate Nietzsche's vision of the secret Dionysian mysteries for being anachronistic and romanticizing: they smack too much of the later, degenerative developments of the Hellenistic age and beyond, with "all their nonsense about mystical vapors, their crude syncreticism," not to mention their affinity with the glazed visions of "Creuzer" and "Schopenhauer" (ibid., 42; cf. ibid., 41). This, of course, does nothing to diminish the force of Nietzsche's critique, insofar as the present is directly continuous with the postclassical past. In other words, Nietzsche has put his finger on a neuralgic issue of classicism. Wilamowitz's point, moreover, is (obliquely) acknowledged already in *BT*. After Euripides (Wilamowitz and Nietzsche agree at least on this much of the chronology of classicism), Dionysianism ("the tragic world view") "had to flee from art into the underworld as it were, in the degenerate form of a secret cult"; "the Dionysian world view . . . lives on in the mysteries and, in its strangest metamorphoses and debasements, does not cease to attract serious natures. Will it not some day rise once again out of its mystic depths . . . ?" (*BT*, §17). The significance of this allusion in Nietzsche can be appreciated only against the kinds of problems we have been considering all along; but see above at n. 12.

22. This and similar reasons tell against arguments for perfectionism in Nietzsche. See Porter 1999.

23. *W*, 1.2, §54; emphasis added. Shortly afterward in the same section, Schopenhauer quotes Goethe's hymn to Prometheus (1774), a poem that is central to *BT* and is likewise quoted in full in *BT* §9. Possibly Schopenhauer is leaning on Karl Philipp Moritz's *Götterlehre* (1795) here; Moritz reports the same evidence of sarcophagi, and earlier quotes Goethe's hymn in full as well (1981, 2: 627–29 and 710–11).

24. Ibid., §58 ad fin. Similarly Lange (1866, vii), although he differs from

Schopenhauer in viewing metaphysics itself, and Schopenhauer's in particula (p. v), as being on a par with religion.

25. Cf. "On Schopenhauer" (p. 355), making light of Schopenhauer's "ini tial *ecstasies* of discovery" (emphasis added).

26. See above, "The Appearance of Metaphysics in *The Birth of Traged* and Beyond," n. 20, on "the will to eternize" as an expression of Apollinianism

27. Cf. *BT*, §21, where myth is acknowledged to be deceptive in essenc albeit a "noble deception," but also a circular one: tragedy deploys myth t "deceive the listener into feeling that the music is merely the highest means t bring life into the vivid world of myth." This has peculiar implications fo music, but the question cannot be pursued here.

28. Cf. *UM*, II:2, which is concerned with the "demand for a monument history" and its limits: "But it is precisely this demand that greatness shall b everlasting which sparks off the most fearful of struggles. For everything els that lives cries No. The monumental shall not come into existence—that is th counter-word. Apathetic habit, all that is base and petty, filling every corner c the earth and billowing up around all that is great like a heavy breath of th earth . . . retards, deceives, suffocates, and stifles it." One should be wary c aggrandizing this urge to impossible greatness; it is an aspiration that blocked by its own improbability, and one that Nietzsche can be more consis tently read as specifically mocking rather than as defending.

Works Cited

I. A. WORKS BY NIETZSCHE IN GERMAN WITH ABBREVIATIONS

BAW: *Friedrich Nietzsche: Historisch-kritische Gesamtausgabe. Werke.* 1933–. 5 vols. Edited by Joachim Mette et al. Munich: C. H. Beck.

KGB: *Briefwechsel. Kritische Gesamtausgabe.* 1975–. Ed. Georgio Colli and Mazzino Montinari. Berlin: Walter de Gruyter.

KGW: *Werke. Kritische Gesamtausgabe.* 1967–. Edited by Georgio Colli and Mazzino Montinari. Berlin: Walter de Gruyter.

KSA: *Sämtliche Werke. Kritische Studienausgabe in 15 Einzelbänden.* 1988. 2d, corrected ed. Edited by Georgio Colli and Mazzino Montinari. Berlin: dtv/de Gruyter. The Colli-Montinari manuscript numeration will be given after volume numbers—e.g., "*KSA*, 7:7[156]"—with page numbers and years appended when greater precision is needed—e.g., "*KSA*, 7:7[156]; 199 (1870/71)."

B. TRANSLATIONS

Beyond Good and Evil: Prelude to a Philosophy of the Future. 1966. Translated by Walter Kaufmann. New York: Vintage.

The Birth of Tragedy and The Case of Wagner. 1967. Translated by Walter Kaufmann. New York: Vintage.

Daybreak: Thoughts on the Prejudices of Morality. 1982. Translated by R. J. Hollingdale. Cambridge: Cambridge University Press.

Ecce Homo: How One Becomes What One Is. 1979. Translated by R. J. Hollingdale. Harmondsworth: Penguin.

The Gay Science: With a Prelude in Rhymes and an Appendix of Songs. 1974. Translated by Walter Kaufmann. New York: Vintage.

Human, All Too Human: A Book for Free Spirits. 1996. Translated by R. J. Hollingdale. Cambridge: Cambridge University Press.

On the Genealogy of Morals: A Polemic. 1969. Translated by Walter Kaufmann. New York: Vintage.

"On Truth and Lying in an Extra-Moral Sense." 1989. In Gilman et al. 1989, 246–57.

Thus Spoke Zarathustra: A Book for All and None. 1966. Translated by Walter Kaufmann. New York: Penguin.

Twilight of the Idols and The Anti-Christ. 1968. Translated by R. J. Hollingdale. Harmondsworth: Penguin.

Untimely Meditations. 1983. Translated by R. J. Hollingdale, with an introduction by J. P. Stern. Cambridge: Cambridge University Press.

The Will to Power. 1968. Translated by Walter Kaufmann and R. J. Hollingdale. Edited by Walter Kaufmann. New York: Vintage.

For a complete list of abbreviations, see "Abbreviations" in the front matter.

II. OTHER WORKS CITED

Adorno, Theodor W. 1966. *Negative Dialektik.* Frankfurt-a.-M.: Suhrkamp (*Negative Dialectics.* 1973. Translated by E. B. Ashton. New York: Continuum.)

———. 1970. *Ästhetische Theorie.* Frankfurt-a.-M.: Suhrkamp.

Allison, Henry E. 1983. *Kant's Transcendental Idealism: An Interpretation and Defense.* New Haven: Yale University Press.

Baeumer, Max. 1976. "Nietzsche and the Tradition of the Dionysian." In O'Flaherty et al. 1976, 165–89.

Bakhtin, M. M. 1981. *The Dialogic Imagination: Four Essays.* Edited by Michael Holquist. Translated by Caryl Emerson and Michael Holquist. Austin: University of Texas Press.

Barbera, Sandro. 1995. "Eine Quelle der frühen Schopenhauer-Kritik Nietzsches: Rudolf Hayms Aufsatz, 'Arthur Schopenhauer.'" *Nietzsche-Studien* 24: 124–36.

Behler, Ernst. 1986. "A. W. Schlegel and the Nineteenth-Century *Damnatio* of Euripides." *Greek, Roman and Byzantine Studies* 27: 335–67.

———. 1989. "Sokrates und die Griechische Tragödie." *Nietzsche-Studien* 18: 141–57.

Benjamin, Walter. 1977. *The Origin of German Tragic Drama.* Translated by John Osborne. London: NLB.

Blanchot, Maurice. 1969. *L'Entretien infini*. Paris: Éditions Gallimard.
Blondel, Eric. 1986. *Nietzsche, le corps et la culture: La philosophie comme généalogie philologique*. Paris: Presses Universitaires de France.
Böning, Thomas. 1988. *Metaphysik, Kunst und Sprache beim frühen Nietzsche*. Berlin and New York: Walter de Gruyter.
Calder, William M., III. 1983. "The Wilamowitz-Nietzsche Struggle: New Documents and a Reappraisal." *Nietzsche-Studien* 12: 214–54.
Cartwright, David E. 1991. "Reversing Silenus' Wisdom." *Nietzsche-Studien* 20: 309–13.
Clark, Maudemarie. 1990. *Nietzsche on Truth and Philosophy*. Cambridge: Cambridge University Press.
Conway, Daniel W. 1992. "Nietzsche's Art of This-Worldly Comfort: Self-Reference and Strategic Self-Parody." *History of Philosophy Quarterly* 9, no. 3: 343–57.
Crawford, Claudia. 1988. *The Beginnings of Nietzsche's Theory of Language*. Berlin: Walter de Gruyter.
Creuzer, Georg Friedrich. 1836–43 [1st ed. 1810–12]. *Symbolik und Mythologie der alten Völker, besonders der Griechen*. 4 vols. in 6. Leipzig: K. W. Leske. Rpt. 1973, Hildesheim: G. Olms.
de Man, Paul. 1979. *Allegories of Reading*. New Haven: Yale University Press.
Deleuze, Gilles. 1983. *Nietzsche and Philosophy*. Translated by Hugh Tomlinson. New York: Columbia University Press. [French original: 1962.]
Diels, Hermann, ed. 1951–52. *Die Fragmente der Vorsokratiker, Griechisch und Deutsch*. 6th ed., edited by Walther Kranz. 3 vols. Berlin: Weidmann.
Diogenes Laertius. 1925. *Lives of Eminent Philosophers*. Translated by R. D. Hicks. 2 vols. Cambridge, Mass.: Harvard University Press.
Fleischer, Margot. 1988. "Dionysos als Ding an Sich." *Nietzsche-Studien* 17: 74–90.
Gerratana, Federico. 1988. "Der Wahn Jenseits des Menschen: Zur frühen E. v. Hartmann-Rezeption Nietzsches (1869–1874)." *Nietzsche-Studien* 17: 391–433.
Gilman, Sander L., Carole Blair, and David J. Parent, eds. and trans. 1989. *Friedrich Nietzsche on Rhetoric and Language*. New York: Oxford.
Goedert, Georges. 1978. "Nietzsche und Schopenhauer." *Nietzsche-Studien* 7: 1–26.
Gründer, Karlfried. 1969. *Der Streit um Nietzsches "Geburt der Tragödie": Die Schriften von E. Rohde, R. Wagner, U. v. Willamowitz-Möllendorff* [sic]. Hildesheim: Olms.
Guthrie, W. K. C. 1965. *A History of Greek Philosophy*. Vol. 2: *The Presocratic*

Tradition from Parmenides to Democritus. Cambridge: Cambridge University Press.

Guyer, Paul. 1987. *Kant and the Claims of Knowledge*. Cambridge: Cambridge University Press.

Hadot, Pierre. 1995. *Philosophy as a Way of Life: Spiritual Exercises from Socrates to Foucault*. Edited by Arnold I. Davidson. Translated by Michael Chase. Oxford: Blackwell.

Hamacher, Werner. 1986. "'Disgregation des Willens.' Nietzsche über Individuum und Individualität." *Nietzsche-Studien* 15: 306–36; translation by Jeffrey S. Librett: "'Disgregation of the Will': Nietzsche on the Individual and Individuality." In *Reconstructing Individualism: Autonomy, Individuality, and the Self in Western Thought*, edited by Thomas C. Heller, Morton Sosna, and David E. Wellbery, with Arnold I. Davidson, Ann Swindler, and Ian Watt, 106–39. Stanford: Stanford University Press.

Hayman, Ronald. 1980. *Nietzsche. A Critical Life*. Harmondsworth: Penguin.

Hegel, Georg Wilhelm Friedrich. 1970. *Phänomenologie des Geistes*. Vol. 3 of *Werke* [1969–71]. Edited by Eva Moldenhauer and Karl Markus Michel. 20 vols. Frankfurt-a.-M.: Suhrkamp.

Heidegger, Martin. 1961. *Nietzsche*. 2 vols. Pfullingen: Neske.

Henrichs, Albert. 1975. "Two Doxographical Notes: Democritus and Prodicus on Religion." *Harvard Studies in Classical Philology*, 79:93–123.

———. 1986. "The Last of the Detractors: Friedrich Nietzsche's Condemnation of Euripides." *Greek, Roman and Byzantine Studies* 27.4: 369–97.

Jacobi, Friedrich Heinrich. 1812–25. 6 vols. *Werke*. Leipzig: G. Fleischer.

Jacobs, Carol. 1978. *The Dissimulating Harmony: The Image of Interpretation in Nietzsche, Rilke, Artaud, and Benjamin*. Baltimore, Md.: Johns Hopkins University Press.

Kant, Immanuel. 1965. *Critique of Pure Reason*. Translated by Norman Kemp Smith. Unabr. ed. New York: St. Martin's Press.

Kaufmann, Walter. 1974. *Nietzsche: Philosopher, Psychologist, Antichrist*. 4th ed. Princeton: Princeton University Press. [1st ed., 1950.]

Kofman, Sarah. 1977. "Metaphor, Symbol, Metamorphosis." In *The New Nietzsche: Contemporary Styles of Interpretation*, edited by David B. Allison, 201–14. New York: Dell.

———. 1979. *Nietzsche et la scène philosophique*. Paris: Union Générale d'Éditions.

———. 1989. *Socrate(s)*. Paris: Éditions Galilée.

Lacan, Jacques. 1981. *The Four Fundamental Concepts of Psycho-Analysis*. Translated by Alan Sheridan. Edited by Jacques-Alain Miller. New York: Norton.

Lacoue-Labarthe, Philippe. 1971. "Le Détour (Nietzsche et la rhétorique)." *Poétique* 2, no. 5: 53–76.

Lange, Friedrich Albert. 1866. *Geschichte des Materialismus und Kritik seiner Bedeutung in der Gegenwart*. Iserlohn: J. Baedeker.

———. 1974. [1873–75]. *Geschichte des Materialismus und Kritik seiner Bedeutung in der Gegenwart*. 2 vols. 2d ed. Frankfurt-a.-M.: Suhrkamp.

Lea, F. A. 1957. *The Tragic Philosopher: A Study of Friedrich Nietzsche*. London: Methuen.

Lloyd-Jones, Hugh. 1976. "Nietzsche and the Study of the Ancient World." In O'Flaherty et al. 1976, 1–15.

Löhneysen, Wolfgang Frhr. von. 1987. "Der Apoll von Belvedere: Kunst als Grund philosophischer Gedanken." In *Schopenhauer im Denken der Gegenwart: 23 Beiträge zu seiner Aktualität*, edited by Volker Spierling, 97–121. Munich: Piper.

Long, A. A., and David Sedley. 1987. *The Hellenistic Philosophers*. 2 vols. Cambridge: Cambridge University Press.

Love, Frederick R. 1963. *Young Nietzsche and the Wagnerian Experience*. Chapel Hill: University of North Carolina Press.

Lucretius. 1910. *On the Nature of Things*. Translated by Cyril Bailey. Oxford: Clarendon Press.

Meijers, Anthonie. 1988. "Gustav Gerber und Friedrich Nietzsche." *Nietzsche-Studien* 17: 369–90.

Moritz, Karl Philipp. 1981. *Werke*. 3 vols. Edited by Horst Günther. Frankfurt-a.-M.: Insel.

Müller-Lauter, Wolfgang. 1971. *Nietzsche: Seine Philosophie der Gegensätze und die Gegensätze seiner Philosophie*. Berlin: Walter de Gruyter.

Nehamas, Alexander. 1985. *Nietzsche: Life as Literature*. Cambridge, Mass.: Harvard University Press.

Nussbaum, Martha Craven. 1991. "The Transfigurations of Intoxication: Nietzsche, Schopenhauer, and Dionysus." *Arion*, 3d series, 1.2: 75–111.

O'Flaherty, James C., Timothy F. Sellner, and Robert M. Helm, eds. 1976. *Studies in Nietzsche and the Classical Tradition*. Chapel Hill: University of North Carolina Press.

Pautrat, Bernard. 1971. *Versions du soleil. Figures et système de Nietzsche*. Paris: Éditions du Seuil.

Plato. 1989. *Symposium*. Translated by Alexander Nehamas and Paul Woodruff. Indianapolis, Ind.: Hackett.

Poliakov, Léon. 1987. *Le Mythe Aryen: Essai sur les sources du racisme et des nationalismes*. Rev. ed. N.p. [Brussels]: Éditions Complexe.

Porter, James I. 1994. "Nietzsche's Rhetoric: Theory and Strategy." *Philosophy and Rhetoric* 27, no. 3: 218–44.

———. 1995. "The Invention of Dionysus and the Platonic Midwife: Nietzsche's *Birth of Tragedy*." *Journal of the History of Philosophy* 33, no. 3: 467–97.

———. 1998. "Unconscious Agency in Nietzsche." *Nietzsche-Studien* 27: 153–95.

———. 1999. "Nietzsche et les charmes de la métaphysique: 'La logique du sentiment.'" *Revue germanique internationale*. 11 ("*Nietzsche moraliste*"): 157–72.

———. 2000. *Nietzsche and the Philology of the Future*. Stanford: Stanford University Press.

Prauss, Gerold. 1974. *Kant und das Problem der Dinge an Sich*. Bonn: Bouvier

Reibnitz, Barbara. 1987. "Nietzsches 'Griechischer Staat' und das deutsche Kaiserreich." *Der Altsprachliche Unterricht* 32.3: 76–89.

———. 1992. *Ein Kommentar zu Friedrich Nietzsche, "Die Geburt der Tragödie aus dem Geiste der Musik"* (*Kap.* 1–12). Stuttgart: Metzler.

Riedel, Manfred. 1995. "Ein Seitenstück zur 'Geburt der Tragödie': Nietzsches Abkehr von Schopenhauer und Wagner und seine Wende zur Philosophie." *Nietzsche-Studien* 24: 45–61.

Russell, D. A. 1981. *Criticism in Antiquity*. Berkeley: University of California Press.

Salaquarda, Jörg. 1978. "Nietzsche und Lange." *Nietzsche-Studien* 7: 236–60

Sallis, John. 1991. *Crossings: Nietzsche and the Space of Tragedy*. Chicago: University of Chicago Press.

Schlegel, Friedrich. 1958– . *Kritische Friedrich-Schlegel-Ausgabe*. Edited by Ernst Behler, with Jean-Jacques Anstett and Hans Eichner, et al. Paderborn: Ferdinand Schöningh.

Schopenhauer, Arthur. 1977. *Die Welt als Wille und Vorstellung*. Vols. 1–4 of *Zürcher Ausgabe. Werke in zehn Bände*. Edited by Angelika Hubscher, Claudia Schmolders, Fritz Senn, and Gerd Haffmans. Zurich: Diogenes.

———. 1989. *Parerga und Paralipomena. Kleine philosophische Schriften*. Vols. 4 and 5 of *Sämtliche Werke*. Edited by Wolfgang Frhr. Von Löhneysen. 5 vols. Darmstadt: Wissenschaftliche Buchgesellschaft. Rpt. of 2nd ed. (1968). Stuttgart.

Shapiro, Gary. 1989. *Nietzschean Narratives*. Bloomington: Indiana University Press.

Silk, M. S., and J. P. Stern. 1981. *Nietzsche on Tragedy*. Cambridge: Cambridge University Press.

Sloterdijk, Peter. 1989. *Thinker on the Stage: Nietzsche's Materialism*. Translated by Jamie Owen Daniel. Minneapolis: University of Minnesota Press.

Stack, George J. 1983. *Lange and Nietzsche*. Berlin: Walter de Gruyter.

Stroux, Johannes. 1925. *Nietzsches Professur in Basel*. Jena: Frommannsche Buchhandlung.

Vaihinger, Hans. 1881–92. *Commentar zu Kants Kritik der reinen Vernunft*. 2 vols. Stuttgart: W. Spemann.

Vlastos, Gregory. 1991. *Socrates, Ironist and Moral Philosopher*. Cambridge: Cambridge University Press.

Wagner, Richard. 1873. *Gesammelte Schriften und Dichtungen*. 10 vols. Leipzig: E. W. Fritzsch.

Warminski, Andrzej. 1987. *Readings in Interpretation: Hölderlin, Hegel, Heidegger*. Minneapolis: University of Minnesota Press.

Warren, Mark. 1988. *Nietzsche and Political Thought*. Cambridge, Mass.: MIT Press.

Waxman, Wayne. 1991. *Kant's Model of the Mind: A New Interpretation of Transcendental Idealism*. New York: Oxford.

Weininger, Otto. 1919. *Geschlecht und Charakter: Eine Prinzipielle Untersuchung*. 18th ed. Vienna: Wilhelm Braumüller. [1st ed. 1903.]

Winkler, John J. 1990. "The Some Two Sources of Literature and Its 'History' in Aristotle, *Poetics* 4." In *Cabinet of the Muses: Essays on Classical and Comparative Literature in Honor of Thomas G. Rosenmeyer*, edited by Mark Griffith and Donald J. Mastronarde, 307–18. Atlanta, Ga.: Scholars Press.

Young, Julian. 1987. *Willing and Unwilling: A Study in the Philosophy of Arthur Schopenhauer*. Dordrecht: M. Nijhoff.

———. 1992. *Nietzsche's Philosophy of Art*. Cambridge: Cambridge University Press.

Zeller, Eduard. 1856–68. *Die Philosophie der Griechen in ihrer geschichtlichen Entwicklung*. 3 vols. in 5. Tübingen: L. F. Fues.

Žižek, Slavoj. 1989. *The Sublime Object of Ideology*. London: Verso.

———. 1999. *The Ticklish Subject: The Absent Centre of Political Ontology*. London: Verso.

Zuckerman, Elliott. 1974. "Nietzsche and Music: *The Birth of Tragedy* and *Nietzsche Contra Wagner*." *Symposium* 28, no. 1: 17–30.

Index

Achilles, 25, 106
Adorno, Theodor, 177, 205
Aeschylus, 82, 103–104, 114, 155, 198–99
Agathon, 112, 115, 119
Alcibiades, 115–16, 118, 134, 202
"all-too-human," 4, 9, 31, 34, 39, 46, 49, 62, 66–67, 125–26, 131, 142, 162, 168, 169, 171, 177–78, 189, 204
Apollo, 4, 22–24, 35–37, 40–42, 44–45, 48–49, 51, 54, 72, 74, 76–78, 82, 84, 87–89, 96, 99–100, 105–106, 110, 113, 116, 120, 124, 139, 143–48, 151–58, 172–74, 178, 181, 183, 186, 188, 189, 193, 195–96, 198, 200, 201, 202, 206, 207, 212
Archilochus, 201
Aristo of Chios, 204
Aristophanes, 94, 104, 112, 113, 114, 117–19, 199
Aristotle, 22, 38, 93, 112, 121–22, 173, 203
Aryanism, 139, 207, 208
atomism
  ancient, 4, 5, 10, 11, 19–20, 36–37, 39, 40, 46, 85, 127–28, 131, 134–35, 168, 171, 172, 179, 180, 187, 188, 205. *See also* Democritus; Epicurus; Leucippus; Lucretius
  of the will, 60–72, 130, 204–205

Bacchants, 78, 200
Bakhtin, M. M., 192
Blanchot, Maurice, 31, 32, 178

centaur, 93, 113, 192, 206. *See also* Chaeremon
Ceres, 138
Chaeremon, author of *Centaur*, 93
Christianity, 7, 154, 194, 196, 210
Cicero, 134, 179, 180
classical antiquity, idea of, 1, 6, 98, 101, 132, 134, 136–37, 141, 148–49, 158, 209
classical ideal, 137, 192
classicism, 137, 143, 148, 172, 181, 207, 210, 211
Cohen, Hermann, 169
comedy, 52, 84, 112–14, 117–19, 131, 201
contest culture, 145–47, 178
Corybantes, 116
Creuzer, Georg Friedrich, 193, 196, 211
Curtius, Ernst, 208
Cynics, 94, 128, 191, 204.

decadence, 24, 34, 85, 88, 90, 102–103, 104–106, 114, 117, 121–22, 139, 146, 152, 154–55, 158, 163, 178, 194, 199, 204, 211
Deleuze, Gilles, 22, 172, 182
De Man, Paul, 79–80, 176–77, 181, 189, 191

Demeter, 155
Democritus, 6–7, 10, 19–20, 27, 37–39, 46, 60, 62, 67, 72, 131–32, 134–35, 169, 171, 179, 180, 193–94, 205, 206
Deussen, Paul, 73, 117, 168, 187, 202
Diocles of Magnesia, 193
Diogenes Laertius, 94, 191, 193
Diogenes of Sinope, 191
Dionysus, xv, 4, 6, 22–24, 26, 35–37, 40–42, 44–45, 48–54, 72–73, 76–78, 81–85, 87–89, 95–97, 99–102, 104–106, 108, 110–15, 117, 119–22, 124–25, 132, 134, 136–37, 138, 139–41, 143–45, 147, 148–49, 151–59, 172, 173, 174, 175, 181, 182, 183, 188, 189, 191, 193, 195–96, 197, 198, 199, 200, 201, 202, 203, 206, 207, 210. *See also* Christianity; mystery cults
Dorian, 146–7, 152, 208

Empedocles, 39, 180, 200
Epicurus, 10, 37, 39, 132–134, 168, 179, 180, 206
Erinyes, 155
Euripides, 88, 103–105, 120, 182–83, 198, 199, 211

gaze, 2, 66, 90, 108–109, 130, 157, 186
genealogy, redefined, 18, 46, 70, 155
Gersdorff, Carl von, 13, 167
Goethe, Wolfgang von, 132, 211

Hamlet, 84, 109
Hecate, 154–55
Hegel, Georg Friedrich Wilhelm, 54, 179, 183, 192–93
Heidegger, Martin, 176
Helen, 146, 209
Heracles, 179, 194
Heraclitus, 131, 176
Hermes, 155
Hesiod, 196, 202
Homer, 93, 106, 112, 151, 173, 196, 197, 198, 202
Horace, 134, 179
horror vacui, 19, 83–86, 109, 113–14, 129, 136, 172, 190, 195
Humboldt, Wilhelm von, 89, 137

ideology, cultural, 10, 20, 141–42, 145, 159, 177, 208
irony, 4, 26, 30, 83–86, 95, 118, 135, 139, 151–53, 159, 171, 190, 202, 207, 209, 210
Isis, 154

Jacobi, Friedrich Heinrich, 168
Julian the Apostate, 134

Kant, Immanuel, 5, 7–8, 10–16, 59–60, 67, 71, 97, 121, 167, 168, 169, 170, 171, 172, 177, 178, 184, 186, 190, 193
Kaufmann, Walter, 3, 22–23, 167, 172, 173, 175, 185, 188, 190, 202
Kierkegaard, Søren, 202
Krug, Gustav, 7, 18

Lacan, Jacques, 186
Lange, Friedrich Albert, 5, 7, 9–17, 45, 50, 59–60, 62–64, 67, 85, 86, 109, 167, 168, 169, 170, 176, 177, 179, 180, 181, 188, 190, 200, 204, 211
Leucippus, 10, 72, 180
Longinus, 180
Lucian, 192
Lucretius, 37–40, 45, 46, 131, 133–35, 138, 142, 171, 179, 180, 182, 188

Marsyas, 115–16
Māyā, veil of, 51, 56, 78, 157, 193
metaphysical recidivism, 14, 31, 98, 195
metaphysics, 2, 4–33, 34–36, 39–40, 43–47, 49–55, 58–62, 64–68, 71–73, 76–88, 92, 95–103, 107–10, 113–14, 120, 122–27, 131, 135, 140, 142, 149, 156,

160–63, 167, 169, 170, 171, 172, 176, 177, 178, 179, 183, 184, 185, 188, 189, 190, 191, 194, 195, 199, 210, 212. *See also* thing in itself
absence of, 19–20, 49, 64, 80–86, 88, 109, 114, 123, 127–29, 135, 156, 171, 195. *See also horror vacui*
"of appearances," 5, 35, 54, 161, 183
as a need, 9, 14, 46, 62, 64–65, 67, 86, 98, 102–103, 125, 154–55, 169, 171, 172, 185, 189, 190
Midas, 134
Mithras, 154
Moritz, Karl Philipp, 211
Müller, Karl Otfried, 208
mystery cults, 102, 181

Neptune, 138

Oedipus, 96, 101, 103–105, 107, 197, 200, 203
optimism, 22, 24–26, 90, 108, 135, 171, 175, 176, 198, 208
Overbeck, Franz, 174, 202

Parmenides, 17
Parrhasius, 56, 156
Persephone, 155
pessimism, 22, 24–26, 57, 71, 103, 122, 174, 175, 197
philology, classical, 1, 93, 132, 150
as cultural critique, 1, 144
Plato, 4–6, 87, 92–93, 94–105, 109, 111–12, 114–19, 120, 122, 131, 155, 157, 160, 191, 192, 193, 194, 195, 196, 197, 198, 200, 201, 202, 204, 206
politics, 141–43, 146–48, 207, 208, 209
Presocratics, 17, 160, 170, 187
Prometheus, 45, 96, 104–105, 155, 200, 211
Protagoras, 10

racism, 129, 147, 208. *See also* Dorian
Raphael, 74, 80
Ritschl, Friedrich, 3, 167, 180, 211
Rohde, Erwin, 93, 180
romanticism, 182, 193
Romundt, Heinrich, 197

Sabazius, 154
satyr, 105, 110, 113, 116, 133, 135–36, 139–40, 142, 159, 199, 201, 206. *See also* Marsyas; Silenus; Socrates
satyr chorus, 54, 84, 104–105, 113–14, 149
satyr play, 112, 114, 121
Schiller, Friedrich, 136, 152, 181, 207
Schlegel, August Wilhelm, 104, 192, 199
Schlegel, Friedrich August, 94, 104, 192, 199, 201, 203
Schopenhauer, Arthur, 5–7, 19–20, 24–26, 46, 50, 54, 57–73, 83, 96–8, 122, 140, 147, 159–60, 162, 169, 172, 175, 182, 183, 184, 185, 186, 188, 189, 190, 191, 192, 193, 194, 195, 196, 199, 204, 207, 208, 211, 212
Semites, 139. *See also* Aryanism
Shakespeare, William, 111
Silenus, 76, 80, 83–84, 101, 110, 114–20, 133–35, 147. *See also* Socrates
slavery, 137, 139, 144, 207, 208
Socrates, 78–79, 81–82, 87–88, 90–95, 98, 100–101, 104–107, 110–12, 114–23, 134, 154, 162, 191, 192, 194, 196, 197, 198, 199, 200, 201, 202, 203, 205, 206
Sophocles, 95, 101–105, 111, 179, 198, 199, 203
sublime, 85, 103, 107, 109, 113–14, 117, 132, 180, 193, 194, 201

Theognis of Megara, 147, 208
thing in itself, 8, 10, 12–15, 26–27, 57, 59–62, 64–65, 67, 69–70, 72–73, 77, 97, 140, 168, 169, 177, 183, 184, 185, 186, 187, 190

Ueberweg, Friedrich, 12–13, 59, 168

Venus, 154
Venus de Milo, 209
violence, critique of, 139, 142, 144, 149, 207–208

Wagner, Richard, 2, 25–26, 32–33, 89, 153, 174, 192, 197, 210
Wilamowitz-Moelendorff, Ulrich von, 41, 180, 211
will to power, 18, 20, 27, 29, 32, 161, 170, 173, 190, 205
Winckelmann, Johann Joachim, 74, 89, 132, 188

Xenophon, 87, 116

Zeus, 45, 118
Zeuxis, 56

Made in United States
North Haven, CT
04 December 2023

45038551R00145